The Sufilive Series

The Sufilive Series
Volume 5

"The Hierarchy of Saints"
Ramadan Series 2010

Spiritual Discourses of
Shaykh Muhammad Hisham Kabbani

PUBLISHED BY
INSTITUTE FOR SPIRITUAL AND CULTURAL ADVANCEMENT

Published and Distributed by:

Institute for Spiritual and Cultural Advancement (ISCA)
17195 Silver Parkway, #201
Fenton, MI 48430 USA
Tel: (888) 278-6624
Fax: (810) 815-0518
Email: staff@naqshbandi.org
Web: http://www.naqshbandi.org

First Edition: May 2011
THE SUFILIVE SERIES, VOLUME 5
ISBN: 978-1-930409-79-8

Library of Congress Cataloging-in-Publication Data

Kabbani, Muhammad Hisham.
Spiritual discourses of Shaykh Muhammad Hisham Kabbani. -- 1st ed.
p. cm. -- (The sufilive series ; v. 5)
"'The hierarchy of saints'. Ramadan series 2010."
Includes bibliographical references.
ISBN 978-1-930409-79-8 (alk. paper)
1. Naqshabandiyah. 2. Sufism. I. Title.
BP189.7.N352K327 2010
297.4'8--dc22
2010044186

PRINTED IN THE UNITED STATES OF AMERICA
15 14 13 12 11 05 06 07 08 09

Mawlana Shaykh Hisham Kabbani inaugurates *Ramadan Series 2010* in the renowned Naqshbandi *zawiya* in Michigan, where, since 1999, he continues the Ramadan tradition of reciting the *awrad* in congregation before sunrise, accompanied by an inspired spiritual discourse. The popular Ramadan program has been broadcast live on Sufilive.com since 2005 and reaches ten of thousands of viewers worldwide. (August 2010)

Table of Contents

About the Author i
Preface iii
Publisher's Notes v
Masters of the Naqshbandi-Haqqani Golden Chain ix
Recitation before Every Association xi
Ramadan Series Introduction: "Purify My House" 1
Characteristics of the Abdal 9
Knowledge of Taste and Knowledge of Papers 19
Saints Dwell in What Allah Likes 25
The Story of Imam Ahmad ibn Hanbal 35
Allah's Possessiveness 43
Follow the Footsteps and Imitate the Pious 51
Changeable and Unchangeable Principles 57
Dhikrullah Is the Main Pillar of Tariqah 63
Characteristics and Levels of Dhikrullah 71
Duties of Guides and Students 79
Types of Baya, Their Conditions and Status 87
The Status of Dhikrullah in Holy Qur'an and Tariqah 95
The Oceans of Sayyidina Ali and Sayyidina Abu Bakr 105
The Four Levels of Dhikr and the Heart of Sayyidina Ali 113
Enter Through the Door and Dwell in the City 121
Secrets of the Two Oceans 129
Levels and Rewards of the Highest Character 139
The High Character and Forbearance of Awliyaullah 147
To Be Rightly Guided, Connect to Your True Fathers 155
The Secrets of Talqin 161
The Divine Dress of Kalimat at-Tawhid 169
The Reality of Tawhid, Allah's Oneness 177
Five Principles of Maqam at-Tawhid 185
Maqam al-Ikhlas, the Level of Sincerity 193
Shari`ah Protects the "Fruit of Islam", Tasawwuf 199
Awliyaullah Teach Tawhid by Example 205
The Secret of the Name "Allah" 213
Series Conclusion: The Ghawth and His Aqtab 221
Glossary 233
Other Publications of Interest 239

About the Author

World-renowned religious scholar, Shaykh Muhammad Hisham Kabbani is featured in the ground-breaking book published by Georgetown University, *The 500 Most Influential Muslims in the World—2009*. For decades he has promoted traditional Islamic principles of peace, tolerance, love, compassion and brotherhood, while rigorously opposing extremism in all its forms. He hails from a respected family of traditional Islamic scholars, which includes the former head of the Association of Muslim Scholars of Lebanon and the present grand mufti (highest Islamic religious authority) of Lebanon.

Shaykh Kabbani is highly trained, both as a western scientist and an Islamic scholar. He received a bachelor's degree in chemistry and later studied medicine. Under the instruction of Shaykh ʿAbdAllāh ad-Daghestani, upon whose personal notes this book is based, he holds a degree in Islamic Divine Law. Shaykh Muḥammad Nazim Adil al-Haqqani, world leader of the Naqshbandi-Haqqani Sufi Order, authorized him to teach and counsel students in Sufism.

In his long-standing endeavor to promote a better understanding of traditional Islam, in February 2010, Shaykh Kabbani hosted HRH Charles, the Prince of Wales at a cultural event at the revered Old Trafford Stadium in Manchester, U.K. He has hosted two international conferences in the U.S., and regional conferences on a host of issues, which attracted moderate Muslim scholars from Asia, the Far East, Middle East, Africa, U.K. and Eastern Europe. His counsel is sought by journalists, academics, policymakers and government leaders.

For thirty years, Shaykh Kabbani has consistently promoted peaceful cooperation among people of all beliefs. Since the early 1990s, he has launched numerous endeavors to bring moderate Muslims into the mainstream. Often at great personal risk, he has been instrumental in awakening Muslim social consciousness regarding the religious duty to stand firm against extremism and terrorism, for the benefit of all. His bright, hopeful outlook, with a goal to honor and serve all humanity, has helped millions understand the difference between moderate mainstream Muslims and minority extremist sects.

In the United States, Shaykh Kabbani serves as Chairman, Islamic Supreme Council of America; Founder, Naqshbandi Sufi Order of America; Advisor, World Organization for Resource Development and Education;

Chairman, As-Sunnah Foundation of America; Chairman, Kamilat Muslim Women's Organization; and Founder, *The Muslim Magazine*. In the United Kingdom, Shaykh Kabbani is an advisor to Sufi Muslim Council, which consults to the British government on public policy and social and religious issues.

Other titles by Shaykh Kabbani include: *At the Feet of My Master* (2010, 2 vols.), *The Nine-fold Ascent* (2009), *Banquet for the Soul* (2008), *Illuminations* (2007), *Universe Rising* (2007), *Symphony of Remembrance* (2007), *A Spiritual Commentary on the Chapter of Sincerity* (2006), *The Sufi Science of Self-Realization* (Fons Vitae, 2005), *Keys to the Divine Kingdom* (2005), *Classical Islam and the Naqshbandi Sufi Order* (2004), *The Naqshbandi Sufi Tradition Guidebook* (2004), *The Approach of Armageddon? An Islamic Perspective* (2003), *Encyclopedia of Muḥammad's Women Companions and the Traditions They Related* (1998, with Dr. Laleh Bakhtiar), *Encyclopedia of Islamic Doctrine* (7 vols. 1998), *Angels Unveiled* (1996), *The Naqshbandi Sufi Way* (1995), *and Remembrance of God Liturgy of the Sufi Naqshbandi Masters* (1994).

Preface

The *Sufilive Series* is based on transcripts of the *suḥbah*, extemporaneous, divinely inspired discourses, of the global head of the Naqshbandi-Haqqani Sufi Order, Mawlana Shaykh Nazim Adil al-Haqqani, and his representative, Mawlana Shaykh Hisham Kabbani.

The Sufilive Series, Volume 5 is a compilation of Shaykh Kabbani's *suḥbah* from "Ramadan Series 2010", devoted to sacred teachings of Sufi masters of the famed Naqshbandi Golden Chain regarding the hierarchy, response-bilities, powers, and character of *awlīyāullāh*, God's saints.

In 2005, Shaykh Kabbani launched Sufilive.com with the goal of bringing the treasures of these discourses to a global audience. Sufilive.com is a free-membership website that features live and recorded broadcasts, and an extensive video archive on a host of topics. A testament to the live broadcasts' popularity, one-hundred volunteer transcriptionists, translators, and editors from around the world help publish Sufilive transcripts in English, Arabic, Turkish, Bahasa (Malay), Bahasa (Indo), Urdu, Farsi, French, German, Spanish, Italian, Dutch, Bosnian, Russian and Cantonese.

Our deep appreciation goes to the hard-working team of English transcribers and editors from across the U.S., Canada, U.K. and Europe, whose valuable contributions have made this collection a reality.

For fifty years, the author has sought to serve his master and promote these sacred teachings in the best way. We hope *The Sufilive Series* reflects this spirit and opens for you a door to the spiritual masters of our time.

Publisher's Notes

This book is directed to those familiar with the Sufi Way; however, to accommodate lay readers unfamiliar with Sufi terminology and practices, we have provided English translations of Arabic texts and a comprehensive glossary. Where Arabic terms are crucial to the discussion, we have included transliteration and footnoted explanations. For readers familiar with Arabic and Islamic teachings, for further clarity please consult the cited sources.

The original material is based on transcripts of a series of holy gatherings which serve as conduits of heavenly guidance. The *ṣuḥbah,* a divinely inspired talk which conveys powerful energy that uplifts the soul, is delivered by the "shaykh," a highly trained spiritual guide. To present the authentic flavor of such rare teachings, great care was taken to preserve the speaking styles of both the author and the illustrious shaykhs upon whose notes this book is based. Please pray that our shortcomings are corrected.

Translations from Arabic to English pose unique challenges which we have tried our best to make understandable to Western readers. In addition, please note the worldwide cultural practice to not include the definite article "the," as in "~~the~~ Prophet," which is a more intimate reference that appears occasionally throughout this work.

Quotes from the Holy Qur'an are offset with chapter and verse cited. The Holy Traditions of Prophet Muḥammad *(āḥadīth)* are offset and cited, in most cases. Historic dates are often referenced as "Hijri" and "A.H." (After Hijri), which is the commencement of the Islamic calendar, when Prophet Muḥammad migrated from Mecca to Madinah in 622 C.E. (Christian Era) to escape religious persecution and form his early nation. A reference calendar has also been provided.

Where gender-specific pronouns such as "he" and "him" are applied in a general sense, no discrimination is intended towards women, upon whom The Almighty bestowed great honor.

Islamic teachings are primarily based on four sources, in this order:

- **Holy Qur'an**: the holy book of divine revelation (God's Word) granted to Prophet Muḥammad. Reference to Holy Qur'an appears as "4:12," indicating "Chapter 4, Verse 12."
- **Sunnah**: holy traditions of Prophet Muḥammad ﷺ; the systematic recording of his words and actions that comprise the *ḥadīth*. For fifteen

centuries, Islam has applied a strict, highly technical standard, rating each narration in terms of its authenticity and categorizing its "transmission." As this book is not highly technical, we simplified the reporting of *ḥadīth,* but included the narrator and source texts to support the discussion at hand.

- ***Ijma*ʿ:** The adherence, or agreement of the experts of independent reasoning *(āhl al-ijtihād)* to the conclusions of a given ruling pertaining to what is permitted and what is forbidden after the passing of the Prophet, Peace be upon him, as well as the agreement of the Community of Muslims concerning what is obligatorily known of the religion with its decisive proofs. Perhaps a clearer statement of this principle is, "We do not separate (in belief and practice) from the largest group of the Muslims."
- **Legal Rulings:** highly trained Islamic scholars form legal rulings from their interpretation of the Qur'an and the Sunnah, known as *ijtihād.* Such rulings are intended to provide Muslims an Islamic context regarding contemporary social norms. In theological terms, scholars who form legal opinions have completed many years of rigorous training and possess degrees similar to a doctorate in divinity in Islamic knowledge, or in legal terms, hold the status of a high court or supreme court judge, or higher.

The following universally recognized symbols have been respectfully included in this work. While they may seem tedious, they are deeply appreciated by a vast majority of our readers.

ﷻ *subḥānahu wa Taʿalā* (may His Glory be Exalted), recited after the name "Allāh" and any of the Islamic names of God.

ﷺ *ṣallAllāhu ʿalayhi wa sallam* (God's blessings and greetings of peace be upon him), recited after the holy name of Prophet Muḥammad.

عليه السلام *ʿalayhi ʿs-salām* (peace be upon him/her), recited after holy names of other prophets, names of Prophet Muḥammad's relatives, the pure and virtuous women in Islam, and angels.

رضي الله عنها / رضي الله عنه *raḍīAllāhu ʿanh(um)* (may God be pleased with him/her), recited after the holy names of Companions of Prophet Muḥammad; plural: *raḍīAllāhu ʿanhum.*

ق represents *qaddasAllāhu sirrah* (may God sanctify his secret), recited after names of saints.

Transliteration

Transliteration from Arabic to English poses challenges. To show respect, Muslims often capitalize nouns which, in English, normally appear in lowercase. To facilitate authentic pronunciation of names, places and terms, use the following key:

Symbol	Transliteration	Symbol	Transliteration	Vowels: Long	
ء	ʾ	ط	ṭ	آ ى	ā
ب	b	ظ	ẓ	و	ū
ت	t	ع	ʿ	ي	ī
ث	th	غ	gh	**Short**	
ج	j	ف	f	ـَ	a
ح	ḥ	ق	q	ـُ	u
خ	kh	ك	k	ـِ	i
د	d	ل	l		
ذ	dh	م	m		
ر	r	ن	n		
ز	z	ه	h		
س	s	و	w		
ش	sh	ي	y		
ص	ṣ	ة	ah; at		
ض	ḍ	ال	al-/'l-		

Masters of the Naqshbandi-Haqqani Golden Chain

May Allāh ﷻ preserve their secrets.

1. Prophet Muḥammad ibn ʿAbdAllāh ﷺ
2. Abū Bakr as-Ṣiddīq ق
3. Salmān al-Farsi ق
4. Qasim bin Muḥammad bin Abū Bakr ق
5. Jafar aṣ-Ṣādiq ق
6. Tayfur Abū Yazīd al-Bistāmi ق
7. AbūlHassan ʿAlī al-Kharqani ق
8. Abū ʿAlī al-Farmadi ق
9. Abū Yaqub Yusuf al-Hamadani ق
10. AbūlAbbas, al-Khiḍr ق
11. ʿAbdul Khāliq al-Ghujdawāni ق
12. Arif ar-Riwakri ق
13. Khwaja Maḥmūd al-Anjir al-Faghnawi ق
14. ʿAlī ar-Ramitani ق
15. Muḥammad Baba as-Samasi ق
16. as-Sayyid Amir Kulal ق
17. Muḥammad Bahaʿuddin Shah Naqshband ق
18. Alaʿuddin al-Bukhāri al-Attar ق
19. Yaqub al-Charkhi ق
20. Ubaydullāh al-Ahrar ق
21. Muḥammad az-Zahid ق
22. Darwish Muḥammad ق
23. Muḥammad Khwaja al-Amkanaki ق
24. Muḥammad al-Baqi billāh ق
25. Aḥmad al-Farūqi as-Sirhindi ق
26. Muḥammad al-Masum ق
27. Muḥammad Sayfuddin al-Farūqi al-Mujaddidi ق
28. as-Sayyid Nūr Muḥammad al-Badawani ق
29. Shamsuddin Habib Allāh ق
30. ʿAbdAllāh ad-Dahlawi ق
31. Khālid al-Baghdādī ق
32. Ismail Muḥammad ash-Shirwāni ق
33. Khas Muḥammad Shirwāni ق
34. Muḥammad Effendi al-Yaraghi ق
35. Jamāluddin al-Ghumuqi al-Ḥusayni ق
36. Abū Aḥmad as-Sughuri ق
37. Abū Muḥammad al-Madani ق
38. Sharafuddīn ad-Daghestani ق
39. ʿAbdAllāh al-Faʿiz ad-Daghestani
40. Muḥammad Nazim Adil al-Haqqani ق

Recitation before Every Association

Aʿūdhu billāhi min ash-Shayṭān ir-rajīm.
Bismillāhi' r-Raḥmāni 'r-Raḥīm.
Nawaytu 'l-arbāʿīn, nawaytu 'l-ʿitikāf,
nawaytu'l-khalwah, nawaytu 'l-ʿuzlah,
nawaytu 'r-riyāḍa, nawaytu 's-sulūk,
lillāhi Taʿalā fī hādhā 'l-masjid.

Atiʿ ūllāh wa atiʿ ūr-Rasūl
wa ūli'l-amri minkum.

I seek refuge in Allāh from Satan, the rejected.
In the Name of Allāh, the Merciful,
the Compassionate.
I intend the forty (days of seclusion);
I intend seclusion in the mosque,
I intend seclusion, I intend isolation,
I intend discipline (of the ego); I intend to travel
in God's Path for the sake of God,
in this mosque.

Obey Allāh, obey the Prophet,
and obey those in authority among you.
Sūratu 'n-Nisā (The Women), 4:59

Ramadan Series Introduction: "Purify My House"

A'ūdhu billāhi min ash-Shayṭān ir-rajīm. Bismillāhi' r-Raḥmāni 'r-Raḥīm.
Nawaytu 'l-arbā'īn, nawaytu 'l-'itikāf, nawaytu'l-khalwah, nawaytu 'l-'uzlah,
nawaytu 'r-riyāḍa, nawaytu 's-sulūk, lillāhi Ta'alā fī hādhā 'l-masjid.
Ati' ūllāh wa ati'ū 'r-Rasūl wa ūli 'l-amri minkum. (4:59)

This Ramadan, *inshā'Allāh*, we will see a lot of changes and especially spiritual changes in the hearts of *murīds* of *awlīyāullāh*; more changes will be in the hearts of *murīds* of Sulṭān al-Awlīyā, Mawlana Shaykh Nazim al-Haqqani ق, who gave permission to speak on his behalf these kinds of lectures or this kind of knowledge, this Ramadan. Mawlana Shaykh Nazim mentioned to me to speak about the importance of *awlīyāullāh* in the life of human beings.

Allāh ﷻ said in the Holy Qur'an:
wa ṭāhhir baytī lil 'akifīn wa-ruka' us-sujūd.
Sanctify My House for those who compass it round, or stand up, or bow, or prostrate themselves (therein in prayer). (Sūrat al-Ḥajj, 22:26)

It means Allāh is giving an order to Sayyīdinā Ibrāhīm ؏, all the way to Sayyīdinā Muḥammad ﷺ, "Purify My House"; purify the status of the House, to make it ready for people to circumambulate it. Everything is pure, even the mass: the mass is what Allāh ﷻ created; this physical body is the mass and the house of the soul. The atom is the house, the mass of the electron, and since the mass is pure, the electrons circumambulate the mass; the electrons will not circumambulate if the mass is not pure or then everything will be still, with no life.

Allāh made everyone circumambulate a purified House of Allāh. The bees circumambulate their queen, birds circumambulate their mother and father, children circumambulate their parents. And Allāh ﷻ has made the soul in the body circumambulate a purified house in the body, and that is why Allāh said, *wa ṭāhhir baytī*, "Purify My House," to Sayyīdinā Ibrāhīm ؏, and Sayyīdinā Isma'īl ؏, and all prophets ؏, for the *tāifīn*, those who circumambulate the House, and the *'akifīn*, those who withdrew from *dunyā* or something they like, and everyone likes *dunyā*. But the *'akifīn* that Allāh mentions in Holy Qur'an are those *awlīyāullāh* who are away, but they are *ʿakifīn*; it means they sit and withdraw from *dunyā*.

The first level of *awlīyāullāh* is comprised of those who circumambulate in constant motion around the House. Those who are on a lesser level are withdrawing and doing *dhikrūllāh*, remembering Allāh through their hearts, but not circumambulating and standing. And the third level are those who are in *rukʿū* and prostrating in *sujūd*. "Clean My House," is meant for those who are in these three categories: who circumambulate continuously, who are not in *dunyā*, sitting, and those who are in *rukʿū* and *sujūd*.

That message applies to the House of Allāh ﷻ. Allāh made his angels make *sajdah* to whom? To make *sajdah* for the light of Sayyīdinā Muḥammad ﷺ that appeared in the forehead of Sayyīdinā Adam ؑ. That is why Imām Malik ؓ said to the *amir* of that time, "Don't turn your face to the *qiblah* in Madinah, turn it to the Prophet ﷺ, the one who took you to Allāh's House." So turning your face to Prophet ﷺ is the place where *awlīyāullāh* are circumambulating.

The *Ṣaḥābah* ؓ circumambulated the Prophet ﷺ, as his heart is the House of Allāh. The revelation of the message didn't come on the Ka'aba, it came on the heart of the Prophet, so that heart is what Prophet has given pure for the *ummah* to circumambulate.

Awlīyāullāh are inheritors from the Prophet ﷺ, so they have a direction for their *murīds* to run to them, to circumambulate their hearts, as it is the House of Allāh.

Prophet ﷺ said in Ḥadīth Qudsī:

qalb al-mu'min baytu 'r-rabb.
The heart of the believer is the House of the Lord.

mā wasiʿanī arḍī wa lā samā ' ī lākin wasiʿanī qalbi ʿabdī al-mu'min.
Neither Earth nor Heavens contained Me, but the heart of the believer contained Me.

So your direction is to find one of these purified hearts that you can withdraw from *dunyā* and do *murāqabah*, meditation, to them and they will take you to presence of Prophet ﷺ, and you must always keep their respect. An example of that is, someone asked one of the *awlīyāullāh*, "Can you tell me about the level of Sayyīdinā Abdul Qadir al-Jilani? What is his *maqām*?"

And he said, "One time Sayyīdinā Abdul Qadir al-Jilani was asked, 'Who is your shaykh?'"

man lā shaykha lahu shaykhahu 'sh-Shayṭān.
Who doesn't have a guide, his desires will be Shayṭān.

Because without a shaykh you cannot decide; you might see something wrong as correct and the correct as wrong. Sometimes the shaykh tells you, "Do this," and to you and to many others it is not correct, but to the shaykh it has *ḥikmah*, wisdom. You don't know the wisdom and they can see farther than you, and you will know the wisdom later, so don't object. What do we do? We complain and object; that order doesn't click in our mind. We think, "Why is he telling me to do this? It is *ḥarām*." Do you know better than the shaykh if it is *ḥarām* or *halāl*? No. So what must you do? Surrender!

So one time they asked Sayyīdinā Abdul Qadir al-Jilani ق, "Who is your shaykh?"

He said, "A long time ago I had a shaykh, Sayyid Hammad ad-Deebaas, but today it changed." Because Sayyīdinā Abdul Qadir al-Jilani ق kept respect to his shaykh, and he went very high, and after his shaykh left *dunyā* he became an inheritor and he reached higher levels. He said, "Today I am receiving knowledge from two oceans."

Look at how *awlīyāullāh* receive knowledge; not like us, because their hearts are purified. They buy machines today, saying, "This machine is a purifier." Purifier of what? Purifier of the pet dander that you cannot see, but they are there; it means the bad desires. You need a purifier to purify that animal dust and take it out, and then you need a humidifier to give you a nice breeze. So the heart of a *walī* purifies and humidifies the *murīd*, giving them that cool breeze at the end after purifying them. The shaykh knows the hearts of his followers. He might look at you and see that you need to do and he wants to empty your heart, though it might not coincide with what you believe. So he asks you to do something specific as he wants to take that away.

So Sayyīdinā Abdul Qadir al-Jilani ق said, "I receive from two oceans, Baḥr an-Nubūwwah, "the Ocean of the Heart of Prophet ﷺ," and from Baḥr al-Futūwwah, "the Ocean of Chivalry."

One is from the ocean of the Prophet ﷺ and one is from the ocean of Sayyīdinā ʿAlī ؓ, as Prophet ﷺ said:

la fatā illa ʿAlī wa lā sayf illa dhul-fiqār.

There is no chivalry except with Sayyīdinā ʿAlī and no sword except Dhul-fiqār (his sword from Heavens).

That means he was most powerful against his ego with his sword, not only on unbelievers. Mawlana Shaykh always tells us a story about Sayyīdinā ʿAlī ﷺ, when he was in battle, one of the unbelievers, a very strong wrestler, called Sayyīdinā ʿAlī bad names. Then they fought in one-on-one combat and afterwards the armies fought directly, not like today when soldiers don't even see the enemy. There is no chivalry today; they blow them up from far away. That is not chivalry, it is cowardice. And so, Sayyīdinā ʿAlī put him down and in war when you put someone down you have the right to kill him. So that wrestler said, "Okay, kill me!" and then he spat in the face of Sayyīdinā ʿAli. Immediately Sayyīdinā ʿAlī threw the sword down.

Again he said, "Kill me!"

Sayyīdinā ʿAlī ﷺ replied, "I cannot as I became angry and then it will not be for sake of Allāh."

Then that wrestler said, "If your religion is like that, then I will become Muslim." Then he took from the heart of Prophet ﷺ and the heart of Sayyīdinā ʿAlī ﷺ!

So there was a question that remained, just as today it stays in the hearts of *murīds*. They ask, "What is your shaykh's level?" We answer, "It is Sulṭān al-Awlīyā and he takes from the heart of the Prophet ﷺ." So that questioned remains until now.

They asked Sayyīdinā Imām Abu 'l-Hasan al-Shādhilī ق, a very famous *walī* buried in Egypt, "Who is your shaykh?" and he said, "My shaykh was Sayyīdinā ʿAbd as-Salam ibn Mashīsh ق," a very famous shaykh from Morocco, a big *walī*. "I used to receive knowledge from his heart and circumambulate his heart and sit looking at him, and I withdrew from *dunyā* looking at him and making *rukʿū* and *sujūd* in his presence. But today I am receiving from ten different oceans."

You don't understand how *awlīyā* are speaking; it depends on the time they are in. Today more *raḥmāh* is coming as we are in time of *fitna*. More of that power is coming to the *ghawth* and passing to the five *quṭbs*, and that makes us able to see with his light, as he is taking from Prophet ﷺ, who is ascending so high. By looking with the power in their eyes, they can turn bad into good! With their strong laser-like vision they can purify people from all their diseases and clean them only by looking, hearing, or touching.

Then they asked him, "Who is your shaykh today?"

"It was ʿAbd as-Salām ibn Mashīsh, but today I am taking from ten oceans: five from Heavens and five from Earth. I am receiving from their hearts directly."

He was taking from the heart of Abū Bakr aṣ-Ṣiddīq ق whatever Prophet ﷺ poured in his heart. And from Sayyīdinā ʿUmar al-Farūq ؓ, who fought *bātil,* of which there is too much today. And from Sayyīdinā ʿUthmān ؓ and from Sayyīdinā ʿAli, *karamAllāhu wajah wa ʿalayhi 's-salām,* taking from five.

About Sayyīdinā ʿAli, Prophet ﷺ said:

'ana madinatu 'l-ʿilmi wa ʿAliyyun babuha.
I am the city of knowledge and ʿAlī is its door. (al-Ḥākim, Tirmidhī)

And he ﷺ said, "Whatever I received, I poured in the heart of Abū Bakr." And ʿUmar was the one distinguishing *ḥaqq* from *bātil.* And Sayyīdinā ʿUthmān had two lights, two daughters of Prophet ﷺ and he was so generous.

Allāh ﷻ said:

taʿruju 'l-malā'ikati wa 'r-rūh u ilayhi fī yawim kāna miqdārahu khamsīn alfa sannah.
The Spirit and the angels ascend to Him in a day whose length is fifty thousand years. (Sūrat al-Maʿarij, 70:5)

He is receiving revelation from Jibrīl ؑ, and from Mikā'īl ؑ who sends rain, from Isrāfīl ؑ who blows the trumpet (it means he receives the power of that), and from Azrā'īl ؑ he receives power of the Afterlife, and from "*Rūh,*" the Angel of Souls, who carries all these souls. So this is how *awlīyā* receive their knowledge; they purified their hearts so their *murīds* can reach and take from that fountain in their hearts. And we have to know that to every *walī* Allāh ﷻ gave *khuṣūṣīyyah,* a specialization, a special job or way, unique to that *walī*; it is not the same to another *walī.*

Everyone has a different way, a different *mashrab,* fountain, and that fountain is like *naqsh ʿalā hajr,* engraving on stone, which is permanent and never disappears. So one *walī* knows another from what is engraved on his heart. That is why there are Ninety-nine Beautiful Names and Attributes, and from them the names of high-level *walīs* are engraved on his heart. So like *Allāhu lā ilāha illa Hūwa 'r-Raḥmānu 'r-Raḥīm,* Abdur-Raḥmān is receiving that knowledge from that secret of the Divine Name, "Ar-Raḥmān," and Abdur-Raḥīm is receiving from the Divine Name, "Ar-Raḥīm." We will explain them later, one by one.

As their hearts are purified, Allāh ﷻ is throwing in their hearts from 'Āḥadīyya, "the Ocean of Unique Oneness," and Wāḥidīyya, "the Ocean of Oneness." And especially in Ṭarīqah Naqshbandiyyah, we are receiving from an ocean that takes you to Maqām al-Fanā, "the Station of Annihilation," which Sayyīdinā Shah Naqshband ق pulled from heart of Prophet ﷺ.

That is why the *ṭarīqah* takes from his name, as he was able to take from secrets of these engravings, that every *walī* has a name, and he exposed them from a level we can understand, and it is a different level for each *walī* depending on the level in which he receives knowledge. There are *awlīyā* that stand at the feet of prophets, which means they receive directly from hearts of prophets. There are 124,000 prophets and there is a *walī* receiving from each prophet, and there is one receiving from the heart of Prophet Muḥammad ﷺ.

This is an introduction to what we will be speaking about this Ramadan, and I hope we can continue as much as we can.

So during this discussion, they asked Sayyīdinā Abdul Qadir al-Jilani ق from where he received his knowledge, and they asked Sayyīdinā Abū 'l-Ḥasan al-Shādhilī ق, and then they asked Sayyīdinā Abū Madyan ash-Shādhilī ق, who said, "I have *juld,* I traveled in knowledges of Allāh's Kingdom, and that is 101 oceans of knowledges. And Grandshaykh ق said what we will explain tomorrow *inshā'Allāh,* "To *awlīyāullāh* in this time, on every letter of Holy Qur'an, Allāh ﷻ opened from 12,000 to 24,000 oceans of knowledge that He will open to your heart and guide you through spiritual navigation."

As you navigate today with GPS, Allāh will navigate you with heavenly navigation, but only your soul knows, not your body, as they cannot open those secrets to our bodies. So that is coming to the hearts of *murīds* like a drizzle, dripping from different sides like a shower, so you get heavenly knowledges they throw in your heart to navigate you. Your soul understands, as you have *baya*ʿ with the shaykh, so Mawlana Shaykh is navigating our souls, but not openly; some are getting like a drizzle, some like a shower, and some receive like a thunderstorm.

May Allāh ﷻ forgive us and may Allāh bless us.

Wa min Allāhi 't-tawfīq, bi ḥurmati 'l-ḥabīb, bi ḥurmati 'l-Fātiḥah.
And with Allāh is success. For the sake of the Beloved, for his sake we recite the opening chapter of Holy Qur'an.

Characteristics of the Abdal

A'ūdhu billāhi min ash-Shayṭān ir-rajīm. Bismillāhi' r-Raḥmāni 'r-Raḥīm. Nawaytu 'l-arbā'īn, nawaytu 'l-'itikāf, nawaytu'l-khalwah, nawaytu 'l-'uzlah, nawaytu 'r-riyāḍa, nawaytu 's-sulūk, lillāhi Ta'alā fī hādhā 'l-masjid. Ati' ūllāh wa ati'ū 'r-Rasūl wa ūli 'l-amri minkum. (4:59)

Allāh ﷻ created His *awlīyāullāh*, saints, of different ranks. No *walī* crosses his limits; he knows where he stands and he is happy with what Allāh gave him. Why don't they cross their limits? There is wisdom there. Allāh puts in their hearts that they have reached the top level, the top point, and they feel they are at that highest level. Although they might be in a lower level, to them it looks like the highest level. That is why they keep content and happy, or else there would have been a kind of unaccepted complaint from that *walī*, that he wants to go to see the rank of the other one. So Allāh ﷻ hides them from each other and gives them the feeling that they have reached the highest station.

That is why you see there are 124,000 *walīs* and everyone thinks he is taking directly from Prophet ﷺ. But in reality they are taking from the one directly above them in rank, and they are all eventually receiving from the *ghawth*, the "al-Fard al-Jami'," who brings everyone together. There cannot be two or three who bring everyone together, there can only be one. And then going down to the level that Allāh ﷻ showed the beauty of the world of Jamāl, the Beautiful; when it is opened, they see beauty in everything, not only on Earth but in the universe, and when they reach it they cannot look at anything else but that beauty.

People here say there is competition in the arts, who is the best artist. From their drawings you can see this artist is better than that one. When *awlīyāullāh* see the beauty of what Allāh ﷻ created, they can no longer see that anything is not beautiful, so they are attracted to that beauty that Allāh ﷻ put in Earth and in Heavens.

When you admire people, when you open your heart to love people because you see that beauty, you are welcoming them through your arms and you are extending what you can give them in their lives. That beauty you see in them is the seed Allāh put, that small *tajallī* appearing through them. That is why the *walī* will be a magnet to them and even one look from him to them will take away their difficulties. And that *walī* will transfer that beauty to their hearts and give them a spiritual injection, so on the Day of Judgment they are under his control.

Not only did Allāh ﷻ give them that beauty to use in order to reach the maximum number of people, but He makes them travel throughout his universes and this Earth, from one place to another, to see more and more of those people who are lost or not lost, to bring them to Hazīrat al-Jamāl "the Garden of Beauty." If anyone enters that Garden of Beauty, they cannot come out of it.

That group of *awlīyāullāh* who are under the *ghawth* are five *quṭbs* (poles) that Allāh ﷻ established in *dunyā* to attract as many people as possible through their travels. They have power to travel through spiritual dimensions and they have power to travel through Earth. They can move through heavenly and earthly power and according to *ḥikmah* (wisdom) of Allāh ﷻ, they follow these two ways. Allāh ﷻ has made their hearts the place in which they can see His secret, *wa atlaʿtahum ʿalā shams asrārahum.*

In every secret there is a sun shining and every secret has been given to one of them. You cannot get the same secret the other one has, or else it is not a secret. Allāh ﷻ gave each one a certain secret he has to follow in order to reach *ʿirādatullāh* (Will of Allāh). He made their souls holy and he made their bodies heavenly. These *awlīyāullāh* have a pure heavenly, subtle body so that they are able to receive these secrets from the Heavens. And they have an earthly body through which they deliver the message that Allāh is sending to them through Prophet Muḥammad ﷺ.

Allāh ﷻ gave those five *quṭbs,* with the *ghawth,* who is the sixth at the top of them, the ability to mine. When you are searching for diamonds, you mine. You might go underground three-hundred feet or three-thousand feet to find diamonds. Allāh ﷻ gave them that power of mining in the hearts of people, to take away what is bad and evil and to put inside what is good.

Don't underestimate the power of a *walī;* they are able to reach from anywhere to anyone, but they prefer to show mostly their physical appearance, to see more people in need for support, and they support them. Allāh ﷻ gave them Quwwat al-Mujāhadah, the Power of Struggling, by putting Shayṭān down and putting *ḥaqq* (truth) in the hearts of people. Their lives are a struggle. They do not just sit, like many people who are lazy and their concern is only for this life, with no concern for the other life. So Allāh ﷻ has put in the hearts of these five *quṭbs* the Power to Struggle, to fight against Shayṭān, to remove *bātil* (falsehood) and to put *ḥaqq* in the hearts of people, and they can do this with the power of their eyes.

Sayyīdinā Aḥmad al-Badawī ق covered his eyes because anyone looking into his eyes fainted. When he reached the highest level possible, a *quṭb* came to him and said, "*Yā* Aḥmad! You need your trust, the key to that door. I have it."

He said, "I don't need the key from you, I need the key from Allāh."

The *quṭb* said, "Okay, try to get it on your own!"

He asked for that key and that *quṭb* disappeared. Finally, Aḥmad al-Badawī ق was hearing a voice coming to his heart, saying, "*Yā* Aḥmad! If you want that key, My key is with that *quṭb*. Go find him." And he went for six months looking for that *quṭb* and he didn't find him. That *quṭb* didn't appear; he was near him but Aḥmad al-Badawī was not seeing him. That *quṭb* didn't give him his key; instead he took all Aḥmad al-Badawī's knowledge, because it was based on his ego.

Show me today anyone who is not basing his knowledge on his ego. *ʿUlamā* today are so proud of their knowledge that they want to put in front of their names the title "Doctor." They want this not just for medical doctors, but so they are all *ʿalāmah*, a *pir*, a professor, a doctor, and that is from the ego. So most of today's *ʿulamā* are building their knowledge on their egos. *Awlīyāullāh* are building their knowledge on the Oceans of Prophet ﷺ that Allāh ﷻ is giving to him.

That is why Imām Muḥammad al-Busayrī ؓ said that everyone is taking from the Ocean of Prophet ﷺ. This is where we put our back, that is where our *ʿitimād* is: our support comes from Prophet ﷺ, our backbone, he supports us.

So these *aqtād* are highest in their levels. We won't elaborate that now; we will go through something else *inshā'Allāh*, but they are the highest of *awlīyā*, and when one goes his seat has to be filled immediately; it cannot remain empty. These five are: Quṭb, Quṭb al-Bilād, Quṭb al-Aqtāb, Quṭb al-Irshād, Quṭb al-Mutaṣarrif. With the eyes of their hearts and their head, all their attention is continuously focused on the *ghawth*. They take their daily assignments from him and he connects everyone to him, and he is taking orders from Prophet ﷺ.

And that is why, as there are five *quṭbs*, there are also five groups of *awlīyā* under them: Budalā, Nujabā, Nuqabā, Awtād, and Akhyār. They are looking at the *quṭb's* order, to execute it. Allāh ﷻ made them Āhlu 'l-Fadl, the People of Favor, and Allāh favors His servants. Therefore, they have to reach and share those heavenly favors with everyone.

So there is the *ghawth,* five *quṭbs,* and under the five *quṭbs* are five different groups. First of them is "Budalā," whom Allāh ﷻ made Āhlu 'l-Fadl and He made them so generous. They have to give to everyone, and they don't ask (about the state of that person); whether someone is saying the truth or not, they give *fi sābīlillāh,* in Allāh's Way.

They are always on *istiqāmah,* the Right Path. If you see something from them that you don't understand, don't object or you will lose, because they might do something your mind may not accept. But they know there is wisdom in it and their goals are there, because they are always on *istiqāmah,* the Right Path, so they know.

You might not always be on the Right Path; you might be on the diversion or the exit. The highway is straight and there are many exits. If you exit, you are not on the highway anymore. You cannot see what *awlīyāullāh* are seeing. You are exiting, maybe on the first or the second or the third exit. *Awlīyāullāh* don't exit. They stay on the straight highway, the Straight Path, Ṣirāṭ al-Mustaqīm.

So when you exit, you are looking from far away, and you might not see what the *walī* on the highway is seeing. Don't try to balance what the *walī* knows to your mind. Because Allāh made these *'abdal* to save themselves from imaginations, *khayāl. Takhallasū min al-khayālāt,* "They freed themselves from imagination." We normal people are full of imagination, like in the desert you see a mirage and you think you see an oasis of water, but you run and then you don't see anything. This is *wahm,* imagination, *khayāl.* A *walī* will see there is nothing there. That is why you need a guide; you cannot be alone.

Allāh ﷻ gave them four different assignments that are physical and four hidden ones that are spiritual. The first physical one the *abdal* have is to keep quiet; they don't talk. It is like what Sayyīdinā 'Alī ؓ said. "To save yourself (from sin), first is not to talk, *aṣ-ṣamt.*" When you talk you begin to show you know nothing. What is not to talk? It is not only not to talk to people, but to make your heart not to talk against people by throwing them with *sūw al-khāṭir,* bad thoughts. It means not only through your tongue, but *ṣamt* has to be through your tongue and your heart.

How much do we accuse people through our hearts and speak badly about them? Always these *Shaytanic* gossips come to our hearts or our minds, and we begin to say things that violate the rights of others. So Allāh ﷻ gave the *abdal* the physical power to keep quiet and that is why you don't know them. They might be in your physical presence but you don't know them, it might be they come in the appearance of a man you know or you don't know, and they keep quite.

And second, Allāh gave them power of *sahr,* to stay up all night, not to sleep. Can you stay up all night? It is not only physical sleep, but also their hearts do not sleep; their hearts remain continuously in divine service.

As related by Aḥmad in his Musnad, Prophet ﷺ said, "When you are in the jungle or desert and feel afraid, call on *ʿibādAllāh, abdal,* the Substitutes, *rijālAllāh,* and they will come and support you."

Everywhere is a jungle; to be around people or in gatherings is a jungle of people with different beliefs, thoughts, actions, behaviors, and ideas, and it is a jungle of bad, low desires. Allāh ﷻ gave the *abdal* power to go everywhere, because everywhere is a jungle; today there is no place pure on this *dunyā.*

Balad al-Ḥarām in Mecca is pure, and in Madinah it is pure, and in Masjid al-Aqsa it is pure, and in Shām (Damascus) it is pure; Allāh ﷻ gave us these. But even in these pure places, today people are not behaving correctly. It is a jungle, so they need *awlīyāullāh, abdal,* to reach them. They are taking orders from *quṭbs* and they do that. "Go here, go there, appear in this place and appear in that place." Sometimes they use normal, physical means and sometimes they use spiritual means. They don't like to show *karāmah,* miracles, they want to show normality to everyone.

Allāh ﷻ gave them the power of *sahr ʿalā rāḥat an-nās.* If a baby is sick in the hospital, you stay with her all night. They look after everyone through their spiritual means in order to lift up that one who is losing his faith or losing his duties during the day. They reach him and they don't differentiate from one to another, as they have orders to reach everyone in need.

Always, if there is food they eat and if there is no food, they don't care, they don't eat. *Al-jūʿ* is one of their characteristics, hunger. They want to feel with everyone, that there are poor people with no food, to sympathize with them, they do not eat. And this I saw in Grandshaykh ق and in Mawlana Shaykh Nazim ق; they don't eat, but we run to fill our stomachs and graze.

They always seclude themselves. They have this characteristic of being away from people. When they need to appear, they appear, but otherwise they seclude themselves.

So they carry these characteristics, especially *aṣ-ṣamt,* which is to keep quiet. Their speech is only *dhikrūllāh.* You see always Allāh's Name on their tongue, either *dhikr* of *Allāh, Allāh,* or *lā ilāha illa-Llāh,* or *ṣalawāt* on Prophet ﷺ.

They don't sleep because they are busy during the nights reaching people when everyone is sleeping. And also, the spiritual meaning of sleeping is *ghaflah,* to be heedless, and they don't allow themselves to be heedless. They are always looking at the five *quṭbs,* and the five *quṭbs* are always looking at the *ghawth,* who is always looking at Prophet ﷺ.

These characteristics of the *abdal* are important to understand, how *awlīyāullāh* interact and react. Some people like stories and some like something else, but since we entered this ocean, we have to finish it.

The characteristics Allāh ﷻ gave them is from the inner circle of *abdal,* as the *abdal* range in number—some *aḥadīth* say they are forty, some say seven. The highest level of *abdal* travel from their places, leaving behind their bodies, taking out from their bodies another copy, and they travel *dunyā* looking for people that need help and they help them. That is why when you see a *walī* who looks like they are sleeping, their soul left their body. In that state, don't wake them up, otherwise you will make a mistake, unless they instruct you, "Wake us up at that moment." That means you are calling them back; when they tell you, "Wake us up," it means, "Call us back;" then you are like an alarm for them, but if they don't say anything to you, don't wake them up.

I saw this with Grandshaykh ق and Mawlana Shaykh Nazim ق. One time I was passing by the window of Grandshaykh's ق room, going where there was *dhikr* and a window. One self was telling me to look and one self was telling me not to look, because when you witness certain things you cannot control yourself, but if you don't look you miss the opportunity.

So I looked and I saw Grandshaykh ق sitting like that and opening his mouth. And I was shocked to see that, you know on cold days when you go out and you blow and you see fog coming out? What was coming out was light. And from his head a greenish color and from his mouth, white color was coming up and they were mixing, like a rainbow. The whole ceiling disappeared and you saw it going up through this universe until you cannot see it anymore. And at that moment I was shaking.

"Why are you looking at something that does not belong to you? Run from here." *Alḥamdulillāh* I took the opportunity to see that, I didn't miss it. Keep him supporting us, *yā Rabb,* and give Mawlana Shaykh long life.

So when you see *awlīyāullāh* on the bed or floor or chair as if they are laying down sleeping, don't touch them or wake them up as they are not present there. For seven days Grandshaykh ق in seclusion left his body and went when Sayyīdinā Shah Naqshband ق appeared to him in a vision in *khalwah*. He left his body for seven days, no movement.

And his wife ran to Grandshaykh Sharafuddīn ق, Grandshaykh's uncle, and said, "ʿAbdAllāh Effendi died."

He said, "No, he didn't die. Leave him, he will be back in seven days."

Awlīyā have that power. If they tell you, accept. If they don't tell you, you are free to do what you like. But *al-amru fawq al-adab,* "the order is above good manners." If it is good manners not to drink from a cup, and if Shaykh tells you "drink", you do it. Don't say, "O Shaykh, it is your cup, it is not my cup." If the shaykh says go to this place, you go. Don't say, "I don't." Go! That is an order above good manners. In his heart it is higher than what you are thinking. There is wisdom to do that. And that is why you see them and always they know if there are objections. And

Grandshaykh ق said, bless his soul, "I never give an order except to two of my students. He used to say Nazim Effendi, Ḥusayn Effendi. They never have doubts. When Shaykh gives you an order, don't try to balance it in your balance. Don't say, "I have this, that, busy here or busy there." No, do it. One day he said to me, "I want you to take me downtown in the car." Grandshaykh ق. And it was a very new car. I will cut the story short. Would you like to hear it? (Yes, sir.) I said it before, where did I say it?

Alḥamdulillāh, my elder brother and my father liked to drive cars and so always we had the latest cars, ten cars. And every year we had new cars. One year we bought a very fancy car, very expensive, a sports car, and it was a Jaguar. And my brother and I said, "Let's go to visit Mawlana in this car." So we arrived and went up to visit him.

He said, "Today I like to go with you to the market, so you take me down."

We said, "OK." So we were happy, since it was a fancy car, and it was a small car, a sports car.

He came down and said, "What is this? This is garbage. Do you think this is a car? Naqshbandis must have the best. Change it, go get a big car."

So we went down to the market and it was small.

He said, "I want to buy wood."

You know, they cut the wood there and sold it. So Mawlana Shaykh filled the car with wood and all the dirt that comes from the wood was coming in the small trunk and on one of the seats.

And he said, "Next time don't come with that car, bring a big car." He was teaching, "Don't have love of *dunyā* in your heart."

Now, according to our minds, this was the best car. But he was giving to our mind that *dunyā* must not be *akbar hamminā,* most of our attention. So the next time, our father bought a Lincoln Continental, a big car with beige seats.

We said, "*Alḥamdulillāh,* we will take this car." We went to Syria.

Grandshaykh ق said, "*Yā, awlād,* I want to go buy something from the market." So we took him in that car and he said, "This is a car for the Naqshbandi." So they like students to be the best. If you are poor, no problem, but act and speak the best, then people will see this *ṭarīqah* as something great.

Don't look poor! That means don't look poor in your appearance, look rich, *mutaḥammis,* to have zeal, *yazal,* showing that you are great with this *ṭarīqah,* that you are not a stinky person, a poor person in your manners. Have rich manners: accept and not deny, give and not be greedy, love and extend your hand to everyone! Even if you receive from others what you don't like, don't give it back.

Keep good relationships. For seven years Prophet ﷺ had a neighbor throwing garbage on his door, and he never complained. Every morning at Fajr time, he saw the garbage and he took the garbage and didn't tell anyone. And finally that neighbor was dying, after seven years and he went to see him. And that neighbor said, "O *Rasūlullāh,* seven years I am giving you a hard time. If this is Islam, then I accept Islam." That is the teaching of *awlīyāullāh.*

So we took Grandshaykh ق and he said, "Take me to the charcoal market." There are two kinds of charcoal, the wood one, the long one, and there is the coal from inside the ground, which has a lot of dust. He bought bags of charcoal and said to the merchant, "Put it in the trunk," and that trunk became dusty black. And that was not enough; he put charcoal on the seats and he beige, clean color became all-black. And he was happy, looking at us to see what we were going to say. What you can say? And so they tell you, "Don't look at our actions; there is wisdom in it." It means don't make your heart dirty like charcoal dust; keep your heart clean." If they say, "Do this," do it. "Don't do this," don't do it. Then you will be successful.

We will continue later. May Allāh ﷻ forgive us and keep us under the mercy of His Prophet, Sayyīdinā Muḥammad ﷺ, and under Allāh's mercy, and the mercy of *awlīyāullāh.* Without that we are lost.

Sayyīdinā Muḥammad al-Busayrī ق said, *Tūba lana ma'ashar-Islāmi inna lana min al-ināyati ruknan ghayra munhadim,* "Good tidings for us, the People of Islam!"

He ﷺ said, *ma'ashar al-Islām,* "People of Islam", not, *ma'ashar al-muslimīn,* "Muslims". It means People of Islam are those who accept Islam with its perfection. Muslims are not in perfection, so Muslims are not in good tidings. Those who are perfecting their Islam have good tidings. Those who are not, who backbite, do not receive good tidings. He said, "Good tidings to the People of Islam. *Inna lana min al-inayāti,* "Allāh ﷻ granted us from His endless blessing a supporting pole that is never falling down." That means the Prophet ﷺ.

O Muslims! As Mawlana says, O Attenders! If we lose love of Āhlu 'l-Bayt, then we lose love of Prophet Muḥammad ﷺ, as it says in Holy Qur'an:

Qul lā asalukum 'alayhi ajran illa 'l-māwaddata fi 'l-qurbā.
Say: "No reward do I ask of you for this except the love of those near of kin."
(Sūrat ash-Shūrā', 42:23)

Say, O Muḥammad, "I am not asking any return for what *dawa* I am delivering to you. I am not asking anything, I will give you everything. But I only ask one thing: love my family. Keep *wud,* compassion, emotions, love for my family."

Where is love for Prophet's family today? Where are you, Ahl as-Sunnah wal-Jama'ah, showing love to Prophet's family? That is what we are ordered to do. Allāh is saying in Holy Qur'an, *Qul lā asalukum 'alayhi ajran illa 'l-māwaddata fi 'l-qurbā.* "I am not asking anything for what I do for you, but to love my family and care for them," to the Day of Judgment. Are you looking? Where are Āhlu 'l-Bayt? Write his name, write his email, and make a collection of Āhlu 'l-Bayti families. There must be millions in this time from Āhlu 'l-Bayt! Do you have a relationship with them?

That is what Prophet ﷺ is asking, "I am asking only to keep love to them." That means you must look for them, and especially some Āhlu 'l-Bayt who are *awlīyāullāh.* Do you look for them?

And that is our message: Allāh ﷻ put *awlīyāullāh* everywhere in the world to guide us to Āhlu 'l-Bayt, to see them and to take *barakah* from them. Most, if not all *awlīyāullāh* are from Āhlu 'l-Bayt. Look at Sayyīdinā Salman al-Farsi ؓ, who is not from the blood of Prophet ﷺ, but whom Prophet made to be from his family because of his love for him, and they considered him to be from Āhlu 'l-Bayt.

Prophet ﷺ left an authentic *hadīth,* "I am leaving behind two things, that you never lose the way: *kitābullāh,* the Book of Allāh, and *ʿitratī,* my family." He put his family up with the Book of Allāh. Look after Āhlu 'l-Bayt. If you are really *ʿulamā* you know that He honored them to be from Āhlu 'l-Bayt. Not everyone is from Āhlu 'l-Bayt. Allāh ﷻ gave them that love from Prophet ﷺ, and everyone has to respect them. May Allāh ﷻ give us the respect that is needed for Āhlu 'l-Bayt, and may Allāh bless us.

Wa min Allāhi 't-tawfiq, bi ḥurmati 'l-ḥabīb, bi ḥurmati 'l-Fātiḥah.
And with Allāh is success. For the sake of the Beloved, for his sake we recite the opening chapter of Holy Qur'an.

Knowledge of Taste and Knowledge of Papers

Aʿūdhu billāhi min ash-Shayṭān ir-rajīm. Bismillāhi' r-Raḥmāni 'r-Raḥīm. Nawaytu 'l-arbāʿīn, nawaytu 'l-ʿitikāf, nawaytu'l-khalwah, nawaytu 'l-ʿuzlah, nawaytu 'r-riyāḍa, nawaytu 's-sulūk, lillāhi Taʿalā fī hādhā 'l-masjid. Atiʿ ūllāh wa atiʿū 'r-Rasūl wa ūli 'l-amri minkum. (4:59)

Man dhāqa ẓafar, wa man lam yudhiq khasir, "Who tastes will succeed or win, and who does not taste will lose, and between succeeding and losing there is no description and no resemblance." The one who succeeds will know the purity and the taste of that food. The one who is not tasking is like a patient who has lost taste in his mouth. Whatever you give him of the best food or grass, it is the same.

If you give grass to the one who has the ability to taste, he will not take it, he will say, "No, give me the best of what you have. I am looking at your generosity, give me from the best." The other one is sick, a patient, so whatever you give him he will take, because he just wants to fill his stomach as he has no taste. It is like feeding someone by a stomach tube to keep him alive. But the one you are feeding through the mouth is far better, because he has the sense of taste and he will appreciate what Allāh gave him.

Awlīyāullāh are the ones who have taste. For those who are not reaching that level, it is very difficult to explain it to them because they don't feel it. It only becomes like ʿIlm al-Awrāq, Knowledge of Papers, with no more knowledge of taste. And not everyone can reach ʿIlm al-Adhwāq, Knowledge of Taste, because there is a problem within us that we are not able to overcome: we allow our ego ride us. However, *awlīyāullāh* are able to ride their egos. Allāh said in Holy Qur'an:

> *Wa aʿaida lahum mastaṭaʿtum min quwwatin wa min ribāṭ al-khayli turhibūna bihi ʿadūwuallāhi wa ʿadūwakum.*
> *And prepare against them all you can of power, including steeds of war, to strike terror into (the hearts of) the enemies of Allāh and your enemies.*
> (Sūrat al-'Anfāl, 8:60)

Electricity has power that if you touch, you can faint or maybe die. Power is a strong support that Allāh is sending to us. When Allāh is saying, "Prepare for them power," that means power to make your enemy faint or be killed. When Allāh orders something, it means he is giving support for that and the support is there. *Awlīyāullāh* take that support, not accepting their own power, but to take from Allāh's Ocean of Power, Baḥr al-Qudrah. When they take from there, they are supported against their Shayṭān who keeps running after everyone. Prophet ﷺ said, "I am the only one on earth that *aslāmtu* Shayṭān, I made my Shayṭān surrender to me."

Who is the biggest enemy to Prophet ﷺ? It is the one who refused to make *sajdah*. When Allāh ordered angels to make *sajdah* to Adam ؏; he refused due to seeing that light of Muḥammad ﷺ in Adam's forehead. Out of jealousy he refused, claiming, "Why he has to take Maqām al-Maḥmūd and not me?" and so Allāh cursed him. Prophet said, "I made my Shayṭān surrender." That means, "I made Iblīs surrender to me." It means, "O Iblīs! You have to know I am Muḥammad; Allāh gave me Maqām al-Maḥmūd, and He sent me as a mercy to humanity! As much you run after people of my *ummah*, they are mine and you will not succeed because the *ummah* is for me! Whatever you make them do, I am taking them to Paradise." For sure Prophet ﷺ will not allow that anyone will go without *shafā'a*. He said:

Shafa'atī li ahl al-kabā'ir min ummatī.
My intercession is for the big sinners of my nation. (Tirmidhī)

This means the small sinners are already included, because all of us do sin. Although Allāh gave Prophet *shafā'a* and he will take the *ummah* with him to Paradise, we must still struggle to make our Shayṭān surrender, we must not leave it loose. Don't leave your horse loose. You cannot hold the horse, you have to keep the reins in your hands. Allāh ﷻ said:

Wa a'idda lahum mastaṭa'tum min quwwah.
Against them make ready your strength to the utmost of your power.

"Whatever you can prepare, whatever you are able to, do it!" That means Allāh will not burden you with more than you can carry. Allāh is "al-Ghafūr" and "*Arhamu 'r-rāhimīn*." Whatever you can do, struggle against Shayṭān! People are not your enemy. Today they say, "This country is an enemy to us." They want to make enmity.

Wa jazāu sayyi'atin sayyi'atun mithluhā faman 'afā wa aṣlaḥa fa-ajruhu 'ala Allāh. innahu lā yuḥibbu 'ẓ-ẓālimīn.
The recompense for an evil is an evil like thereof, but whoever forgives and makes reconciliation, his reward is due from Allāh. Verily, He likes not the oppressors. (Sūrat ash-Shūrā', 42:40)

Why make enemies? If I make a rocket, you make a rocket. If I make an atomic bomb, you make an atomic bomb. For what? This is arrogance, to say, "I am stronger than you and I want you to be under my feet." In this way they create enmity. Allāh ﷻ is telling you your enemy is Shayṭān, no one else. So if you want to succeed, prepare whatever power you can for that struggle. It is like struggling to start a car in winter. You want to run it, but on cold days it doesn't start. You try and try, and then after a while, it starts. You keep trying until the battery finishes. Allāh is saying to keep struggling until your battery is finished; then you have surrendered to Allāh ﷻ. Don't lose hope! Allāh said, *min ribāṭi 'l-khayl,* "prepare reins." He didn't say, "Prepare horses only." You need a horse to fight your enemy, which means you need a vehicle.

O Muslims! You have to know that every word in the Holy Qur'an has a meaning; not the meaning that comes to your mind, but thousands of meanings! He told you to prepare your power and then prepare your vehicles, horses. You must prepare your reins. How do you control that horse? You need a vehicle that will take you wherever you are going and which is under a command. In a car you have brake, whether it is a stick shift or automatic. You have everything on an airplane to make sure you are running it well. You cannot run a car without a steering wheel. Allāh is saying that you have to prepare horses, but you have to be ready with reins.

And the example of that is, one of the *awlīyāullāh,* Sayyīdinā Abāyazīd al-Bistāmī ق, who reached a highest level in his time. He was able to hear heavenly voices coming. He was in the Kaʿaba holding the round chain that opens the door to the Kaʿaba, saying, "*Yā Rabbī*! Give me permission, only five minutes to catch Iblīs. I will catch him and chain him so that he cannot run after *Ummat an-Nabī.*" One *walī* has that power, so what do you think of other *awlīyā*? Allāh gave them power as they prepared themselves.

A voice came to his heart, "*Yā* Bayāzīd, why are you asking? Do you think I cannot stop Iblīs? Without a second or a moment, with no time, if My Will comes to stop it, immediately he is melted! He will disappear from this universe. *Yā* Bayāzīd! Look up above you at the *multazam,* at the door of Kaʿaba."

He looked up and fainted. Allāh left him in that state, and after a while he came back to normal, and began to crawl around the Kaʿaba saying, "*Yā Rabbī ʿafwak wa riḍāk,* Your forgiveness and Your mercy! I made a mistake to interfere in Your Will. I am asking forgiveness."

Allāh ﷻ said, "*Yā* Bayāzīd! What you saw is My manifestation of My mercy descending on My House."

Ṭāhhir baytī li 'ṭ-ṭā'ifīn wa 'l-ʿakifīn wa 'r-rukaʿi 's-sujūd.
That they should sanctify My House for those who compass it round, or use it as a retreat, or bow, or prostrate themselves (therein in prayer).
(Sūrat al-Baqarah, 2:125)

"I am sending that mercy on my House. *Yā* Bayāzīd! If you catch Iblīs that means no one is going to struggle, and I give My mercy to those who are struggling. If there is no Shayṭān, it is as if people are living in Paradise, then all are on the same level. But I let them struggle to manifest on them My mercy. And when My mercy is manifested, those who receive more are more near, those who receive less are farther away."

That is why *awlīyāullāh* are able to prepare that power, that possibility of, "prepare your power". Sometimes you see on a remote control or in cars, or anywhere else, a button labeled "power". If you don't press that button, nothing works, although you continue to play with the remote. Press the power button and all the other buttons will work, even thousands of buttons. Look at a space shuttle, how many thousands of buttons it has? But they need one button in the beginning. If you open that one button, then everything opens to you and then you can taste everything. There is a button with 10 watts or 20 watts, or 30, 240, 360, 1,000 volts, 10 megavolts, or 100 megavolts; it depends on how strong your button is.

Allāh ﷻ said, "O Bayāzīd! However much I am sending and people are taking by struggling against their egos and purifying themselves, they are going to receive that *raḥmāh*!"

Why Allāh sent *Ummat an-Nabī* or all of humanity to circumambulate His House? Why do we have to go there to circumambulate, are we going to circumambulate the walls? What is inside? Some people go inside, and they find it just like the outside. The inside is not visible, it is like an X-ray, not visible to your eyes but visible to the eyes of the machine. Are the eyes of a machine better than your eyes? No. So why can't our eyes see, and the eyes of the machine can? Because the button for our eyes is not pressed. You press the button on the machine to give it power. *Awlīyāullāh* have pressed that button already.

That is why they are explaining about those five different types of *awlīyā* and the many different groups. But all of them come under a leader, as all prophets come under the Seal of Messengers, Sayyīdinā Muḥammad ﷺ. All *awlīyā* come under the *ghawth,* who inherits from the heart of Prophet. His button is huge, and under him are the five *quṭbs,* and under them are five groups of *awlīyāullāh.* We mentioned the five *quṭbs:*

Quṭb, Quṭb al-Bilād, Quṭb al-Mutaṣarrif, Quṭb al-Irshād, and Quṭb al-Aqtāb. And under each there are five groups and under them, there might be up to 70,000 *awlīyā*. Under each *quṭb* there is a head of each group; head of Budalā, head of Nujabā, head of Nuqabā, head of Awtād, and head of Akhyār. And under each of them come 70,000 *awlīyā* that are spread out, and all have power buttons. Some have more, some have less. They have prepared themselves, they have that power.

But without a vehicle you cannot move; their guides as their vehicle. That is why it is very important to have a vehicle. You need to have *quwwah, wa aʿidda lahum,* and He added on that *wa min ribāṭi 'l-khayl,* "from reins of horses." That means you need a vehicle with reins that takes you to safety. *Turhibūn bihi ʿ adūwullāh wa ʿadūwakum,* "(You will) strike terror into (the hearts of) the enemies, of Allāh and your enemies." Who is Allāh's enemy? Allāh's enemy is Iblīs. And who are human beings' enemies? They are devils and evil *shayṭāns,* and Iblīs. How do you terrorize them? By not listening to them; then they become upset with you and come more heavy on you. That is what happened with Sayyīdinā Abū Yazīd al-Bistāmi ق.

One time he was visiting Madinah al-Munawwarah, the *maqām* of Prophet ﷺ, and it was raining heavily. He saw someone holding a lot of reins and passing them to people who were also there to visit. He was putting a rein on every one's mouth. Abū Yazīd ق looked at him with a normal look; he is a man, giving them reins like we put on horses. Then he looked with heavenly power and saw that is Iblīs. There is a place in everyone's heart where he can enter. *Thumma āmanū, thumma kafarū.* One time we are in belief, one time we are in unbelief; one leg here, one leg there. We hope we are always on the good side and for when we are on the bad side, we hope Allāh forgives us.

Abū Yazīd ق said, "Do you have reins for me?"

Iblīs replied, "O Bayāzīd! For all of these I have reins, but you I will ride without reins!"

For that one moment of heedlessness, it came. *Awlīyāullāh* are not *maʿsūm* (innocent) like prophets. One moment made him fall.

He said, "I don't need reins to ride you, these are easy."

And Abū Yazīd ق cursed him saying, "O you *malʿūn*!"

For the next few days it rained constantly. You know the Earth there doesn't swallow rain water for the benefit of people, to make streams to run. Madinah was flooded, water was coming up to the necks of people. I saw that one time in Mecca. Entire Mecca was flooded and in the Kaʿaba water reached to your neck. This was when we were doing *ṭawāf* with Mawlana Shaykh Nazim ق in 1979. We did the first *ṭawāf,* then the second, the third, and at the beginning of the fourth *tawaf,* Shaykh Nazim ق stopped.

He raised his hands and said, "O Allāh! We are coming all the way here. Send us Your mercy, send us the rain." And he made a *du'ā* that I had never heard before, a very strong one. When he finished his *du'ā* we began the fourth *ṭawāf.* As soon as we passed Hajar al-Aswad, clouds came from everywhere, formed a thunderstorm, and it began to rain. There was no possibility for the rain water to drain. The Ka'aba was filling up, the Ḥarām filled with water up to our necks. I experienced that.

So when the water filled up in Madinah, Abū Yazīd ق saw an old man in trouble, and he asked that one, O! May I help you?"

He said, "I have to cross from here to there."

So Abū Yazīd ق said, "Okay, I will carry you," and he climbed on Abū Yazīd's back.

When they reached the other side and Abū Yazīd helped him to dry ground, that one turned smiling and said, "You see Abū Yazīd! I told you I will ride you without reins!"

From one moment of heedlessness he had to pay that big invoice, that big price. Allāh ﷻ gave *awlīyāullāh* that power to prepare their strength in order to defeat Shayṭān for the benefit of the *ummah.* That is what we were describing yesterday, the Budalā, the first of these *awlīyā* after *quṭbs.* There are too many powers, spiritual and physical, that we explained some yesterday. This is an abbreviation between two brackets, only to understand that we are explaining, reading, or teaching from papers, but Mawlana wants us to taste what he wants to say. It is very hard to understand how these *awlīyā* work. So now between the brackets there is an insert to show you that there are such men to whom Allāh gave authority for the benefit of all humanity. May Allāh ﷻ forgive us and bless us.

Wa min Allāhi 't-tawfiq, bi ḥurmati 'l-ḥabīb, bi ḥurmati 'l-Fātiḥah.
And with Allāh is success. For the sake of the Beloved, for his sake we recite the opening chapter of Holy Qur'an.

Saints Dwell in What Allah Likes

A'ūdhu billāhi min ash-Shayṭān ir-rajīm. Bismillāhi' r-Raḥmāni 'r-Raḥīm.
Nawaytu 'l-arbā'īn, nawaytu 'l-'itikāf, nawaytu'l-khalwah, nawaytu 'l-'uzlah,
nawaytu 'r-riyāḍa, nawaytu 's-sulūk, lillāhi Ta'alā fi hādhā 'l-masjid.
Ati' ūllāh wa ati'ū 'r-Rasūl wa ūli 'l-amri minkum. (4:59)

Two or three days ago, Mawlana Shaykh gave a *ṣuḥbah* in which he said, "I have to go down to that level so we can learn where we are standing. However high you think of yourself, you are never going to see yourself higher than a president or a king of a country." He said, "O presidents, O kings of countries! Where do you think you are flying?"

There is nothing higher than that in *dunyā,* in the ego realm. This is important for us to learn, to understand later what are the meanings of the various levels and ranks, and I will repeat them another time. There is the level "Ghawth", and under him the five *quṭbs*: Quṭb, Quṭb al-Bilād, Quṭb al-Aqtāb, Quṭb al-Irshād, and Quṭb al-Mutaṣarrif. Under every one of these there are the five different groups of *awlīyā;* Budalā, Nujabā, Nuqabā, Awtād, and Akhyār.

It is difficult to understand their levels or what they do, because if we meet one of them, we see something of *mughayyar at-tafkīr*, contrary to what we think. You think this way, that is correct, but that *walī* is acting differently and you protest, complain, and sometimes you run away and say, "What is he doing?" You don't know; it might be a test for you.

Allāh ﷻ gave a big example in Holy Qur'an of Sayyīdinā Mūsā ﷺ, who came with Sharī'ah, the heavenly constitution. Allāh sent him to one of His servants, Sayyīdinā Khiḍr ﷺ, to whom He gave a different kind of knowledge, and Sayyīdinā Mūsā was not able to keep patience with that one. *innaka lan tastaṭi' ma'īya sabra.* He (Khiḍr) said to him (Mūsā), "You cannot be patient with me." If he was patient, the knowledge would have opened up, but Allāh wants us to learn, so He used this as an example for us.

To go along with someone to whom Allāh ﷻ has given a knowledge different from yours, you will not meet (come to terms), because their knowledge is the destruction of the ego, they want to destroy your ego and kill it. So what did Sayyīdinā Khiḍr ﷺ do first?

Fantalaqā ḥattā idhā rakiba fi 's-safīnati kharaqahā. Qāla akharaqtahā li tughriqa āhlahā. Laqad ji'ta shayan imrā.
So the two set out until, when they were in the ship, he made a hole in it. (Moses) said, "Have you made a hole to drown the folk therein? Verily you have done a dreadful thing!" (Sūrat al-Kahf, 18:71)

When they went on the boat, what did he do? *Allāhu Akbar*! He made a hole. It might be that he had some kind of drill at that time, so he drilled it. How did he make the hole? It didn't mention in Holy Qur'an that he had equipment. If there was equipment, it was a very old kind of equipment and it would take a long time to make a hole. But with the heavenly power Allāh ﷻ gave to him, *wa 'alamnāhu min ladunna 'ilma,* "We have taught him from heavenly knowledge." (18:65) By looking, he made a hole. So what happened? *Qāla akharaqtahā li tughriqa āhlahā,* Sayyīdinā Mūsā ؑ asked, "Did you make a hole in order to make it sink and drown the people within it?" Of course, that is the Boat of Safety. What is the boat? It is to take you from a shore to another shore. But that vehicle you went on is your ego. That is why *awlīyā* want to make a hole in your ego. They want to suck away your ego, to throw it out and then you don't need it anymore. Even if there are hundreds of holes, the body will fly, as when Sayyīdinā Jalāluddin ar-Rumi ق was whirling, he was rising and was lifted up as gravity was no longer able to pull him down.

Sayyīdinā Mūsā was unable to accept that hole, and he complained. Sayyīdinā Khiḍr said, "I told you, you are not patient." How did Allāh ﷻ give Sayyīdinā Khiḍr, *al-jassāra ḥattā yukhāṭib Mūsā bi hadha 'l-khiṭāb*? He gave him that bravery or courage to speak like that to Sayyīdinā Mūsā, who is *ūlū 'l-ʿazam,* one of the five highest prophets. Sayyīdinā Khiḍr must be bowing to Sayyīdinā Mūsā, giving respect and honor to Sayyīdinā Mūsā. But Allāh ﷻ gave him that courage to teach, not Sayyīdinā Mūsā, because it may be Sayyīdinā Mūsā was hiding his reality from Sayyīdinā Khiḍr to teach us, so we may learn.

He said, "Why did you do that?"

So Khiḍr said, "I told you, you will not be patient with me! Wait for the second step."

That first incident is easy. The second one was, they left the boat and it was sinking, sinking, sinking. When they reached the other shore, Sayyīdinā Khiḍr killed a boy.

F'anṭalaqa ḥattā idhā laqīya ghulāman fa qatalahu qāla aqtalta nafsan zakīyyatan bi ghayri nafsin laqad j'ita shayan nukrā.

Then they proceeded until, when they met a young man, he slew him. Moses said, "Have you slain an innocent person who had slain none? Truly a foul (unheard of) thing you have done!" (Sūrat al-Kahf, 18:74)

Sayyīdinā Mūsā ﷺ said, "How? First we understand the boat, but now you are killing someone who did no sin."

Sayyīdinā Khiḍr ﷺ repeated, "I told you that you are not going to be patient with me."

That is why it is very difficult to go along with these *awlīyāullāh*. Yesterday they were telling me there were viewers on Sufilive who could not go along. They love the shaykh, but they said, "We see things around the shaykh that we don't understand." They are around the shaykh but cannot understand how he does not object. He is in complete submission to Allāh's will, whatever Allāh put for him. For such people, whatever comes or goes, they submit.

People cannot accept or understand, so they complain. But they have to know that the *walī's* knowledge is not equal to the knowledge of normal people. If Allāh ﷻ doesn't give you that knowledge, you cannot understand the work of someone who has that knowledge. It is like what happened with Sayyīdinā Mūsā ﷺ, who is not a normal person—he is a prophet and a messenger—but Allāh ﷻ didn't give him that knowledge, to show him, "What I give you, I give you. What I give someone else, don't try to ask about it."

And then Khiḍr did the third thing for Mūsā.

F'anṭalaqa ḥattā idhā ātayā āhla qaryatin istaṭ'amā āhlahā fa abaw an yuḍayyifūhumā fawajadā fīhā jidāran yurīdu an yanqaḍḍa fa aqāmahu qāla law sh'ita lattakhadhta 'alayhi ajrā.

Then they proceeded until, when they came to the inhabitants of a town, they asked them for food, but they refused them hospitality. They found there a wall on the point of falling down, but he set it up straight. (Moses) said, "If you had wished, surely you could have exacted some recompense for it!"

(Sūrat al-Kahf, 18:77)

The third incident was, they entered a village and saw a wall completely falling apart and the treasure that was under it was going to be exposed. So Sayyīdinā Khiḍr ﷺ immediately restored the wall, although when they entered they asked people to host them and they refused. This means that when someone harms you, return it with goodness. And Sayyīdinā Mūsā ⌘, in his Sharī'ah, constitution, it is written, *Al-'ayn bi 'l-'ayn*, "An eye for an eye." If someone pokes your eye, you poke his eye. *Wa 's-sin bi 's-sin*, "and a tooth for a tooth." If someone broke your tooth, you break his tooth. In another Sharī'ah of Sayyīdinā 'Īsā ⌘, whoever hits you on your right cheek, turn the left for him to hit.

In the Sharī'ah of Prophet ⌘, the highest level of *iḥsān* is to submit. If they hit you, don't move, because when you turn, as Sayyīdinā 'Īsā ⌘ said, "When they hit you on your right, turn for them your left," ego is there. It is saying, "I am better than you. You are hitting me on my right, and I am turning for you my left, beat me also." There is some kind of egoism there. But in the Maqām al-Iḥsān as taught by Prophet, you submit. They beat you on the right, they beat you on the left, they beat you on the head, wherever they beat you, you are submitting.

To understand *awlīyāullāh* is very difficult. But we are giving these examples so that even if we can't explain, at least we can understand their powers. So Mawlana Shaykh Nazim ق said, "O presidents and kings! I am sorry to say this," and I am quoting, "but I have to say it. You are sitting in your big palaces and sometimes meeting other presidents. And then a bell is ringing. What do you do? You leave the important session entirely and run, responding to that bell. Because that place is calling you, 'Come, come to me, I am waiting. I love you. I want to see you there. I cannot be without you. Leave your palace and come to my toilet quickly!' So you leave your palace and go down to that place." Especially if you have a bad stomach, it keeps ringing and you might cancel all your meetings!

Allāh is showing no matter how you can be the highest, don't think you are the highest. "I made you to be in need for the lowest." Don't see your ego. *Awlīyāullāh* don't like you to *as-sima'*, listen to your ego or to something coming out of your ego; they want you to listen only to what Allāh and His Prophet are ordering you.

Man yuṭi'i 'r-rasūla faqad atā'ullāh.
Whoever obeys the Prophet obeys Allāh. (Sūrat an-Nisā, 4:80)

Mā atākumu 'r-rasūl fakhudhūhu wa mā nahākum 'anhu fantahū.
Leave what Prophet forbade and take what he ordered. (Sūrat al-Hashr, 59:7)

So, in order to understand, Imām Shādhilī ق said, *alfaw ābāuhum ḍāllīn*, "They followed traces and footsteps of their ancestors who are on the wrong way." Don't follow their footsteps or their traces, they are *ḍāllīn*, "on the wrong path;" they deviated from the right path. Prophet ﷺ said, "We are, *naḥnu ummatan wasaṭan,* a moderate nation, in the middle, not on the two extremes." We are not on the right side too much and not on the left side too much, but in the middle. We are not so liberal; we have to know our limits. Know your limits, like in a country you have laws and you have to know your limits, you cannot trespass them.

Why do some people say, "You have to be liberal, if you are liberal your Islam is good." No, that is not correct. You are liberal in the meaning of what Islam is giving you, in the knowledge of the constitution. And you are liberal in the meaning of what your country's constitution is. You cannot trespass against it. Can you trespass against the police and say, "I don't want to give my ID or my driver's license." What will happen? You will go to jail. If the police say, "Give me your ID," what do you say? "Yes, sir! This is my ID." Be moderate. Don't say, "no," or you will end up in jail.

Awlīyāullāh look at you and they know what is your ID. If they say, "Give us your ID," you don't say, "no." This means you have to submit. When you don't submit to your shaykh, you're finished. Even if you do whatever you like to do, you cannot be raised up. *Al-amru fawqu 'l-adab. Amr,* the order of the shaykh, is above your knowledge, even if you are the biggest scholar. How a scholar of Islam, those who knew that matter, came to the *shuyūkh* and it might be that the shaykh is not on the academic level of the scholar, but he is a *walī* in spiritual, heavenly knowledge, which is better. You have to surrender to him even if you are the biggest scholar and you know everything. No, you know everything by *awrāq,* papers, but you don't know everything by taste. Taste is different. Even if he gives you a small sip of taste, any, it is enough for you to save you on the Day of Judgment, because he gave you something that refreshed your body Today they say an "energy pill" gives you energy.

So Imām Shādhilī ق said, "Don't follow your ancestors who deviated; if they were wrong, don't follow them."

> *Innahum alfaw ābā'ahum ḍāllīna fahum ʿalā 'āthārihim yuhraʿūn.*
> *Verily, they found their fathers on the wrong path, so they (too) made haste to follow in their footsteps!* (Sūrat aṣ-Ṣāffāt, 37:69,70)

They followed the footsteps of their ancestors, but they were wrong. But as we said, when the *walī* gives you an order, the *walī* is above your decisions and knowledge, so even if you think it is wrong, you must do it.

Of course Sayyīdinā Khiḍr knew you cannot make a hole in a boat. But he made a hole, as there was wisdom in saving that boat from the king who was a tyrant. He was taking the boat of every poor person. Allāh didn't show that knowledge to Sayyīdinā Mūsā, but showed it to Khiḍr. So when they asked Imām Shādhilī ق about *sim'a,* hearing, he said, "Be careful of what your ego wants you to hear. Only hear what Allāh wants you to hear. Ego likes you to hear itself and it doesn't allow you to hear what Allāh wants."

And he said, *rā'ita bi 'l-manām ka-annī bayna yadayya kitāb al-faqīh ibn 'abd as-salām. wa fi yadihi 'l-yusrā awrāqan min ash-sha'r. fa tanāwala ustādhī al-kitābayn minnī wa qāla lī ka 'l-mustahzī ata'dilūna 'ani 'l-'ilm az-zakīyya,* "I saw in a dream, as if between my hands is the book of one of the famous scholars, al-'Izz Ibn 'Abd as-Salām. And in the left hand, *awrāqan min ash-sha'r,* 'papers of poetry.' One is a book of a very scholarly *walī*; he is a scholar and a *walī* at the same time. And in the left hand is a book or papers of poetry."

Today they study Sayyīdinā Jalāluddin Rumi's ق poetry. Do they know more than that? They explain but do not understand the taste of his knowledge; they read it as poetry.

Imām Shādhilī ق continues, "I saw my teacher standing and saying, *fa tanāwala kitāba faqīhihi bi-yamīnihi wa awrāq sha'ar bi yassārih.* "I saw the books of Abdus-Salām in his right hand and in his left hand, a book of poetry. And he said sarcastically, *ata'dilūna 'ani'l-'ilm az-zakīyya fa ashār ila awrāq ash-sha'r fa ramāhā fi'l-arḍ,* 'Are you balancing? What kind of value are you giving? Do you prefer the poetry over the scholarly writings of that *faqīh*?' And he took the poetry and threw the papers on the floor. He said, *fa man akthar min hadha fa-hūwa 'abda hawwāhu wa asīru shahwatahu wa munāhu,* 'Who will give more attention to these papers of poetry,' (opposed to the real knowledge of *awlīyāullāh), fahuw 'abdun marqūqan li 'l-hawwā,* 'he is slave of his desires,' *wa asīran li shahwatih,* 'and he is a prisoner to his bad desires and he is also a prisoner to what is *munā,* something that is good, but he became a prisoner to that arrogance or pride of that kind of knowledge that is in poetry.' And he said, *yastariqūn qulūb al-juhalā,* 'This poetry is only to attract the hearts of heedless people.'"

When they write these songs and sing them, it is not in Allāh's Way. It is describing *dunyā* and making all children, youth, and adults run to it. They don't listen to Imām al-Busayrī ق, they say it is *bid'a.* When someone is describing Prophet ﷺ and something heavenly, they say, "That is *bid'a.*" They run after their desires.

Imām Shādhilī ق continues, "They have no will to do goodness or to reach Gnosticism. They will never reach what the People of Vision will reach." Allāhu Akbar! They sway when they hear Shakespeare. You see how they go and dance, especially to songs of Hollywood and the Middle East. There are more cable stations now for Arabic popular music than stations teaching *irfān*, Gnosticism, real spirituality!

They are only listening, and they think what satisfies their egos is all there is. But they are not able to visualize that what they are hearing is what Allāh wants. Allāh wants you only to hear *dhikrūllāh.* He wants you to hear only His Name and to be remembering Allāh and his Prophet ﷺ.

alā bi dhikrūllāhi taṭma'inu 'l-qulūb.
In the remembrance of Allāh do hearts find satisfaction. (Sūrat ar-Raʿd, 13:28)

And that is what Grandshaykh ق is mentioning:

Wa ṭāhhir baytī li 'ṭ-ṭā'ifīn wa 'l-ʿakifīn wa 'r-rukaʿi 's-sujūd.
And sanctify My House for those who compass it round, or stand up, or bow, or prostrate themselves (there in prayer). (Sūrat al-Ḥajj, 22:26)

Allāh has *ghīra,* possessiveness. He wants His servant to be for Him only, not for Iblīs or Shayṭān. He wants you to be only for Him! When Prophet ﷺ demonstrated he was for Him, Allāh raised him, calling him for Miʿrāj. He raised him by putting his name with His Name before all Creation, because He loves him. He doesn't want anyone to share that. What are we doing? We are running after ourselves and our desires and excitement. *Lā in lam yantahi ẓāliman lā,* "If that oppressor who does not follow the footsteps of Prophet ..."

Qul in kuntum tuḥibbūn-Allāha fattabiʿūnī yuḥbibkumu Allāhu wa yaghfir lakum dhunūbakum w'Allāhu ghafūrun Raḥīm.
Say, "If you love Allāh, follow me (Muḥammad). Allāh will love you and forgive you your sins, for Allāh is Oft-Forgiving, Most Merciful."

(Sūrat 'Āli 'Imrān, 3:31)

Don't listen to what is coming to your ear. You have to check, as you are not yet ready. If you don't have a real shaykh but only a fake shaykh, what comes to your ear might not be correct. A real shaykh can correct you from far away and even fix your hearing. Allāh said if you are an oppressor, not listening to what He likes, he will flip you upside-down. Heavens will be Earth and your Earth will be Heavens.

He said, "No, it is not what you are explaining." See how the shaykh interferes quickly. *idhā kānat ar-rū bi-amṭāri 'l-ʿulūmi dāratun wa 'n-nafs bi ṣāliḥati nabātatun,* "If the soul has been showered with heavenly rain, the rain of knowledge, it is going to be *dāratun,* like pearl, glowing and shining, and whatever the ego is doing will come out from it, as when grass grows it comes up and grows under the rain of that knowledge. That is okay. That is why, with the knowledge that Allāh showered on Sayyīdinā Khiḍr ﷺ, he was under it. Whatever his *nafs* did, whatever he did, was okay. Although he made a hole in the boat, killed the boy, and built the wall, it was okay. Meaning he gave you a vehicle with a hole, it cannot reach anywhere. But even if it has a hole, the way you are going has lots of holes and will make all your good *ʿamal* disappear.

You must be careful. Then when you are careful, kill the boy (the ego). And when you submit, *ʿallamnāhu min laddunna ʿilma.* When he stopped Shayṭān from attacking the treasures of your heart, he made it safe for you in a safety box so Shayṭān cannot touch it.

Therefore, if the showers on the soul are *dāratun,* showering you with that knowledge, the soul will grow, and then the heavenly self will do what is written according to Allāh's will. Then *thabat al-khayr kullih,* "Confirm whatever you do."

But what if the self was successful, *wa 'r-rūḥu maghlūbatan,* and the soul is defeated by the ego? That is why you have to be careful of what you listen to. Today when they go to the music areas, they sway. So he said, *idhā kāna an-nafs ghālibatun illa ḥaṣal al-qaḥṭ wa 'l-jadab,* "If the ego was successful, then there will be no crops and there will be famine and drought." Everything will be finished. Whatever you do will not be fruitful. *Fa anqaḍa al-amr wa jā ash-sharr kullāhu,* "then the issue will be delivered and complete evil will ensue. Therefore, we say *al-amr fawq al-adab,* do what they say." Don't say, "What is this or that?" Kill the boy, kill the boy!

Sayyīdinā Mūsā ﷺ is teaching *Ummat an-Nabī* that if you allow the soul to be conquered, all of your affairs will be upside-down and evil will come. So then what do you need? You need Allāh's words that will guide you, and the words or knowledge of His Prophet ﷺ that will cure you. Allāh ﷻ guides and Prophet cures. Allāh shows you the way; that is His will, and Prophet shows you what you need. *Awlīyāullāh* take from the heart of Prophet ﷺ as he guided the *Ṣaḥābah* ﷺ. *Awlīyāullāh* can follow the way of *Ṣaḥābah* ﷺ, how they interacted with Sayyīdinā Muḥammad ﷺ, the Seal of Messengers.

wa āhlu 'l-ḥaqq idhā samiʿū al-laghwa ʿariḍū ʿanhu. wa idhā samiʿū al-ḥaqq aqbalū ʿalayh.
And if People of Truth hear nonsense they leave it, and if they hear words of truth they run to it.

wa man yaqtarif ḥasanatan nazid lahu fīhā ḥusnā.
And if any one earns any good, We shall give him an increase of good in respect thereof. (Sūrat ash-Shūrā', 42:23)

"And those We reward more and more."

So these are some of the characteristics of *awlīyāullāh. Inshā'Allāh* in this series we will explain more, and describe the levels of different *awlīyā.*

Wa min Allāhi ʿt-tawfīq, bi ḥurmati ʿl-ḥabīb, bi ḥurmati ʿl-Fātiḥah.
And with Allāh is success. For the sake of the Beloved, for his sake we recite the opening chapter of Holy Qur'an.

The Story of Imam Ahmad ibn Hanbal

*A'ūdhu billāhi min ash-Shayṭān ir-rajīm. Bismillāhi' r-Raḥmāni 'r-Raḥīm.
Nawaytu 'l-arbā'īn, nawaytu 'l-'itikāf, nawaytu'l-khalwah, nawaytu 'l-'uzlah,
nawaytu 'r-riyāḍa, nawaytu 's-sulūk, lillāhi Ta'alā fī hādhā 'l-masjid.
Ati' ūllāh wa ati'ū 'r-Rasūl wa ūli 'l-amri minkum. (4:59)*

*I*f some people don't have eyeglasses they can't see, and with eyeglasses they see. So eyeglasses are important for those who don't have perfect vision, and if they don't have perfect vision, they are nearsighted, measuring minus one, minus two, three, or four, up to minus twenty, which is total blindness. And also a person might be farsighted. If you can't see, you need eyeglasses, which means you need someone to show you the way. And that's why Abū Yazīd al-Bistāmi ق, one of the greatest *awlīyāullāh*, said, *man lam yakun lahu ustādh fa imāmahu 'sh-Shayṭān*, "Who doesn't have a guide, his *imām* is Shayṭān, the devil." And it is said, *man lam yakun lahu shaykh fa-shaykhahu 'sh-Shayṭān*, "Who doesn't have a shaykh, his shaykh is whatever gossips come to his heart, and he will follow that."

So *awlīyāullāh* reach that station not because of their progress in scholarly matters, but because their guides guided them. So the importance is on the guide: how strong he is and how much power he has to guide those who are listening and following his teachings. That is very important to know and understand. It's not so easy that you will be able to reach higher stations by reading books and studying, but it's important to reach when your guide is teaching, and Allāh ﷻ guided everyone to something or someone. He guided the *Ṣaḥābah* ؓ and *Ummat an-Nabī* to Prophet ﷺ, who said, "Whoever you follow from my *Ṣaḥābah*, you will be rightly guided."

This is an example from one of the biggest scholarly shaykhs and many people follow his *madhhab*, that in his time two big *imāms* of Islam were following, like teacher and student: Imām Shafi'ī ق and Imām Ahmad ibn Ḥanbal ق. Imām Aḥmad ibn Ḥanbal was following Imām Shafi'ī, and after Imām Shafi'ī passed away, Imām Aḥmad ibn Ḥanbal established his own school of thought, which today many people follow. He was a very scholarly person, and all of the *a'immah* (Imāms) were, but this is one example.

One time Imām Aḥmad ibn Ḥanbal was in an association with Imām Shafi'ī and suddenly one *walīyullāh* came, whom Imām Shafi'ī respected a lot. And I heard from Grandshaykh ق, and it is very well established in Sharīʿah that the water from ablution is dead water because it takes all your sins and illnesses. The water of *wuḍū* cleans you and then it becomes dead and you can't use it. That's why some people throw it in the garden or outside, because you can't consume it. So they were discussing some issues and Grandshaykh ق said, "When that *walī* came to Imām Shafiʿī 's association, not talking, only listening, people didn't give attention to him. But when he made ablution, Imām Shafiʿī used to drink that water, although he knew in Sharīʿah you can't drink it, but he drank it for *barakah*. That was Shaybān ar-Rāyy ق, a very high *walī* who was also *ummi,* illiterate, but Allāh ﷻ doesn't look at who is literate or illiterate, and He made his heart and tongue connect.

So Shaybān ar-Rāyy ق came and sat with them in their association and at that moment Imām Aḥmad ibn Ḥanbal looked at Imām Shafiʿī and said, "O my shaykh! *li unnabīh hādha ʿalā nuqsāna ʿilmihi.* I want to emphasize and bring to the attention of that person!" He didn't call Shaybān ar-Rāyy by name, he only said, "that person," not giving importance. "He must complete his knowledge as he doesn't know anything!" Then he pointed to Shaybān ar-Rāyy, saying, "I want to bring to his attention that he is lacking *ʿilm, li yashtaghil li tahsīli hādha 'l-ʿilm,* so he will go and learn a little bit."

Today they say you need a certificate, a paper that says you are an *ʿālim,* or else they consider you are nothing. How do they know you are nothing? Shaybān ar-Rāyy ق didn't know how to read or write, and Imām Aḥmad ibn Ḥanbal ق wasn't giving him importance.

Imām Shafiʿī ق said, "Wait, don't say anything or he will humiliate you!"

Aḥmad ibn Ḥanbal insisted, "No! My duty is to make him aware that he has no knowledge!"

Today if you don't have doctorate, if you are not a PhD, they think you don't know anything; for them, you have to be a doctor of Sharīʿah, but that *walī* is not a doctor in Sharīʿah. That means *awlīyāullāh* don't know that (knowledge from papers), only Allāh ﷻ chooses them. When Allāh chooses them, it is finished.

Wa 'anā 'khtartuka fastamiʿ limā yūḥā.
I have chosen you; listen then to the inspiration (sent to you).

(Sūrat Ṭāhā, 20:13)

Allāh ﷻ said to Sayyīdinā Mūsā ؑ, "If you know Sharī'ah or not, I choose you." Allāh chooses His *awlīyā*, and not everyone becomes *walī*. But when Allāh chooses, the matter is finished. Allāh said, *anā 'khtartuka fastami' limā yūḥā*, "Listen to what I am giving you and go and deliver it."

Bismillāhi' r-Raḥmāni 'r-Raḥīm.

> *Yā ayyuha 'l-muddaththir, qum fa andhir wa rabbaka fakabbir wa thīyābaka faṭāhhir wa 'r-rujza fahjur.*
> *O you wrapped in your cloak! Arise and warn! Your Lord magnify, your garment purify, and pollution shun.* (Sūrat al-Muddaththir, 74:1-5)

"O Muḥammad! You, the one who is covering yourself." Prophet ﷺ was shivering at that time, *qum fa andhur*, "Wake up, go and deliver the message, and glorify your Lord." *Wa thīyābaka faṭahhir*, "And go purify your clothes." Which clothes; what we wear, or the clothes of the heart? They cover this physical body, which is the cover of the heart, a piece of flesh, but what is inside it? Can Allāh not put inside the flesh what He put inside Ka'aba? What is inside Ka'aba? It is four walls and inside are *asrārullāh*, Allāh's secrets, and what He manifested on that House no one knows, just as what He put in the heart of Prophet no one knows!

> *Fa-kayfa idhā ji'nā min kulli ummatin bi-shahīdin wa ji'nā bika 'alā hā ūlā'i shahīdā.*
> *How then if We brought from each people a witness, and We brought you as a witness against these people!* (Sūrat an-Nisā, 4:41)

"When we have brought from every *ummah* a *shahīd*, witness." That means Allāh chose a witness from every *ummah*. *Wa ji'na bika 'alā hāūlā'i shahīda*, "And We have brought you, O Muḥammad, as a witness over all of them." That means, "We brought these prophets first and then *awlīyāullāh* as witnesses on their followers that are on the right path and rightly guided, and We are not confirming that until you, *yā* Muḥammad, make witness on all of them, the prophets and the *awlīyā*!"

Was Sayyīdinā Mūsā ؑ educated? No. It means if Allāh ﷻ chooses, He chooses. And Sayyīdinā Muḥammad ﷺ is *nabī al-ummī*, the prophet who never opened a book or read. Today, what is knowledge? Show me what do they teach in Azhar ash-Sharīf, in Shām, Morocco, or Hijāz? They teach what is in books and no longer give importance to spiritual knowledge. Let the shaykhs of Azhar go to where Imām Shafi'ī ق is buried there.

This story is from two main scholars, Imām Shafiʿī and Imām Aḥmad ibn Ḥanbal. Imām Shafiʿī was following Shaybān ar-Rāyy and said to Imām Aḥmad, *lā takūn jassūran,* "Don't encourage yourself to question him as he will humiliate you.

He said, "No, no, no! My job is to tell him he needs this kind of teaching and to go and learn.

And Imām Shafiʿī said, *lā tafʿal,* "Don't touch on that subject; leave him alone."

And Imām Aḥmad asked Shaybān ar-Rāyy, *madhā taqūl fiman nasīya ṣalātuh min aṣ-ṣalawāt al-khams fi 'l-Islām, fi 'sh-sharīʿah,* "What is the judgment of someone that the time of the prayer passed and he didn't pray, he forgot?" It needs knowledge. Today there are too many different schools of thought and they give different answers. Like the Wahhabis and Salafis say, "Don't repeat it as the time is gone, so even if you pray *qadā,* make it up, it is not accepted."

They believe there is no *qadā,* but other schools of thought say it is an obligation to make it up, and they believe that *qadā* prayer it is not perfect, but nevertheless you have to make it up so you will learn discipline. Those are two different schools.

So Imām Aḥmad was checking Shaybān ar-Rāyy and said, "You don't know anything! What is the *ḥukum*? Give me the judgment of Sharīʿah. What do we say to this question? Give me a *fatwa.*" Shaybān ar-Rāyy laughed and Imām Aḥmad became more frustrated, he wanted to humiliate him in front of Imām Shafiʿī .

Shaybān ar-Rāyy answered, "*Yā* Aḥmad! Are you challenging me?"

Aḥmad ibn Ḥanbal began to shake, and Shaybān ar-Rāyy said, "Your question is like that of a child. How dare you ask me such a question? Don't you know you are ignorant for asking that? *Yā* Aḥmad, *qalbun ghafala ʿan Allāh fa yanbaghī an yu'addab ḥattā la yaʿūd ilā ghaflatihi,* a heart that becomes heedless of Allāh's Presence for one moment must be disciplined. That means you must be disciplined when you come and ask such a question. How dare you ask someone whose heart is with his Lord in every moment, that if he misses a prayer what he has to do! If you miss a prayer you have to be disciplined, *ḥattā la yaʿūd ilā ghaflatihi.* That means, don't ask that childish question! Your heart has to be in Allāh's Presence, if your heart is there you will never miss a prayer."

That is like someone who has no heart, what will happen? Throw him in the grave. That heart must be disciplined so you don't become heedless another time. And at that moment Imām Aḥmad fainted, he had a heart attack from the power of those words of Shaybān ar-Rāyy.

Imām Shafi'ī said, "Leave him until he comes back to normal and leaves asking such childish questions." When he woke up, Imām Shafi'ī said to him, *alam aqul laka lam tata'arad lahu*, "Didn't I tell you not to bother him? So don't bother him! If you bother him, this is your end."

Don't bother *awlīyāullāh*; don't come against them or they will make you to faint. What happened to Sayyīdinā Mūsā ؏? He fainted! He said, "O my Lord, let me see You." You cannot; when Allāh ﷻ wills, you will see without questioning. Allāh made him faint to make him learn. That is why *awlīyāullāh* are always fainting in Allāh's Divine Presence, surrendering. So don't come to a *walī* and criticize; they will humiliate you from their powers.

And I heard the continuation of this story from Grandshaykh ق: When Imām Aḥmad woke up he crawled on his chest to Shaybān ar-Rāyy, asking for forgiveness and seeking his guidance.

So two *imāms* were taking from Shaybān ar-Rāyy, and he was illiterate! Also, Imām Abū Ḥanīfa bin Nu'man ق took knowledge from Bishr al-Hāfi ق. If an *ummī*, one who cannot read or write, is a powerful *walī* that is able to put down Imām Aḥmad ibn Ḥanbal, what do you think about a *walī* who is literate, who knows everything? What about his power; what can he do? If you see that one *ummī* from *awlīyā* has this power, what do you think if Allāh gives them heavenly knowledge, then what can they do? They can make a hole in the boat!

> *Fantalaqa ḥattā idha rakiba fi as-safinati kharaqaha. Qāla akharaqtaha li tughriqa ahlaha. Laqad ji'ta shay'ān 'imrā.*
> So the two set out until, when they were in the ship, he made a hole in it. (Moses) said, "Have you made a hole to drown the folk therein? Verily you have done a dreadful thing!" (Sūrat al-Kahf, 18:71)

What did Sayyīdinā Khiḍr ؏ do? He made a hole in the boat, then killed the boy, and then he built the wall. So he drowns you to take all your bad characteristics, and then he kills your ego, and then he builds the wall of treasures in your heart. So don't bother *awlīyāullāh*, because they have many ways to bother you. In every moment of your life they can bother you!

Grandshaykh ق said, "Every day the shaykh has to look at the *murīd* three times. When he looks he doesn't send candies, but he sends him poison, to check if they are handling difficulty or not." So when you get in difficulty remember that your shaykh is looking at you, and don't get angry. I am not speaking about business difficulties, I am talking about *murīd*-to-*murīd*, or people-to-people, who get angry with each other, who lie about what they are doing, and this and that. Be careful and remember at that moment the shaykh is observing you. That is why today, I am going to tell these two *(murīds)* not to go back home, but to stay here! (laughter)

So that is why they said, *laylī bi wajhika mushriqun wa ẓalāmahu fi 'n-nāsi sāri*, "My night in your face is daylight," or, "When I am looking at your face, O my shaykh, my night is daylight shining. Even if it is night, when I look at your face in dark nights I see that *ḍīyā*, that shining of the sun on Earth. Your face is shining, *wa ẓalāmahu fi 'n-nāsi sāri*, but the darkness of the night in the faces of the people is dark, but in your face it is sunlight. *Wa 'n-nāsu fi sadaf aẓ-ẓalāmi*, and the people are in darkness, *wa lākin naḥnu fi ḍaw an-nahār*, and we are with you, O our shaykh, O our *walī*, in the daylight." That means, "When you are among us it is daylight, but when we are with people it is darkness." That is why we always have to watch what we are doing, what we are saying, and what we are putting in our hearts.

It is said that Rābiʿah al-ʿAdawiyyah ق got sick. They asked her, "What is the cause of your illness? Why are you sick?" She didn't have the flu, a heart attack, or any physical sickness, but spiritually she was depressed. They asked her, "Why are you depressed?"

Today if you ask people, "What are you doing?" they will answer, "I am getting counseling from a psychologist." He is a psychologist who himself needs a psychiatrist! If you need a psychologist, go to a *walī* because he knows your needs.

Rābiʿah al-ʿAdawiyyah ق said, "Oh, I have a major problem."

They said, "You, a lady saint?"

And ladies complain they have no saints! There are many. The Prophet's wives are Ummuhāt al-Mu'minīn, "Mothers of All Believers" ﵅.

No one can reach their ranks, or the ranks of the lady Companions of Prophet ﷺ or the lady teachers after them. But this psychological problem is in the minds of ladies because of the rudeness of men.

They said, "Why are you depressed? Did anyone from the *jamaʿat* bother you?"

She said, *wa lākin naẓartu ilā 'l-jannata bi 'l-qalb*, "No. I gazed at the Heavens with my heart. I was in a trance, a spiritual state, and that opened, and I looked at the Heavens through my heart."

To us that is good, but for her it was not good, because she made a mistake according to her rank. *Fa ghāra ʿalayya qalbī,* "My heart got jealous from me, because my heart doesn't want to have partners or have anyone other than Allāh ﷻ. It asked, how am I looking through my heart to Paradise when I have to look with my heart to Allāh ﷻ? I fell into this big sin, this mistake."

Look how they are so sensitive when their heart moves a little bit! Although she was looking at the Heavens, she moved one second to heedlessness. For us it is perfect, but for her it was a heedless moment that her heart went to look at Paradise and left looking at Allāh ﷻ.

Her heart asked, "How do you dare look at Paradise? I (your heart) has to always be in that Divine Presence!" That's why Prophet ﷺ said:

lī wajhun maʿ Allāh wa lī wajhun maʿ al-khalq.
I have one face (presence) with Allāh, and I have one face with the ummah.

That means, "I don't let anything interfere," *yaghār ʿalā awlīyā'ihi wa anbīyā'ihi.* Allāh ﷻ doesn't like to share anyone with His servants! We will continue tomorrow about Ḥaqīqat al-Ghīrah, the Reality of Jealousy, and what is the jealousy that *awlīyāullāh* are trying to get rid of. So it means, be aware of the power of your shaykh. Don't let anyone share with you your love to your shaykh. Your love must be to your shaykh, from your shaykh to Prophet ﷺ, and from Prophet to Allāh ﷻ.

So Shaybān ar-Rāyy ق scolded Imām Aḥmad ق, saying, "Why are you asking me about missing prayers when every moment I am in prayer? How can you miss a prayer when you are always in that Presence? That prayer time is heavenly time." Shaybān ar-Rāyy is showing him, "Not only am I praying in *dunyā* time, but in heavenly time also. Do you know heavenly time, O Aḥmad?"

"No, I only know *dunyā* time."

One time Grandshaykh ق and Mawlana Shaykh ق said that Sayyīdinā Bilāl ؓ was standing to call *adhān*, and Prophet ﷺ said, "Wait," and as soon as he said, "Don't call *adhān,*" he said, "Call *adhān.*" Sayyīdinā Bilāl was surprised. Prophet explained, "The moment from when I said 'wait' to the time I said 'call', the sun moved fifty thousand years." That means in that moment the Bayt al-Mā'mūr moved. The reality of Kaʿaba is the reflection of Bayt al-Mā'mūr, the real House of Allāh ﷻ located in the Fourth Heaven, where Prophet ﷺ prayed with all prophets in Laylat al-'Isrā' wal-Miʿrāj.

So *adhān* is not on our time, it is on the time that Prophet accepted in the holy night; he established the times and we pray on the time of Bayt al-Mā'mūr in Mecca and Madinah. It is not when we pray Dhuhr in America, for (by then) already it was prayed in the Heavens! But the right time was what Prophet ﷺ established. Allāh ﷻ (accepts our prayer) as made at the right time, but in reality, the right time is when Prophet prays.

Who can give you such knowledge if not an inheritor of the secrets of Prophet? You don't know how *awlīyāullāh* act and what they know, from knowledge they inherited from the heart of Sayyīdinā Muḥammad ﷺ! That is why we must not object on how they do things; what they do is according to the Prophet ﷺ, who did not pray except on the right time.

According to a *ḥadīth* in Bukhari and Muslim, it was near the time of Maghrib, and Prophet asked Sayyīdinā ʿAlī ؓ, "Did you pray ʿAṣr?" He said, "*Yā Rasūlullāh,* I did not." So Prophet ﷺ stopped the sun for Sayyīdinā ʿAlī ؓ until he finished praying, and then it went to sunset. So Prophet's power is but a drop and he gives drops to *awlīyāullāh.* All of them have one drop from that ocean of Prophet's knowledge, and that keep things moving until the Day of Judgment.

May Allāh bless us, forgive us, and grant our shaykh long life, and make all of us happy, healthy and wealthy.

Wa min Allāhi 't-tawfiq, bi ḥurmati 'l-ḥabīb, bi ḥurmati 'l-Fātiḥah.
And with Allāh is success. For the sake of the Beloved, for his sake we recite the opening chapter of Holy Qur'an.

Allah's Possessiveness

A'ūdhu billāhi min ash-Shayṭān ir-rajīm. Bismillāhi' r-Raḥmāni 'r-Raḥīm. Nawaytu 'l-arbā'īn, nawaytu 'l-'itikāf, nawaytu'l-khalwah, nawaytu 'l-'uzlah, nawaytu 'r-riyāḍa, nawaytu 's-sulūk, lillāhi Ta'alā fī hādhā 'l-masjid. Atī' ūllāh wa atī'ū 'r-Rasūl wa ūli 'l-amri minkum. (4:59)

Who does not have a shaykh, his shaykh is Shayṭān; he comes at the right time to deviate us from the real path. People ask, "Why are we speaking of Shayṭān and devils? We are praying, fasting, doing this and that." It is true, we are praying and fasting in our eyes, but in Allāh's eyes, Shayṭān is still playing with us, as he played with Adam ﷺ in Heavens. Isn't Shayṭān able to play with us on Earth then? He can. That is why you always need a guard.

Today if you travel to Malaysia or Indonesia, you see a hired guard at the entry to every house. Why? Although Malaysia is a country with not too much crime, but still they are hiring guards because they don't want to fall into a heedless moment and suddenly something happens, so they are taking care. Likewise, we have to take care by understanding and knowing that at any moment we might fall into heedlessness and if we don't have a shaykh to guide us, we fall into the miseries of this *dunyā.* Allāh ﷻ sent messengers. He has messengers and He has prophets. A Prophet is not a messenger. A messenger is a Prophet and a messenger at the same time, *Sahib ar risalah.*

> *wa mā arsalnā min rasūlin illa li yutā'a bi idhnillāhi wa law annahum idh ẓalamū anfusahum jā'ūku fastaghfarullāh wa 'staghfara lahumu 'r rasūla la-wajadūllāha tawwāban raḥīmā.*
>
> *We sent an apostle, but to be obeyed in accordance with the Will of Allāh. If they had only, when they were unjust to themselves, come unto you and asked Allāh's forgiveness, and the messenger had asked forgiveness for them, they would have found Allāh indeed Oft-Returning, Most Merciful.*
>
> (Sūrat an-Nisā, 4:64)

The messenger has a message to deliver so you have to obey his message. A prophet does not have a message to deliver. He obeys the messenger of his time or the messenger that came before him. So any prophet who is not a messenger must obey the messenger that came before or the messenger who is in his time.

Allāh has appointed many prophets. What is the *hikmat* (wisdom) of appointing many prophets if they don't have a message? Why did they become prophets? We understand that a messenger has a constitution and Sharīʿah, and Allāh sent him with that message to follow it. But a prophet can be in the same time of a messenger. So who follows whom? A prophet follows a messenger, a messenger doesn't follow a prophet. So every messenger that came, was a cycle of this lifetime. Allāh sent messengers and ended them with the seal of Messengers, Sayyīdinā Muḥammad ﷺ. That is why Islam orders us to accept all the messengers that came before the Prophet.

Wa mā arsalnā min rasūlin illa an yutāʿa bi idhnillāhi. He didn't say, "we didn't send a *nabī*," He said, "we didn't send a messenger until he will be obeyed." So Prophet wrapped all messengers that came before. But it is not necessary to accept prophets that came before as you have Sayyīdinā Muḥammad ﷺ as a messenger. But prophets are appointed to accept the messenger that came before them and in their time. Why? Because we have must have a role model. If there is a messenger in the east, there was no technology at that time, it was not opened yet, it opened in the time of Prophet. There was no tech to reach (far) and so Allāh sent messengers and prophets; "prophets" means *ʿibādAllāh aṣ-ṣāliḥīn,* servants that are symbols, role models for everyone.

Prophet ﷺ mentioned "Maqām al-Iḥsān," to worship Allāh as if you are seeing Him. And if you are not seeing Him, know that He is seeing you. So Allāh sent prophets as role models to be symbols for the community around them.

> *Yā ayyuhalladhīna āmanū ittaqūllāh wa kūnū maʿ aṣ-ṣādiqīn.*
> *O you who believe! Fear Allāh and be those who are pious (in word and deed).* (Sūrat at-Tawbah, 9:119)

So that is an indicator to be with prophets in the time before the Prophet. They are trustworthy ones, and thus are symbols and examples for their communities in their time, as *awlīyāullāh* are today. There are no more prophets or messengers after Sayyīdinā Muḥammad ﷺ. There are inheritors of the pious and sincere people, the prophets, and they are *awlīyāullāh.* Some *awlīyāullāh* carry knowledge they take from the heart of the Prophet and that is how they guide their followers. Some take with a prophet who had no message but who was pious. So they dress in that piety and become a role model between their communities.

This is a very, very important point in our understanding and the teaching. That is why Allāh ﷻ said, as mentioned by Prophet ﷺ:

Min al-mu'minīna rijālun ṣadaqū mā ʿaḥadullāha ʿalayh. Fa minhum man qaḍā naḥbahu wa minhum man yantaẓir wa mā badalū tabdīla.
Among the believers are Men who accepted and did what they promised of the Covenant they took with Allāh. Of them some have completed their vow (to the extreme), and some (still) wait, but they have never changed (their determination) in the least. (Sūrat al-'Aḥzāb, 33:23)

They are men who kept their covenant and did their best in *dunyā.* Some of them left and some are living. They are passing away slowly with time and others are coming in their turn. They are the real models whom we can learn from. Not every *murīd* is a *walī* or a role model. The shaykh picks up or appoints some role models because he wants the *barakah* to be spread. These people might not have knowledge to guide, but the shaykh appoints them as they are sincere and pious to do *dhikrūllāh,* as when Prophet ﷺ was asked by one *Ṣaḥābī*:

Yā Rasūlullāh, inna sharīʿah al-islām qad kathurat ʿalayya, "The rules of Islām became heavy on me." Prophet ﷺ said, lā yazāl lisānak raṭban bi-dhikrillāh, "Make your tongue wet (alive) with dhikrūllāh."(Tirmidhī)

So those who make themselves busy with *dhikrūllāh* are pious ones. They are not necessarily *murshidīn* to guide you through knowledge, but they are like blending a beautiful smell, as when someone with a nice scent comes in and makes everyone smell that way. It is like a rose that makes everyone in its environment smell nice. One of these *awlīyāullāh* is appointed by the shaykh.

That is why Sayyīdinā Abū Yazīd al-Bistāmi ق said, "Who has no shaykh, Shayṭān is his shaykh." Why? Because Shayṭān will bring him stinky roses and will guide him not to remember *dhikrūllāh.* The one who does *dhikr* will have a nice smell. The Prophet ﷺ said, "The smell of a fasting person's mouth is better than the smell of Paradise." Because the angels approach the fasting person and reflect their smell on them. So the person disobeying Allāh will smell of Shayṭān, bad smell. This is *ʿilmu 's-sulūk,* knowledge of that journey where you are going, to Allāh's Divine Presence. *as-sālik* is the one who is following the path.

Each one of us has a different way or journey. Our journey is full of miseries because we are blending it with *dunyā* work. But *awlīyā's* journey is perfect. If you follow that *walī* or that role model, you will reach your destiny and he will bring you to the Divine Presence. That is why a guide is important in the lives of people. As we said, there are two types of guides; the one spreading the teaching of Prophet ﷺ and Islam, and the one who is a role model, who guides through his behavior. He has Maqām al-Iḥsān, the Station of Perfected Character. You like his ways and you follow him. He doesn't need to say anything to you.

That is why you have many different kinds *awlīyāullāh.* They are, Budalā, Nujabā, Nuqabā, Awtād, and Akhyār. They are everywhere to guide the *ummah* through their destinies. So Allāh ﷻ has chosen, as He chose His prophets and His messengers, from *Ummat an-Nabī* ﷺ guides that carry and inherit knowledges continuously from the heart of Prophet and spread it.

Some are only to be role models for others and Allāh loves them. He doesn't like their love to be for other than Him; it has to be to Him only. That is why in *ṭarīqah* there is *gharīh,* not in the meaning of jealousy, but *karāhat mushārakat li-ghayrih* (hatred of sharing with anyone else), but possessiveness. You dislike that someone shares the love of your beloved. If you love someone, you want that one to be to yours only, and it is not jealousy. You feel, "I don't like anyone to share that love except me."

Let us give an example. A husband doesn't like to share anyone with his wife and a wife doesn't like to share anyone with her husband; that is *ghīrah.* So in another meaning, Allāh chose his saints and He doesn't like His saints to share their love with anyone, it must be exclusively to Him. The students of the shaykh have to know that the final level of their love is to reach the Divine Presence and love to Allāh ﷻ! That is why we say *maḥabbat ash-shaykh* guides you to *maḥabbat an-Nabī* ﷺ, which guides you to *maḥabbat Allāh,* which is the last landing. This means that you don't see anyone in your life. In every *ʿamal,* action, you do or every moment of life passes, you have to see the Will of Allāh ﷻ, no one else. If you don't do that as a *walī,* Allāh doesn't like it. He likes His *walī* only to be to Him. That is why He likes the heart of His servant not to be attached to anyone.

When Rābiʿah al-ʿAdawiyyah ق got sick, they asked her, what is the problem? She said, "I looked at Paradise with my heart. That was a mistake. I looked with my heart at something created and my heart must be only for my Lord." Maqām al-Wilayat it is not easy to reach. That is why these *awlīyā,* Aqṭāb, Budalā, Nuqabā, Nujabā, Awtād, and Akhyār, have excellent characteristics. We are only able to speak about it, but they are able to taste it. We are not tasting, we are only listening and reading, but they are listening and tasting. Adam ﷺ listened to Iblīs and he lost. That is why Prophet ﷺ said:

Ḥubbuka li shay ya'mī wa yaṣum.

O my Lord! Your Love to someone will make that one blind and deaf.

Your love to someone or to any of your Creation, will make that one blind and deaf. It means Allāh has *ghīrah;* He doesn't like anyone to share His servant and wants the love of that servant directed only to Him. And when He loves that servant completely, that servant becomes blind and deaf to this *dunyā;* he cannot see and hear anything of this world, he only hears and sees Allāh ﷻ. That is why Prophet ﷺ said:

Lī sa'atun ma' al-khāliq wa lī sa'atun ma' al-khalq.

I have a picture or an hour with My Lord in which no angels can be in the middle of that relationship.

Prophet Muḥammad's ﷺ heart is completely blind from *dunyā,* although he is not, but in the meaning and he is deaf and blind from *dunyā.* That is why he was invited to Mi'rāj, where no angel reached. At (the station of) *qāba qawsayni aw adnā,* he is not seeing or feeling anything but the Divine Presence of His Lord. Grandshaykh ق said Allāh asked him there, "Who are you?" and Prophet said, "I am You."

There is the real *tawḥīd* for the Prophet! He understood the level of Oneness, that in the Divine Presence everything was not existing, and *awlīyāullāh* quench their thirst from that ocean. When you are near, you are not seeing anything except Holy Divine Attributes that Allāh will be manifesting on you. *Wa al-ḥaqqu anna al-ghīratu lillāh ḥaqqan,* "The reality is, Allāh has the right not to share anything of His servants with Him." Allāh ﷻ said:

Awliyāī taḥta qibābī la ya'lamahum ghayrī.

My awlīyā are under My domes; no one knows them except Me.

(Ḥadīth Qudsī)

Man 'adā lī walīyyan faqad ādhantahu bi 'l-ḥarb.

Whoever comes against a walī (friend) of Mine, I declare war on him.

(Ḥadīth Qudsī)

That is *ghīrah.* So Allāh's servants have no right; all their actions, all their breaths, and all their remembrance must be only for Allāh ﷻ. When someone has *ghīrah,* it means he loves someone and doesn't want to share. This shows there is love there. *Ghīrah* takes you to love. When you become pious, *ghīrah* to Allāh comes to you and when that happens, *maḥabbatAllāh* blows to you. So then you enter the first level of *maḥabbatAllāh, maḥabbat al-*

habīb, and maḥabbat al-shaykh, which leads to *hudūr,* and then that leads to annihilation.

It is said, *al-ghīra ghīratān,* possessiveness, jealousy, is of two kinds: *ghīrat al-bashar ʿalā an-nufūs wa ghīratallāh ʿalā al-qulūb,* the possessiveness of the self, the body loves the ego and the ego leads to bad desires. When body is attached to the ego, then you are making a detour and that is why we call it *al-ghīrat al-bashariyya ʿalā an-nufūs.* The body doesn't want to share anything with the self. The ego must be "for the body only" and that is where Shayṭān can play.

But there is the second part; *ghīratallāh ʿalā al-qulūb,* the heavenly *ghīrah* which is on the hearts, as it is said, *ma fi qalbī illa-Llāh,* "There is nothing in my heart except Allāh." So the heart is the House of Allāh ﷻ. Constantly for twenty-four hours that heart is in *dhikrūllāh.* If you put a speaker on the heart, you can hear it saying, *Hū, Hū, Hū.* You see these palpitations in this sound. That is a sound that has been coded and covered.

Everyone has a code in their heart; if they open it, they will understand what kind of *dhikr* their heart is doing. And every person's *dhikr* doesn't resemble the *dhikr* of another. Even if both say *Hū,* each one will be different from the other or else, that will diminish Allāh's Greatness. Just as every angel has a different *dhikr,* each person's heart has a *dhikr,* voluntary or involuntary. The human being is born on *fitrah,* on the natural way, but his parents make him either Christian, Jewish, or Zoroastrian. But you are born on *fitratu 'l-Islām,* and that is the light put in the heart of people.

Inna ad-dīna ʿind-Allāhi al-Islām.
The religion before Allāh is Islām. (Sūrat 'Āli 'Imrān, 3:19)

All religion ends up in Islam, even from Adam ﷺ and Ibrāhīm ﷺ, who said:

innī wajahut wajhiyya lil-ladhī fatar as-samawāti wal-ʿarḍa hanīfa muslimān.
I have directed my face to the One Who created Heaven and Earth, and I am Muslim.

It is from that time. So the religion to Allāh is Islam as it came last, but it came with Ibrāhīm ﷺ and ended with Prophet ﷺ wrapping everything together. The hearts of human beings are created and born on Islam, that is why it is voluntary or involuntary, and that is why it is making that *dhikr* by pumping. When the heart stops pumping, you are finished. If the brain stops you are still alive, but if the heart stops you are dead. Allāh doesn't like His servant's heart doing anything other than remembering Him. When Allāh loves someone, He wants that one to be for Him only.

One of the *awlīyā* said, "Why did Allāh send Adam on Earth?"

Al-Qushayrī ق said, "The example of this is Adam whose homeland was Paradise living there eternally, with all its delicious tastes, then Allāh became possessive of him. Adam loved to be live for eternity in Paradise, which Allāh did not accept. To show him that Allāh does not accept his self to love other than Him. Allāh does not become harmed by someone but you will be harmed by losing Allāh.

And he said, "When Ibrāhīm became so fond of Ismāʿīl, Allāh said to go slaughter him," as there can be no competition, no love for anyone else in the hearts of His servants. Prophets have no love except to their Creator, and here we are speaking of real love. When Ismāʿīl was born, Ibrāhīm was so happy that his love went to Ismāʿīl. That is why today humans are receiving that kind of love for their children, which is okay. But for Ibrāhīm, Allāh said, "Go and slaughter your son, Ismāʿīl."

So Allāh told Ibrāhīm to slaughter Ismāʿīl, and when Ibrāhīm took the knife to slaughter Ismāʿīl, at that moment Allāh ﷻ took his love for ʿIsmāʿīl out of his heart, then He sent the lamb to be slaughtered. But Adam ؑ wanted to be eternally in Paradise. So for Ibrāhīm ؑ, Allāh accepted his intention to slaughter, saying, "That is enough for Me."

Dhikrūllāh is important. That is why the guidance of *shuyūkh* took their followers to *dhikrūllāh*. Mawlana Shaykh Nazim ق says that even if two people have homes next to each other, both do *dhikr* to increase the *tajallī*."

May Allāh give long life to Mawlana Shaykh Nazim ق!

Wa min Allāhi 't-tawfīq, bi ḥurmati 'l ḥabīb, bi ḥurmati 'l-Fātiḥah.
And with Allāh is success. For the sake of the Beloved, for his sake we recite the opening chapter of Holy Qurʾan.

Ittiba and Taqleed: Follow the Footsteps and Imitate the Pious

Aʿūdhu billāhi min ash-Shayṭān ir-rajīm. Bismillāhi' r-Raḥmāni 'r-Raḥīm. Nawaytu 'l-arbāʿīn, nawaytu 'l-ʿitikāf, nawaytu'l-khalwah, nawaytu 'l-ʿuzlah, nawaytu 'r-riyāḍa, nawaytu 's-sulūk, lillāhi Taʿalā fī hādhā 'l-masjid. Atiʿ ūllāh wa atiʿū 'r-Rasūl wa ūli 'l-amri minkum. (4:59)

A*wlīyāullāh, qaddas-Allāhu Taʿalā arwāḥahumu zakīyya wa nawwar-Allāhu Taʿalā aḍriḥatahum al-mubāraka*, may Allāh ﷻ bless their souls, those who passed away and those living. *Awlīyāullāh* always cared for their followers. As we said yesterday, if Allāh likes His servant He is possessive of that one; He doesn't want His servant to go anywhere. That is why the end-goal of a servant is to be in the Divine Presence and the shaykhs have to do their best for their followers to reach there, as this is their duty. And *awlīyā* were not able to become *awlīyā* except by *inkisār*, to lower themselves to be like Earth for their followers.

If you step on the Earth, it doesn't complain; if you drill it, take its treasures, mine it, or throw garbage on it, it doesn't complain. A *walī* is like the Earth; he doesn't complain. He wants those whom he is guiding to benefit and they didn't reach that level except through humiliation and humility.

Humility means to show they are like normal people. I am speaking of the Naqshbandi Ṭarīqah and other *ṭarīqahs*. In the Naqshbandi Ṭarīqah, the shaykh doesn't show himself with any abnormality, he always shows himself as normal, in order to make familiarity with followers. They even joke with their followers, as they are following the footsteps of the Prophet.

He used to sit privately with *Ṣaḥābah* ‎ and joke and eat with them to make them feel easy-going. It is not like visiting a government minister, when you have to follow many protocols, although the minister might stand at the door of the Prime Minister like nothing. A Prime Minister might even kick the minister, and we might shake in front of the minister. Even to his doorman we say, "Yes sir." Do we say it (among ourselves)? Never.

Awlīyāullāh don't have that behavior or characteristic because they want to show how they are easy-going with followers, and that is how their followers are attracted to them. *Murīds* have to show discipline to their shaykh by keeping the *adab* of following. That is why people say, *hal atabiʿuka.* Mūsā ﷺ, who is *ūlū 'l-ʿazam,* one of the five highest prophets and messengers, said, "Can I follow?" *Ittibaʿ* means to follow, or "footsteps". That is why *ʿulamā* said you must have *ittibaʿ*, not like today as the Salafi *ʿulamā* say, *lā tatatabiʿ*, "Don't follow, do what you like." No, you have to follow! Sayyīdinā Mūsā ﷺ asked permission from Sayyīdinā Khiḍr ﷺ, "Can I follow you?" Khiḍr said, "I don't know, you might not be able." But Mūsā asked; he came with discipline and knocked on the door.

So *ʿulamā* must understand, as Āhlu 's-Sunnah wa 'l-Jamaʿah, we have to follow the pious ones who came before us, and imitate them, *taqlīd.* Today they refuse *ittibaʿ* and *taqlīd,* and Allāh ﷻ said He chose messengers and put them among the community for people to follow their footsteps. People look at them and say, "That is a pious one. I have to imitate his way." So that is *ṭarīqah*: to make *taqlīd* and *ittibaʿ*, which is the order in the Holy Qur'an.

So Sayyīdinā Khiḍr said, "If you want to follow me I accept, but you have to be patient." You have to follow a shaykh, yes; you took his hand, you gave initiation, then what is your duty? To follow. One simple example is when Sayyīdinā 'Ubaydullāh al-Ahrār ق said to his *murīd,* "Go to the mountain and wait, I am coming." What did he do? He went to the mountain and he stayed all day; Maghrib came and shaykh didn't come. But he was a clever *murīd* and his heart is connected. He said to himself, "O! Shaykh said, 'I am coming.' Why do I have to listen to the ego and go home?" So he stayed and waited and the second day he waited and shaykh didn't come, one week, one month, no more food, the fruit on the trees finished. He didn't say, "I have to go home to sleep," he waited. One year passed, and no shaykh. Then Allāh ﷻ sent a deer to him, because he kept the word of the shaykh, who said, "I am coming, wait for me." That is *ittibaʿ*, to follow.

Sayyīdinā Khiḍr ﷺ said to Sayyīdinā Mūsā ﷺ, "You may follow, but don't object against me."

Qāla innaka lan tastatiʿ maʿiya sabra.

(The other) said, "Verily you will not be able to have patience with me!"

(Sūrat al-Kahf, 18:67)

Don't object. When you object it means there is no *ittibaʿ*. The first step in *ṭarīqah* is *ittibaʿ* and *taqlīd,* and unfortunately today *ʿulamā* are saying, "Don't follow." The principle of Āhlu 's-Sunnah wa 'l-Jamaʿah is to follow and take the consensus of the *ʿulamā*! That *murīd* waited seven years until his shaykh came, saying, "O my son! Where were you? I might have died and you didn't come to see?"

The *murīd* answered, "If I left, then you would not be here now by order of Prophet." He reached a high level.

What happened yesterday? I said I am coming at 12 o'clock, and you ran away, you didn't wait even half-an-hour! This one (*murīd*) ran away. What kind of notes are you taking?

Whoever doesn't follow Allāh's orders first, then Prophet's ways and orders, and *awlīyāullāh's* order and ways, *fa laysa fī yadihi shay*, then he will not achieve anything. Sayyīdinā ʿAlī ؓ said, "The reality is within three things:

> *al-haqīqatu fī thalāth: Man lam yakun ʿindahu sunnatullāh wa sunnat rasūlihi wa sunnat awliyāihi fa laysa fī yadihi shay.*
>
> *If someone doesn't have respect for Allāh's way, the Prophet's way and awlīyā's way, he or she can't achieve anything.*

Prophet ﷺ said:

> *'ana madīnatu 'l-ʿilmi wa ʿAliyyun babuha.*
> *I am the city of knowledge and ʿAlī is its door.* (al-Ḥākim, Tirmidhī)

His Companions ؓ said, "Tell us what we have to do."

He said, "Allāh's Way is *kitmān as-sirr*, keep the secrets." Don't expose them, keep hiding secrets. That has two meanings here: it means keep whatever Allāh gives you in the way of your journey, don't expose it, or you will feel arrogant and you lose. Don't say, "I am speaking with *jinn*, I will send *jinn* on you, or I will do this and I will do that." No, show humbleness in every situation (as if you know nothing; that way you will not show yourself as arrogant. And *kitmān as-sirr*, don't expose your brothers' and sisters' mistakes. Both of these ways are exposing.

If you get secret of what Allāh opened to your heart, you go and say it, especially if they saw a dream. What do they do? They are so happy to tell about their dream. If Allāh wants to show that dream to everyone He can, but He sent it to you. If you want to say it, say it to your shaykh directly, not to people. They come and say to each what they have seen in dreams and expose it on the Internet even, saying, "I have seen a dream." If it is nice a one, keep it for yourself, and secondly, don't expose to your brothers and sisters what Allāh ﷻ gave you. What do we do? We expose them! So what we said about, *anā madinatu 'l-'ilmi wa 'Alīyyun bābuhā*, and what *ṭarīqahs* came from Sayyīdinā 'Alī ؓ? Don't expose secrets that Allāh has given to you, keep it to yourself. If you did good for humanity, keep it to yourself. If you gave of what Allāh gave you, don't say to people, "I gave." Don't say it, keep it to yourself.

And they asked, "What about the *sunnah* of Prophet, *wa mā hīya sunnat ar-rasūl?*" And this is what *'ulamā* have to know the importance of, and all politicians have to go back to Muslim sources, and extract from pious people what they said, and not to listen to those who are extreme in their understanding.

They asked Sayyīdinā 'Alī ؓ, "What is Prophet's way? We understand Allāh's way to veil what happened to you, but what is the way of Prophet?"

Sayyīdinā 'Alī said, *al-muḍārātu li 'n-nās*. That is very important. "O politicians! That is what Islam is based on."

He took from the *sunnah* of Prophet ﷺ and he didn't say, "Explode yourself with suicide bombings," as we see Muslims killing Muslims now. He said, *al-muḍārātu li 'n-nās*, to be able to take everything balanced, to be caring for everyone, how to deal with him to keep him happy. It means whoever you meet. And he said, *li 'n-nās*, "to humanity," not *li 'l-Muslim*, "Muslims (only)." Prophet's way is to make everyone feel they have been cared for. Prophet took everyone into consideration, and this is not easy, but this is what we have to tell people Islam is based on, to take consideration for everyone's needs. Prophet ﷺ gave everyone what he or she needed, but who doesn't have a mind or a heart doesn't understand.

They asked, *Qīla wa mā sunnata awlīyā-ih*, "What is the *sunnah* of the saints?"

Sayyīdinā 'Alī ؓ said, "One of the most difficult is *ihtimālu 'l-adhā*, to carry peoples' harms."

What is their harm? It is not that they speak bad about the *walī*, as today they say, "There are no *awlīyā*." It is for the shaykh to carry the harm, the mistakes and the sins of his followers, and clean them by taking their mistakes on his shoulders and giving them from his good deeds and good tidings that he dressed them with. He is sacrificing himself for the benefit of his followers. That is a *walī's* job and that is a *walī*, what he gave him from the beginning.

And so when Sayyīdinā Mūsā ؑ asked Sayyīdinā Khiḍr ؑ, "Can I follow you?" he said, "Yes, but you have to be patient. I am not going to expose my secrets and I am carrying the harm and difficulty, taking into consideration my prophet will carry the burden and make people happy." That is why he took responsibility when he put a hole in the boat, as he didn't want the king to take the boat from the poor fisherman; then he took responsibility when he built the wall to save the treasure for its rightful heirs, and he took responsibility for that child that was harmful to his parents.

So our responsibility in *ṭarīqah* is to carry each other and not to criticize each other, and our way is not to advocate separation. And today all technology is the worst, as Mawlana said yesterday, because people are using it for destruction. You are destroying the morality of people on the Internet by saying things or showing things. And these three ways Allāh made under three actions. If you follow them, as Sayyīdinā ʿAlī ﷺ said, Allāh will give you support, Prophet will give *shafāʿa,* and *awlīyā* will accept you as followers.

The first *ʿamal* is to do for *ākhirah;* always do your best for the Hereafter, don't do the best for *dunyā. Man ʿamal li 'l-ākhirah kafā-Allāhu dunyā hu,* "Whoever does his best for *ākhirah* will make people help him for his *dunyā."* He doesn't need to work even, from everywhere help will come. If you are doing for Allāh ﷻ, Allāh will make people come to help you. But we are not doing enough for *ākhirah* and that is why we are running after our *dunyā,* to be able to eat and drink!

And I can see and I observed and experienced how Mawlana Shaykh, may Allāh give him long life and may Allāh bless the soul of Grandshaykh, how they were only working for *daʿwah.* Allāh made people to come and serve them, their homes were never empty from anything. *SubhānAllāh*! Grandshaykh's home was so humble but three times a day food was served. If any guest came food was served and not one day there is no food in his house. *SubhānAllāh.* Allāh sent people to serve. And similarly with Mawlana Shaykh Nazim, may Allāh give him long life.

Grandshaykh ق one day said to me and my brother, "Who followed me, Allāh and Prophet promised to me in my visions, 'O ʿAbdAllāh Effendi! Anyone who follows you will not see *fi 'd-dunyā sharr aw fi 'l-ākhirah,* never in *dunyā* will he see any harm and never in *ākhirah,* and his pocket will never be empty of money.' Allāh gave every *walī* a specialty, anyone who follows me will never see harm in this life or the Next Life and their *rizq* will always be there." Their doors are always open and that is why whoever does for *ākhirah,* Allāh will give him whatever he needs in *dunyā.*

Wa man aḥsana sarīratahu aḥsan Allāhu ẓāhirah, "The one who rides his ego and perfects his inside, Allāh will perfect his appearance." When he appears, any spot will be a spotlight, in any assembly or meeting or association, people will run to him because of that light that Allāh and his Prophet and *awlīyā* have put in his forehead. They run to him and they feel attracted like a magnet. That is why *awlīyāullāh* are like magnets; Allāh gave them that secret speciality. You cannot perfect your outside; that has to come from them. It is not perfecting outside by wearing nice clothes, but you need that heavenly light to be put and people will be attracted to that heavenly light.

So try to fix what is between you and people. These are major issues that if we follow, we succeed. *Awlīyā* succeeded, because they follow these ways. They began to know *'irfān,* Gnosticism. Allāh gave them the knowledge. They fixed that pipe between them and Allāh, and Allāh made people run to them!

May Allāh ﷻ forgive us.

Wa min Allāhi 't-tawfīq, bi ḥurmati 'l-ḥabīb, bi ḥurmati 'l-Fātiḥah.
And with Allāh is success. For the sake of the Beloved, for his sake we recite the opening chapter of Holy Qur'an.

Changeable and Unchangeable Principles

A'ūdhu billāhi min ash-Shayṭān ir-rajīm. Bismillāhi' r-Raḥmāni 'r-Raḥīm. Nawaytu 'l-arbā'īn, nawaytu 'l-'itikāf, nawaytu'l-khalwah, nawaytu 'l-'uzlah, nawaytu 'r-riyāḍa, nawaytu 's-sulūk, lillāhi Ta'alā fī hādhā 'l-masjid. Ati' ūllāh wa ati'ū 'r-Rasūl wa ūli 'l-amri minkum. (4:59)

Alhamdulillāh that Allāh ﷻ has connected us with people to whom He granted heavenly support. As followers or *murīds*, it is necessary for everyone, if he wants to find his journey and reach his goal, to know where he is putting his foot. To know where he is stepping, his intention has to be clean, that he is following the path of Āhlu 's-Sunnah wa 'l-Jama'ah, the path of Āhlu 'l-Bayt, and his intention has to be *Ṣādiq*, pure, on his journey. Because today people are connecting with so many *'ulamā* and different scholars, leaving the reality of Islam behind them and not giving importance to or even speaking about Maqām al-Iḥsān, the station where thoughts and characters are pure, and moral values are carried within you, which takes you to your goal and destiny.

Awlīyāullāh say that every person likes to reach somewhere. The goal is to reach Allāh's love and Prophet's love, but unfortunately, it is like a pipe with many holes, so water leaks through the holes and doesn't reach the end of the pipe, so you don't receive anything. *Qālū innamā kharam al-wusūl,* "They pierce their way by putting many holes in it," and they lost the *usūl,* the main principles of Islam, which is Maqām al-Iḥsān.

People say they want Maqām al-Iḥsān, but already they have put too many holes in their pipe, so how will they reach it? They will not. *Awlīyā* say you have to be careful. One of the big Sufi *'ālims,* Imām 'Abd al-Karīm ibn Hawāzin al-Qushayrī ق (d. 1074, Persia), said, "It is not good to follow someone who is not from this path (Āhlu 's-Sunnah wa 'l-Jama'ah and Āhlu 'l-Bayt; the Sufi path) as it might take you somewhere unaccepted. Today (700 years ago) people are on two ways and you have to avoid these two ways."

It means, not avoid them completely, but find someone who carries them and carries the reality of Maqām al-Iḥsān. "People today are people of footnotes and hearsay. They copy; they don't depend on what is new coming to hearts, refreshing their hearts. They copy what has been written, as this is their knowledge. They know what others wrote, but they don't progress to reach their destination. *aw imma aṣḥāb al-qawl wa 'l-fikr,* They are people of thoughts: academia and intellectuals. You have to be careful about them. They are thinking with the mind, and Allāh ﷻ cannot be known by the mind, He is known by hearts."

So today people copy and paste and if that knowledge is not footnoted, they don't accept it! So they copy what came before them or they use their mind to make "reforms," as if Islam needs reform. No, Islam doesn't need reform but Muslims need to reform, by returning to the tradition of Prophet ﷺ and his Companions ؓ! So the first group copy and paste and the second group are thinking people, like socialists who came at the beginning of the 20th century, Maududi, Syed Quṭb and many others, saying, "We have to reform Islam." No, you have to be very careful about what your mind is thinking.

Awlīyā take from the heart of Prophet ﷺ, and in that there are two principles: *thawābit*, firm, fixed elements that you cannot play with or change, and *mutaghayarāt,* changeable. The *thawābit* principles are not changed from copying and pasting, nor through academia thinking, but there has to be an inspiration from the heart of Prophet. Allāh ﷻ sends to Prophet, and Prophet sends to the hearts of *awlīyā*. This is why Jalāluddin Rumi ق brought so many changeable principles that he dressed on *thawābit,* firm principles, because firm principles can be dressed with whatever dress you like.

Allāh ﷻ is known through His Beautiful Names, so His Beautiful Names can be dressed. Allāh will manifest on His Prophet with His Beautiful Names, and He can dress on anyone from His Beautiful Names and grant them to know what name they are under. And there are many Names. Like *tajalli 'Ismullāh al-'Aẓam,* the manifestation of the Name encompassing all Names, "Allāh". How will it be manifested? For example, it will be manifested on "one," as in Holy Qur'an it is mentioned:

> *Wa annahu lamma qāma 'abdullāhi yad'ūhu kādū yakūnūna 'alayhi libada.*
> *Yet when the Devotee of Allāh stands forth to invoke Him, they just make round him a dense crowd.* (Sūrat al-Jinn, 72:19)

When Allāh's servant, the only one mentioned in Holy Qur'an as "AbdAllāh'," which means He dressed Prophet ﷺ with His Beautiful Names and with *'Ismullāh al-'Aẓam,* the Name encompassing all the Beautiful Names and Attributes, "Allāh".

Prophet ﷺ is the only one on whom Allāh ﷻ manifested His Beautiful Names and Attributes, because he reached the highest rank and highest *shān*, prestige, the reality and certainty of the manifestation of His Highest Beautiful Name, "Allāh". That is why he was able to go in 'Isrā' wal-Miʿrāj. If Allāh ﷻ did not dress him, he would have been completely annihilated! Allāh dressed him so he can come back. So Imām al-Qushayrī ق said, "When the servant of Allāh asks through prayers, that Name was for Prophet and his inheritors," who are Ghawth, Aqtāb, Budalā, Nujabā, Nuqabā, Awtād, Akhyār.

So the reality is not changeable. They can be dressed by *mutaghayarāt,* changeable principles, and in this way you can give every reality a colorful dress that you can follow. He continues:

> *wa law istaqāmū ʿalā aṭ-ṭariqati lā asqaynāhum mā'an ghadaqa.*
> *If they kept straight forward on the way, ṭarīqah, we would shower them with blessings.*

"If they stay on the Way, Ṣirāṭ al-Mustaqīm," this is a fixed principle. But you can dress that principle, that anyone can go on that path, in a different manifestation, with different dresses, with different shuyūkh, with different *dhikr*. The road doesn't change, but your technique as you go from one shaykh to another is a dress that can be changed. Allāh said in Holy Qur'an: *wa law istaqāmū ʿalā aṭ-ṭariqati lā asqaynāhum mā'an ghadaqa.*

Today they know now where rain comes from and to where it goes. The reality of the rain doesn't change. There are lakes or equatorial areas to where water evaporates, that is unchangeable, but where that rain is sent is changeable.

> *Wal baladu 'ṭ-ṭayyibu yakhruju nabātuhu bi-idhni rabbihi wa'Lladhī khabutha lā yakhruju illa nakidan kadhālika nuṣarrifu 'l-ayāti li-qawmin yashkurūn.*
> *From the land that is clean and good, by the will of its Cherisher, springs up produce, (rich) after its kind, but from the land that is bad, springs up nothing but that which is begrudging. Thus do we explain the signs by various (symbols) to those who are grateful.* (Sūrat al-Aʿrāf, 7:58)

The clouds are there, but Allāh ﷻ moves them as He likes by wind, which is in hands of angels, which is changeable. The principles of evaporation are unchangeable. For example, if you drop water on the floor, in ten or fifteen minutes it evaporates. If you go to the sauna, you sweat. Similarly, you have to sweat in the way of *ṭarīqah*. If you don't sweat, what is the benefit? Do you want to sit on the throne and for them to carry you? *nuqsānīyyah*, you have deficiencies they must work on for you to improve. For example, you don't like watermelon, so they give you watermelon; that is a bitterness, a sweat. This one likes to sleep too much, so they keep him awake! So everyone has to sweat and in a different way.

So a big *walī* said to someone who is higher than him but he didn't know, and *awlīyā* like to joke with each other, "Do you like to see Him, *aturīdu an tarāh.*" The same question applies to everyone here: do you like to see Him? Yes, of course! Why are you coming to make *dhikrūllāh*? To see Him, to be more near Him. That *walī* answered, "No, I don't like to see Him."

If they ask us, we would run to see Him! Sayyīdinā Mūsā ﷺ asked to see Him! So this *walī* was careful. And so he said no. They said that is strange.

He continued, *unnaziḥu dhāk al-Jamāl ʿan nadhari mithlih,* "I exalt that Beauty from Someone who has my eyes," meaning, "I am not worthy; I don't want my dirty eyes to see that Beauty, because that Beauty is exalted." To see that Beauty requires clean eyes. Can we say that?

They said, "When do you relax?" Today they say when you relax, take a massage. (laughter)

He said, "No, *mā dumtu lahu dhākiran,* as long as I am remembering Him, I am relaxing. When I am heedless from His remembrance, I will not find any relaxation; I am sweating."

So you see the difference between them and us? Imām al-Qushayrī ق said, *wa law istaqāmūʿalā at-ṭarīqati lā asqaynahum mā'an ghadaqa,* "If they knew the variants (*utaghayarāt*), they would have succeeded."

Light is a constant speed, traveling at 300,000 Km/s. The moon has many variations in density between it and Earth; that is *mutaghayarāt*. That is why the speed of light coming from the moon is less than 300,000 Km/s, as there is a lot of friction taking place within that distance. So in this galaxy with so many stars—some farther than the moon, the sun, or the polestar—your destination on this path is farther than any star in this universe. And a lot of variations might drop your power to move forward. That is why the guide will teach you what *awrād* to say, to make you move depending on your capacity. If you connect a 500-watt lamp to a 100-watt power source, the light, the lamp, and the wire will burn. But if you connect a 50-watt lamp to a 100-watt power source, neither the lamp nor the wire will burn. So the shaykh knows the capacity your heart can carry; he connects you, and your light is not burned out, and you move on that path. What the shaykh gives is *mutaghayarāt*, something that changes. He might give you a 50-watt or a 100-watt connection.

So Allāh ﷻ said in Holy Qur'an, "If he would stand on the path, we would order angels to send these clouds of mercy and put in their hearts. We would shower them with 'un-understandables' (unique knowledge)."

Support comes from Allāh ﷻ. If you are on a track ready to move, as you are given awrād from your shaykh and you do it, then mercy, *ināyatullāh,* comes to push you like the wind blowing the clouds of rain. That is *rīḥ aṣ-ṣibā,* "cool breeze from Heavens" that moves you forward. Like a carriage on a track only needs the first push and it keeps going like a roller coaster. It might find a hill but it will go slowly up and then will go down quickly.

Allāh ﷻ said, *inna maʿ al-ʿusri yusrā,* "With difficulty comes ease." (94:6) He didn't say, "With ease comes difficulty," no, with difficulty there must be ease. So you face difficulty first, then you reach ease, as Allāh ﷻ confirmed:

alam nashraḥ laka saḍrak, wa wadāʿnā ʿanka wizrak.
Have We not opened your breast for you and removed from you your burden.
(Sūrat al-Shahr, 94:1-2)

Then, when you are steady on path, He sends angels to move these clouds of mercy and you quickly reach your goal. Today people are so interested in *an-naql wa 'l-athar,* "This one said this and this one said that." If you don't say the transmission of that knowledge, it is not acceptable. But everything is changeable, as today there are *awlīyāullāh* inspired from the heart of Prophet ﷺ, who said, "I left behind the Book of Allāh and my Way," and, "I left behind the Book and my Family."

Put these two different *ḥadīth* in an equation with the first side *kitābullāh wa sunnatī — kitābullāh wa ʿitratī.* Remove what is common on both sides, *kitābullāh,* so what is left? *Sunnatī — ʿItratī.* So you have to look, those who are on his way are from his Family. Who are his Family? Many are from his blood family and also there is his spiritual family, like Sayyīdinā Salmān al-Fārsi ؓ. *Awlīyā* are the ones who can take you forward to understand *kitābullāh,* the Book of Allāh. Others only say, "He said this and he said that," but they do not understand what is coming new. That is *ʿilm al-ghuyūb* for you, but for them that is *ʿilm aẓ-ẓuhūr,* knowledge appearing for them.

So follow those who are receiving divine inspiration in their hearts, *shuyūkh aṭ-ṭā'ifah,* shaykhs of that particular group. Who are they? They are *awlīyāullāh.* If you follow others, you are in a maze. So *awlīyā* take you out of that maze. *Awlīyāullāh* are all on the similar way. Think-tank intellectuals believe if they study four years, they become a doctor and put that certificate. No, *awlīyā* are those who take you through your life, the past, future and present, giving you precisely what you need at any given moment. Now the intellectuals are coming to reform Islam. Islam is perfect like the full moon! You cannot reform Islam with ideas of Marx, Lenin, or socio-political movements such as communism, socialism, or even democratic or liberal ideologies. You have to come with something that is more spiritual and in the middle, which everyone can follow.

So Prophet ﷺ mentioned in many *aḥadīth,* and what is revealed in Holy Qur'an, that the best way to reach that is through *dhikrūllāh* and different ways of *dhikr*. Allāh ﷻ describes Himself for us with Ninety-nine Beautiful Names. You can go to infinite Names to remember Him and you have to know the highest is *'Ismullāh,* "Allāh," and when the servant of Allāh ﷻ stood up to pray, he is the one whom Allāh ﷻ dressed with all the Beautiful Names and Attributes. Abdus-Salām is under the *tajallī* of the Divine Name "as-Salām," but "'AbdAllāh," Allāh's Servant, is under the *tajallī* of all the Beautiful Names and Attributes!

So *awlīyā* are changeable, based on what is dressing them. So may Allāh ﷻ clean us with His endless power.

Be careful on that verse, *wa law istaqāmū 'alā aṭ-ṭarīqati la asqaynāhum mā'an ghadaqa.* May Allāh ﷻ fill our hearts with all His Names and Attributes.

Wa min Allāhi 't-tawfiq, bi ḥurmati 'l-ḥabīb, bi ḥurmati 'l-Fātiḥah.
And with Allāh is success. For the sake of the Beloved, for his sake we recite the opening chapter of Holy Qur'an.

Dhikrullah Is the Main Pillar of Tariqah

A'ūdhu billāhi min ash-Shayṭān ir-rajīm. Bismillāhi' r-Raḥmāni 'r-Raḥīm. Nawaytu 'l-arbaʿīn, nawaytu 'l-ʿitikāf, nawaytu'l-khalwah, nawaytu 'l-ʿuzlah, nawaytu 'r-riyāḍa, nawaytu 's-sulūk, lillāhi Taʿalā fī hādhā 'l-masjid. Atiʿ ūllāh wa atiʿū 'r-Rasūl wa ūli 'l-amri minkum. (4:59)

Rābiṭah is the connection of the pipe from you to the shaykh. When he takes your hand for initiation, he is connecting you. In the same way you connect a pipe with fittings, he connects all the fittings so there is no leak. And not only does he connect the fittings, but he glues them also so it will never break. So always the *rābiṭah* is the connection with fittings and it is glued so that it is never going to break. And *murāqabah* is to keep observing both from the *walī's*/shaykh's side and from the *murīd's* side. From both sides they are always in observation. *Murāqabah* means to observe like a video camera what is going on, to be vigilant to maintain that pipe with no leakage.

As a *murīd*, from your side you are looking to make sure that if there is a defect you fix it, and from the side of the shaykh, he is looking for any defects to fix. If you want to count the defects between you and your shaykh, you can realize there are a lot of holes and leaks in that pipe and nothing can fix them except heavenly glue; you can't use *dunyā* glue or anything else as it will not work. Heavenly glue is *dhikrūllāh*, and that heavenly backbone or pillar on which you can lean is *dhikrūllāh*.

To do *dhikrūllāh*, you have to be clean. When you do *dhikr* it means you are knocking on the door to be opened for you. Allāh ﷻ said in Holy Qur'an:

> *Alladhīna yadhkurūnullāh qiyamān wa quʿūdan wa ʿalā junūbihim wa yattafakkarūna fī khalqi 's-samawātī wa 'l-arḍ, rabbanā mā khalaqta hadhā bāṭilan subḥānaka fa qinā ʿadhāba 'n-nār.*
> *Those who remember Allāh (always, and in prayers) standing, sitting, and lying down on their sides, and think deeply about the Creation of the Heavens and the Earth, (saying),"Our Lord! You have not created (all) this without purpose, glory to You! Give us salvation from the torment of the Fire.*
> (Sūrat 'Āli 'Imrān, 3:191)

Al-ladhīna yadhkurūnullāh, "Those who mention their Creator, Allāh ﷻ, on their tongues in different ways and positions." So when you mention Allāh ﷻ, you go into that pillar of *ṭarīqah*. *Ṭarīqah* doesn't differ from

Sharī'ah. Sharī'ah is the law and *ṭarīqah* is the way. You cannot change what Allāh ﷻ has ordered for us, the law of Islam, the obligations. *Imān*, what the Prophet ﷺ described, you cannot change. You cannot change the constitution Allāh ﷻ gave to Muslims; the Holy Qur'an and the Holy Ḥadīth of Prophet cannot be changed!

Ṭarīqah is the way to execute these laws. One of the main pillars of *ṭarīqah* is *dhikrūllāh*, and Allāh mentioned, "The best of *dhikr* is to know *lā ilāha illa-Llāh*, which is Maqām at-Tawḥīd, the Station of Oneness of Being." So to glue and restore what is broken, you have to come back to *dhikrūllāh*. I'm not speaking of *dhikrūllāh* that is a public association, but rather *dhikrūllāh* when you are alone, as Prophet mentioned, *ij'al lisānak ratban bi dhikrūllāh*, "Keep your tongue wet with *dhikrūllāh*."

How are we spending our time, in *dhikrūllāh* or in *dhikr ad-dunyā*, in Allāh's remembrance or in remembrance of *dunyā?* As soon as you remember *dunyā*, you need *ghusl* (prescribed shower of purification). You cannot come to Allāh's door bringing your *dunyā* with you! That is *adab at-ṭarīqah*, "principles of *ṭarīqah*." You cannot come to an association of *dhikrūllāh* with no *ghusl*. That is why Sayyīdinā Shah Naqshband ق didn't allow any of his followers in his time to attend his sessions without not only *wuḍū*, but a complete *ghusl*. Do you know why you are required to make *ghusl* after you and your wife are intimate? It is not only to remove *najāsah* (impurity); that act is pure, clean. But you make *ghusl*, saying, "*Yā Rabbī*! I am moving from the desire you put in me for my family to my desire for You." That is why the curtain between you and Allāh ﷻ is very thin. So when you are in *dunyā* and you fulfill Allāh's order, you take *ghusl* when you finish (that act), in order to go back to Allāh's remembrance and open that door.

Al-Qushayrī ﵁, one of the biggest scholars of *taṣawwuf*, said, *Lam adkhul fī ḥudūri 'sh-shaykh illa ṣā'iman mughtasilan*, "I never enter the presence of my shaykh without having taken a shower and observing fast, and whenever I come to his school, I enter, go to the door of the place where he is sitting, and then I back up, respecting him, not coming inside with my ego or my *dunyā* because I am worried."

Today, how do we go to the door of the shaykh? What determines who goes in and who stays out? Who pays more money is allowed in!

Imām Al-Qushayrī ﵁ continues, "If I have the courage and insist to enter, then as soon as I enter I feel numb from the *tajallī*, divine manifestations, coming on my shaykh that make me run away trembling."

This is the beginning of the journey. We are lucky because we are in a time that is full of ignorance. As Grandshaykh ق said, that is why Allāh ﷻ opened more and more His doors of mercy. Because of these doors of mercy there is no more protocol, no more this discipline that is a prerequisite. Like a child that is spoiled, does he have any kind of principles to enter his father's room? Even if his father is president or king, no one will stop him and he enters. We are spoiled today with that *raḥmat* opening from Allāh ﷻ and there are no more restrictions.

So *awlīyāullāh* no longer look at the behavior of their followers; they say, "That is okay." Before, they could not take a step, out of respect and discipline toward the shaykh; a student became numb and went back. Today, no one is asking because of that huge *tajallī* of mercy coming on *Ummat an-Nabī* and on this *dunyā*. When you have a lot of water, you can use it in any way you like, even for irrigation of crops, but if you don't have water you save it. The *awlīyāullāh* used to save the *raḥmat* for their followers, but now it is coming like an ocean. So let them take it; with that *raḥmat* they will be blessed and cleaned.

So if al-Qushayrī ؓ said, "I would not enter my teacher's presence without fasting or taking a shower," oh *murīd*, how then do you dare to knock on the door of Allāh, which is *dhikrūllāh*? How can you go there without fasting from not only food, but also from all desires? You must come clean. As soon as you sit in the association of *dhikrūllāh,* your thoughts interfere and take you right and left, so Allāh ﷻ made *dhikrūllāh* an obligation.

> *Yā ayyuha 'Lladhīna āmanū 'dhkurūllāha dhikran kathīra wa sabiḥūhu bukratan wa aṣīla. Hūwa 'Lladhī yuṣalli ʿalaykum wa malā'ikatahu li yukhrijakum min aẓ-ẓulumāti ila 'n-nūr.*
>
> *O you who believe! Remember Allāh! Continue to mention Him without limit, before sunrise and before sunset. He is The One Who encourages, appreciates, and supports you all, and His angels, and replaces darkness and tyranny with divine Light.*
>
> (Sūrat al-'Aḥzāb, 33:41-43)

This means *dhikr* not only by tongue, but with all your senses, all your organs, all your body, all your soul and with everything possible to use that Allāh ﷻ has given you! You have to mention and continue reciting, not His Name, but entering the Ocean of Vision and seeing defects in your body and soul, and enter to that Presence. Mention to yourself, don't mention to people. *Dhikrun kathīra* means "excessive *dhikr*". How do we do *dhikr?* For ten or fifteen minutes only, but *dhikrun kathīra* has no end; it is non-stopping, a continuous remembrance of Allāh ﷻ, in your day and night! So if you stop, you are coming against His will.

That is the difference between *awlīyāullāh* and people; they are in constant *dhikrūllāh,* while we do *dhikr* for one hour and stop. Their hearts are constantly in remembrance. *kathīra* means, "unlimited". Then, *sabihū bukratan wa aṣīlā.* So first is *dhikrūllāh,* because as Allāh ﷻ said, "And We are nearer to him than his jugular vein." (al-Qaf, 50:16). It means, "Don't leave My Presence!" Allāh is possessive of His servant: He doesn't like the heart of His servant to be occupied or possessed except by Him. So Allāh ﷻ wants *awlīyāullāh* to be exclusively for Him.

> *Qulnā 'hbiṭū minhā jamī'an fa imma yātīyannakum minnī hudan faman tabi'a hudāya fa lā khawfun 'alayhim wa lā hum yaḥzanūn.*
> *We said, "All of you get down from here, and if, as is sure, there comes to you guidance from Me, whosoever follows My guidance, on them shall be no fear, nor shall they grieve.* (Sūrat al-Baqarah, 2:38)

Awlīyāullāh never feel sad because Allāh is taking care of them, making them slaves at His door. So there is a huge gap (in conduct) for *murīds* to be at the door of their teacher.

w'a'dhkurullāha dhikran kathīra wa sabihūhu bukratan wa asīla, "And praise him and glorify him morning and evening." There is morning remembrance and evening remembrance.

> *Yā ayyuha 'Lladhīna āmanū 'dhkurullāha dhikran kathīra wa sabihūhu bukratan wa asīla. Hūwa 'Lladhī yusalli 'alaykum li yukhrijakum min adh-dhulumāti ila 'n-nūr.*
> *O you who believe! Remember Allāh! Continue to mention Him without limit, before sunrise and before sunset. He is The One Who encourages, appreciates, and supports you all, and replaces darkness and tyranny with divine Light.*
> (Sūrat al-'Aḥzāb, 33:41-43)

That is*'imād at-ṭarīqah,* the "pillar of *ṭarīqah.*" Then Allāh brings you to His Presence after you do that continuous remembrance and glorify him morning and evening. Then what? Allāh and his angels will send blessings on you. *Inna Allāha wa malā'ikatahu yuṣallūn,* He will raise you to be connected to the heart of Sayyīdinā Muḥammad ﷺ; as He orders his angels to send blessing on Prophet, He also orders his angels to send blessings on you, to take you up, away from darkness to light. What darkness? Darkness of *dunyā,* which for *awlīyā* is not worth anything. That is why they became ascetics; they left *dunyā* and those who took it made a mistake. Our duty is to leave the desires of *dunyā,* but if Allāh makes *dunyā* a slave running after you, that is no problem.

Hūwa 'Lladhī yuṣalli 'alaykum wa malā' ikatahu li yukhrijakum min aẓ-ẓulumāti ila 'n-nūr. "He is The One Who supports you and takes you from darkness to light." When He takes you from darkness to light, *wa kān bil-mu'minīna Raḥīmā.* "He is showing you His mercy." It means, "You remember Me! I am ordering My angels to pray on you, and send that mercy on you."

So when *awlīyā* see this, they insist *dhikrūllāh* is the pillar of *ṭarīqah.* They don't ask people to do *irshād,* which is not for everyone, but they tell them do *dhikr* so they will benefit.

And Prophet ﷺ said:

yā 'ibn ādam idhā dhakartanī faqad shakartanī kathīran wa idhā nasītanī kafarta, wa bish-shukru tadūm an-ni'am.
O son of Adam! If you mention Me, it means you are thanking Me. By thanking Allāh, favors will not stop reaching you.

And Prophet ﷺ said in a holy *hadīth*:

O son of Adam! If you mention Me you are thanking Me, and if you thank someone he gives you more.

What do you think of Allāh ﷻ? If you thank Him, you get more, so to remember Him is to thank Him.

wa idhā nasītanī kafarta. "And if you stopped remembering Me, you are not becoming an unbeliever." *Kuffār* here does not mean "unbeliever," but rather "to make a mistake," or, "You have ignored My favors on you."

When you don't thank who is generous with you, what will he say? It means you didn't care, you are ungrateful. Here *kafartanī* means "ungrateful"; it does not mean "to become non-Muslim". You are ungrateful when you forget Him, so show gratitude to Allāh!

Prophet ﷺ said:

khayru 'l-'amal dhikrūllāh.
The best of deeds is to remember Allāh.
wa qāl an-nabī li kulli shay'in saqālan wa saqāl al-qulūb dhikrūllāh.
For everything there is a polish and polish of the heart is dhikrūllāh.

Like a diamond is in a rock, and to take it out you must cut the rock and then you polish it. The shaykh polishes us like a rock. Many of us go to the shaykh as tyrants, so what does he do? He has to break you down and hammer on you. They ask, "Why is Shaykh hammering on me?" Because he loves you, and that is to help you. When he shouts at you, don't get upset because he is carrying your problems! For everything there is polish and the best polish for hearts is *dhikrūllāh.*

Prophet ﷺ said:

O my Companions! If you find Riyāḍ al-Jannah, the Heavenly Gardens on Earth, stay there and sit in it and be in it. They asked, "Are there heavenly gardens on Earth?" He said, "Yes, the associations of dhikrūllāh."

It means *dhikrūllāh* of Holy Qur'an, Holy Hadith, the Beautiful Names and Attributes, or of holy prophets. So when you find such associations, go and sit in them as that is Heaven on Earth.

Do you want Heaven on Earth? People go everywhere looking for Heaven on Earth. Go sit with humble, broken-hearted people: sit with people of *dhikrūllāh.* That is what we need. We don't need to sit with presidents or kings. They are leaving whatever they have behind them (when they die). Those sitting in *dhikrūllāh* sessions are finding Heaven on Earth, where they clean their hearts for their Lord, then receive these manifestations.

wa qīla man kāna yurīd an yaʿrif manzilatahu ʿindallāh fal yanẓur ilā manzilatillāhu fī qalbih. "As much as we are keeping Allāh in our hearts, Allāh is keeping us." Say the truth: who are we keeping more in our hearts, Allāh or our children? We are always keeping our children in our hearts.

One of the *awlīyāullāh,* Abū ʿAlī ad-Daqāq ق, said, "*Dhikrūllāh* is *manshūr al-wilāyah,* the proclamation of sainthood." That big proclamation is displayed everywhere, and throughout circles of *dhikr* they know you are a *walī.* Your level can be known there, because you are from ʿAbdal, Nujabā, Nuqabā, Awtād, Akhyār, and Quṭb, Quṭb al-Bilād, Quṭb al-Aqtāb, Quṭb al-Irshād, Quṭb al-Mutaṣarrif. Everyone knows his level. *wa man utīyya dhālika al-manshūr...* "And whoever keeps his *dhikr* has that proclamation," and who has been *sulib,* one who *dhikrūllāh* has been taken from his heart, that means he has been "laid off", he is no more in that heavenly gathering on Earth.

And it is said *dhikrūllāh* is better than *fikr,* to think. With thinking you have to pull information or knowledge, and with your mind you can only pull *dunyā* knowledge, you cannot pull secrets. However, with *dhikr Allāh* ﷻ

opens for you the interpretation of Holy Qur'an and the Holy Hadith, and an understanding of what *awlīyā* have said. *Allāh taʿalā yuṣaf bihi wa lā yuṣaf bil-fikr, "Allāh* ﷻ is not described by thought, but He is described by remembering Him." A mental description is too limited.

Grandshaykh ق said, "The punishment of a *walī* is to be cut from *dhikr,*" because Allāh said:

F'adhkurūnī adhkurkum.
Remember Me and I remember you; mention Me and I mention you.
(Surat al-Baqarah, 2:152)

O students of Mawlana Shaykh Nazim ق! We are lucky and blessed to be connected to such a *walī,* who is connected to the Golden Chain through two big oceans, Sayyīdinā Abū Bakr aṣ-Ṣiddīq ق and Sayyīdinā ʿAlī ؓ, *maraj al-baḥrayn yaltaqiyyān,* "two oceans coming together and between them is a thin divider." Those are two places of knowledge that come together, as mentioned in Sūrat ar-Raḥmān, that He made the two oceans come together with very thin divider between them.

maraja al-baḥrayni yaltaqiyāni baynahumā barzakhun lā yabghīyān.
He has let loosed the two seas meeting together. Between them is a barrier which none of them can transgress. (Sūrat ar-Raḥmān, 55:19-20)

That is the *baḥr,* ocean, of Sayyīdinā Abū Bakr and the *baḥr* of Sayyīdinā ʿAli! The two of them came together in Sayyīdinā Jafar aṣ-Ṣadiq ق. May Allāh bless these two great ones and all *Ṣaḥābah* ؓ of Prophet ﷺ and His deputies ق, and those looking for normal life, not a life of extremism!

Wa min Allāhi 't-tawfiq, bi ḥurmati 'l-ḥabīb, bi ḥurmati 'l-Fātiḥah.
And with Allāh is success. For the sake of the Beloved, for his sake we recite the opening chapter of Holy Qur'an.

Characteristics and Levels of Dhikrullah

Aʿūdhu billāhi min ash-Shayṭān ir-rajīm. Bismillāhi' r-Raḥmāni 'r-Raḥīm. Nawaytu 'l-arbāʿīn, nawaytu 'l-ʿitikāf, nawaytu'l-khalwah, nawaytu 'l-ʿuzlah, nawaytu 'r-riyāḍa, nawaytu 's-sulūk, lillāhi Taʿalā fī hādhā 'l-masjid. Atiʿ ūllāh wa atiʿū 'r-Rasūl wa ūli 'l-amri minkum. (4:59)

Every one of us intend to love Allāh ﷻ, our Prophet ﷺ, our shaykh ق, and to love everyone. But we are weak servants, *pas faible, très faible;* we cannot do more than what we are doing. However, it is nice to know what *awlīyāullāh* think of those things we are heedless about. Their knowledge is very high and ours is very limited.

The Prophet ﷺ said:

innamā al-ʿamālu bin-niyyāt wa innamā li-kulli 'mrin mā nawā.
Every action is by intention and truly to every man is what he intended.
(Bukhari and Muslim)

We were speaking in the previous session about the importance of *dhikrūllāh,* which is important for everyone seeking this path. *Shuyukh aṭ-ṭā'ifa,* which means, "shaykhs of *taṣawwuf*", all of them with their differences and different ways of *dhikrūllāh.* As much as there are differences in that Way it is better, because people are able to find and take from the tap that quenches their thirst. This one makes *dhikr* in this way, this one in that way. It is okay as all of them are making *dhikr* to The One, Whom you cannot describe, the Exalted One. You cannot describe Him through any kind of thoughts in your mind. *lā yaṣifahu bil-fikr.* "You cannot describe Allāh ﷻ through your mind." Only through what Allāh describes Himself you can understand, through His Beautiful Names and Attributes. But you cannot understand the Essence.

Awlīyāullāh are swimming in these oceans to pull out these treasures, and the deeper they go the deeper the water becomes and they cannot reach (an end). *kullamā taqarabū wajad al-masāfa abʿad.* "However nearer they come, the distance increases and to pass it is difficult." In the Miʿrāj, Prophet Muḥammad ﷺ reached *qāba qawsayni aw adnā,* very near, *"two bows' length or nearer."* But with that nearness which is only for Prophet, it is still far to reach the Reality of Allāh's Essence. No one can reach that! How far is the

Divine Presence? Only Prophet knows, but the Essence is much further (beyond that).

That is why Allāh ﷻ is always putting different meanings in the heart of Prophet ﷺ and in the hearts of *awlīyāullāh*. That is why ascensions never end.

wa fawqa kull dhi ʿilmin ʿalīm.
Above every knower is a (higher) knower. (Sūrat Yūsuf, 12:76)

This *ayah* also means that in every moment there is a higher knowledge (revealed). That is why books contain knowledge of the past and knowledge of that time, when written by *awlīyā*, but tomorrow a higher knowledge will be revealed. Grandshaykh ق said, "In the time of Sayyīdinā Mahdī ؏, if you open any book there will be nothing in it; all the writing will have disappeared." All previous knowledge will have passed, but in the time of Sayyīdinā Mahdī ؏ there is new knowledge called, *khāmis al-Qur'an*, "the secret of the Qur'an."

Today no secret of the Qur'an comes out, but then that secret with 12,000-to-24,000 oceans of knowledge will come on every letter of Qur'an to hearts of seekers! Those living in that time will immediately understand and reach their destiny in sainthood.

(An attendee sneezes.) Yarḥamakullāh. I did not hear you say, *'Alḥamdulillāh'*, which is a sin, and we are witness on that. *(Attendee says, "Alḥamdulillāh!")* When someone sneezes, you must say *'Alḥamdulillāh'* and then we respond, *'yarḥamakullāh'*. If he does not say that, we are not responsible to reply. Allāh ﷻ said:

fadhkurūnī adhkurkum, wa ashkurū lī wa lā takfurūna.
Remember Me and I will remember you, and thank Me and don't be ungrateful. (Sūrat al-Baqarah, 2:152)

That specialty is only for *Ummat an-Nabī*. Before, for other nations, it was *adhkurūnī*, "Remember Me." But for *Ummat an-Nabī*, Allāh ﷻ added, *adhkurkum*, "I remember you." Others are under the order to remember Him, what He revealed in another verse:

utlu mā uḥīyya ilayk min al-kitābi wa aqimi 'ṣ-ṣalāta inna'ṣ-ṣalāta tanhā ʿani'l-faḥshāi wa 'l-munkari wa ladhikrullāhi akbaru w'Allāhu yʿalamu mā taṣnaʿūn.

Recite what is sent of the Book by inspiration to you, and establish regular prayer, for prayer restrains from shameful and unjust deeds. And remembrance of Allāh is the greatest (thing in life) without doubt. And Allāh knows the (deeds) you do. (Sūrat al-ʿAnkabūt, 29:45)

Allāh's remembrance is for *Ummat an-Nabī*, but His mentioning of you is higher and greater. How much higher and greater? There is no limit in that greatness! That means in every moment, even if you remember Him one moment in your life, you are *ʿabd*, servant, and your *ʿibādah*, worship, is limited. So if you mentioned Him one time in your life, saying, "*Yā Allāh!*" or, "*lā ilāha illa-Llāh*," Allāh will render it back to you non-stop until the Day of Judgment, and He will assign angels to send praise on you non-stop, without end and with no limits! That is for one time, and it is enough for Allāh ﷻ to send in every moment! Let us say now, *Yā Rabb! Yā Rabb!* O Allāh! O Allāh! That is for you a great blessing.

That is why the association of *dhikr* is a light, as angels are there. It becomes a place of *ʿibādah*, worshipness. Allāh ﷻ is looking and that place becomes a place of worshipness, where angels are all the time. That is why they say to appoint in your home a place only for prayers and *ṣalawāt*. To enter there has to be with *adab*, discipline. You cannot enter there in your normal daily life, as that area becomes special and it has heavenly visitors.

That is why Sayyida Maryam's place became sacred. *kullamā dakhala ʿalayha zakariyya 'l-miḥrāb wajada ʿindahā rizqā*. Whenever Sayyīdinā Zakarīya ؑ entered that place, he found provision there. So there, he asked Allāh to give him a child, and Allāh ﷻ granted him Sayyīdinā Yaḥyā ؑ. So it is nice to have *makān al-ibadah*, a place of worship, and later it becomes a *maqām al-ibadah*, a place of worship where manifestations of angels come on you; angels must be present there.

One of *awlīyāullāh* said, *law lā anna dhikrūllāh taʿālā farḍan lamā dhakartuhu ijlālan lahu*. "If it was not an obligation to remember Allāh, to mention His Beautiful Names and Attributes, or to mention Him in recitation of Holy Qur'an, I would never do it."

It is ordered in the verse of *dhikr* mentioned previously; there might be 50-60 *ayāt* in Holy Qur'an. If it was not an order he will not mention it! Why? This is very significant.

He said, "How do I mention Him?" as when you mention Him you are entering the Divinely Presence. "How am I mentioning His Majesty when I revere Him so much, *ijlālan*. How can someone weak mention Someone

Who created him? I feel ashamed. I have to wash my mouth before I open it *alfu alfu*, a thousand by a thousand (1,000 x 1,000) times of repentance." That means, "Millions of repentances I have to do before I open my mouth to remember Him!"

Today when we come to *dhikr*, we come lazy. Why lazy? Because according to that *walī*, our soul knows that we are weak and our soul is ashamed from the doings of our bodies, which always contradict whatever Allāh wants, so we do the opposite. Our body is absorbed in *dunyā* desire and our soul is absorbed in heavenly desire. So when you come for *dhikrūllāh*, be sure you are very clean. As we said, in previous times they came to *dhikr* only in pure white clothes reserved for that. They had a room to change into their very clean clothes, with no dust. Today they say there are no special requirements, that to just attend *dhikr* is enough. Allāh's mercy is in this time (and standards have dropped).

They asked one person, *a'anta ṣāimun,* "Are you fasting?"

He said, *naʿm anā ṣāimun bi dhikrillāh.* "Yes, I am fasting, as I am remembering Him, making *dhikrūllāh* in every moment. I am not with you, I am in the Divine Presence with My Lord. If I remember anyone other than My Lord, then I break fast."

Not like us; we say we are fasting if we are not eating. Let's count in 24 hours, how much we are mentioning Allāh's Name and how much we are mentioning each other's names? It might be that in 23 hours and 59 minutes we are mentioning *dunyā,* and the rest is mentioning and remembering Allāh, our Creator, and that we are His weak servants (*i.e.,* one minute)!

And a *jawāriḥ* (whose limbs do *dhikrūllāh*) mentioned, "There was a man between us who says *'Allāh, Allāh,'* and one day a tree branch fell on his head and split it open. (There were no stitches at that time to close the wound) and blood was running from his head and gushed on the ground, and it began to write *'Allāh, Allāh.'*" That one was mentioning Allāh 23 hours and 59 minutes, because with him everything was with *dhikrūllāh*.

Also, there was a lady in Egypt who died recently. She never answered any question except with a verse of Holy Qur'an; even she wanted to eat, from Qur'an she mentioned foods and they prepared that food for her. She didn't eat anything that is not mentioned in Holy Qur'an. Allāh mentions in Qur'an that He made *halāl* for you *ibil* and other kinds of meats, and birds, and fruits of the sea. Always she answered from Holy Qur'an and never she opened her mouth to answer from other than that, until she died! Where are such people today?

In previous *ummam*, nations, were prescribed *dhikr* at certain times, but *Ummat an-Nabī* was granted to make *dhikr* at any time, in their heart or by tongue. Allāh ﷻ said in Holy Qur'an:

> *Al-ladhīna yadhkurūnallāh qīyāman wa qu'ūdān wa 'alā junūbīhim wa yattafakkarūna fi khalqi 's-samāwātī wa 'l-arḍ, rabbanā mā khalaqta hadha bāṭilan subḥānaka fa qinā 'adhāba 'n-nār.*
>
> *Those who remember Allāh (always, and in prayers) standing, sitting, and lying down on their sides, and who think deeply about the Creation of the Heavens and the Earth, (saying), "Our Lord! You have not created (all) this without purpose. Glory to You! Give us salvation from the torment of the Fire."* (Sūrat 'Āli 'Imrān, 3:191)

And there is *dhikr* of the heart, *dhikr* of the tongue, and *dhikr* of the soul. When the heart and tongue *dhikr* coincide, that is an opening for the soul to remember Allāh, as in 24 hours when *Ummat an-Nabī* sleeps, their souls ascend to make *sajdah* at the Throne of Allāh. In that *sajdah,* the soul is free to make remembrance of Allāh in the Divine Presence. That is why in Ṣalāt an-Najāt, that *sajdah* is not here in *dunyā,* it is under the Holy Throne. *Awlīyāullāh* take their followers when they go in *sajdah,* to the location in the Divine Presence at the Throne. Your heart must be well connected at that time, not to wander here and there; in this *sajdah* you must be extremely careful with your thoughts, and you must be aware that you are in that Divine Presence! It is very heavy and that makes *awlīyā* shake, to consider how much you wasted your time in *dunyā*! Your *du'ā* there is accepted, so it is essential in that *sajdah* to only make *du'ā* for your *ākhirah,* not *dunyā.* But you may ask for *dunyā* also; ask what comes to the heart, such as:

> *Rabbanā ātinā fi 'd-dunyā ḥasanatan wa fi 'l-ākhirati ḥasanatan wa qinā 'adhāba 'n-nār.*
>
> *Our Lord! Grant us good in this world and good in the Hereafter, and save us from the chastisement of the Fire.* (Sūrat al-Baqarah, 2:201)

When we prayed Ṣalāt an-Najāt behind Grandshaykh 'AbdAllāh ق, we made *sajdah* for one hour! Our foreheads, feet and hands become numb. We could not raise our heads (before Grandshaykh raised his). *Awlīyāullāh* know the importance of being in the Divine Presence, and as he was making *du'ā* and we were saying, *amīn.* The main difference is, his *du'ā* is not like our *du'ā,* because he is there under the Throne. That is not simple!

The first level is *dhikrūllāh* is *bil-lisān, dhikr* by tongue, because the heart is not yet connected. This is considered "the Station of Heedlessness," because your heart is not able to open and that is called the Maqām al-Awwam, "the common people's station, *maqām* of *ghaflah,* heedlessness". Because with your tongue you can say, "*Allāh, Allāh*" and you are watching TV! How many of you are watching TV when doing *dhikr*? And that is also known as *dhikr ul-ʿada,* "the *dhikr* of habit." Like we make our prayers from habit, but it is not real worship. And we ask, "O Allāh! Change our *dhikr al-qalb* to real *dhikr*!"

The second level is to make *dhikr* by tongue and *dhikr* by heart. In the Naqshbandi Order, they train you to do *dhikr* by tongue and *dhikr* by heart, by assigning you to recite daily 2500 times *Allāh, Allāh* by tongue (verbally) and 2500 times *Allāh, Allāh* by heart (silently). As soon as you do that, you feel it. Take your beads or even without beads (*taṣbīḥ*); put your tongue on the roof of your mouth and you find your heart doing *dhikr, Allāh, Allāh.* That is *dhikru 'l-khawāṣ,* "*Dhikr* of the Chosen," assigned to some *murīds* by the shaykh. It is *dhikru 'l-ʿibādah,* "*dhikr* of (real) worship" and its fruit is *wa la-dhikrūllāhi akbar,* "Allāh will remember you in a Presence better than your presence."

Then the third level is, *dhikr al-khawāṣ al-khawāṣ,* "*Dhikr* of the Chosen of the Chosen," or *dhikr al-muḥabbatullāh,* "*Dhikr* of the Love of Allāh," in which all parts of body do *dhikr*. That is only for *awlīyāullāh.* When *dhikr* of the heart and tongue coincide, who does that *dhikr* is able to enter the Divine Presence, which is the best of *dhikr*, as Allāh ﷻ said:

> *w 'adhkur rabbaka fī nafsika taḍaruʿan wa khufiyā wa dūn al-jahri min al-qawl wa lā takun mina 'l-ghāfilīn.*
>
> *And bring your Lord to remembrance in your (very) soul, with humility and in reverence, without loudness in words, in the mornings and evenings, and be not of those who are unheedful.*
>
> (Sūrat al-Aʿrāf, 7:205)

That means, don't make *dhikr* openly, but make it within yourself. Don't show that your beads are moving; that is "showing off," which is ego. One of Grandshaykh's representatives, Shaykh Ḥusayn ق, like Shaykh Nazim ق, I never saw him with beads in his hands during the day. He said, "We don't like to show off. Do *dhikr* at night, up to Ishrāq." They don't show they are carrying beads. Today they show five-hundred beads or even one-thousand beads, so long!

tadaruʿan wa khīfatan wa dūn al-jahri min al-qawl, "Mention your Lord in yourself." Run to Him asking forgiveness, moving by your heart, afraid from losing His love to you, and inaudibly, without making a sound for people to see you are doing *dhikr*. Surrender and don't show off for others, with pride and arrogance.

wa qawlahu ʿalayhis salām khayru 'dh-dhikr al-khafī.
The best of dhikr is the silent. (Ibn Hibbān)

dhikr al-qalb sabaʿ diʿfan bi sabaʿ diʿf.
The dhikr of the heart is 70 times better.

When you multiply 2 x 2 it is 4, and 4 x 4 is 16, and the multiplication increases exponentially. So if you do 1000 *dhikr* of the heart, it is 70 times exponentially more than *dhikr* of the tongue. One-thousand times one-thousand is one-million, and then one-million times one-million is one-billion; that is two *dʿaf*. Three *daʿf* is one-billion times one-billion equals one-trillion. So see how high you go with 70 *daʿf*!

wa la-dhikrūllāhi akbar. This is a huge number; it has a limit, but you are happy with that huge number because Allāh's remembrance of you is without limits! Will He throw that one in the Hellfire? So say, *yā Allāh, yā Rabb*! If you mention "Allāh" one time, He will mention you and that is enough for your entire lifetime.

wa 'dh-dhikr al-qalbi 'lladhī lā yasmaʿu al-ḥafaẓa ʿalā min dhikru 'l-lisān.
The dhikr of the heart is higher than the dhikr of the tongues which the angels hear. (Narrated by Ayesha in Bayhaqī)

SubhānAllāh, the knowledge never stops!

Wa min Allāhi ʿt-tawfiq, bi ḥurmati ʿl-ḥabīb, bi ḥurmati ʿl-Fātiḥah.
And with Allāh is success. For the sake of the Beloved, for his sake we recite the opening chapter of Holy Qur'an.

Duties of Guides and Students

Aʿūdhu billāhi min ash-Shayṭān ir-rajīm. Bismillāhi' r-Raḥmāni 'r-Raḥīm. Nawaytu 'l-arbāʿīn, nawaytu 'l-ʿitikāf, nawaytu'l-khalwah, nawaytu 'l-ʿuzlah, nawaytu 'r-riyāḍa, nawaytu 's-sulūk, lillāhi Taʿalā fī hādhā 'l-masjid. Atiʿ ūllāh wa atiʿū 'r-Rasūl wa ūli 'l-amri minkum. (4:59)

Mawlana Shaykh Nazim ق says that we have to ask *madad* from *awlīyāullāh* every time; it is proper *adab*. *Awlīyāullāh* ask their support from Prophet ﷺ, and so we ask support from Grandshaykh ق, from Mawlana Shaykh Nazim ق, and from every *walī* standing at the door of Prophet. They are our role models and the *murīd* tries to at stand their door to reach the Divine Presence. You cannot reach the Divine Presence without a teacher; they are there already. One of these *shuyukh aṭ-ṭā'ifa*, the shaykhs of *tazkīyyat an-nafs*, is Shaykh Shiblī ق. They are one group but they have different ways, because *awlīyā* are friends with each other and they know their limits.

Shaykh Shiblī said, "I mentioned You, not because I forgot You for the blink of an eye, but because it is easy on my tongue to refresh it and to say Your Name." That means he is speaking with his Lord. *Fa lammā wajadta annaka ḥādiran shahidta annaka mawjūd fī kulli makān,* "When I found that You are present, I testified that You are present in every place. I spoke to everyone without speech. I observed someone without looking through my eyes." They recite this poetry when they are in a trance-like state; then they cannot control themselves anymore and they are always trying to reveal what is in their hearts by expressing themselves.

Many people today remember their Lord when they are in an emotional state. Even if they are not *awlīyā,* when something horrible happens and they are sad, they feel like turning to their Lord and asking from Him, because it is there, but in normal life it is veiled with the darkness of this *dunyā.*

When someone you love dies and you are present there, you feel that majestic manifestation of al-Qahhār, (The Dominant), al-Jabbār (The Compeller), Qābiḍ (The Restricter), "the One in Whose Hand is everything." You feel these attributes and you begin to fear death, and maybe with that fear you cannot enter the deceased one's room as you feel uneasy. So you remember Allāh at that time. *Awlīyāullāh* are always in that state of feeling their return to Allāh. They are not like us; we like to live even longer than Sayyīdinā Nūḥ ﷺ!

One of the conditions of guiding to *dhikrūllāh* is, the *murshid* must be based in Islamic beliefs, *f'il-ʿaqāid wa fi'l-fiqh,* in beliefs and in jurisprudence, so that he can answer his followers' questions. If not, the *murīd* will begin to doubt his shaykh. This is one of the conditions of the shaykh of Ṭarīqat an-Naqshbandiyya as mentioned by Sayyīdinā Khālid al-Baghdādī ق. He must know *sharīʿatullāh.* If not, he must step down and surrender his status of shaykh to someone who knows it. Also, he must be able to perfect and discipline the hearts of followers to the highest level of perfection. He must know all kinds of *afāt an-nufūs,* the sicknesses of the self, and which sickness his *murīd* is in. He must also know the illnesses and how to cure the *murīds* from them. And not only will he guide them through their journey, but also if he found them in need for something, he has to provide it.

Sayyīdinā Khālid al-Baghdādī ق said, *Wa li-kulli min imkānahu la-atāhu min al-māl,* "The shaykh even has to give his *murīds* money to build them up, and he doesn't leave him without money." *Allāhu Akbar*! You can see how Mawlana Shaykh Nazim ق reacts to this. People come to his door for money. We used to say, "Why is Mawlana giving money to *murīds?*" He is not like us; he doesn't mind. He gives like an ocean! Allāh ﷻ gives to him and he gives.

Allāh ﷻ gave that *walī* power to see and observe all *ʿayb,* deficiencies, of his *murīd.* So from his perfection, he never exposes his *murīd;* he never says anything. Someone came complaining to me when I was in England and also by email, saying they have a problem with someone there who considers himself accomplished in everything and he is a senior one. He was begging me to tell Mawlana Shaykh Nazim ق. I said, "Okay, when I go to Cyprus. I cannot talk about these issues over the phone." I was entrusted with that matter, so when I went there I told Mawlana Shaykh Nazim ق. It was so simple. He said, "No, I never saw or heard that. I don't believe it. If it is true, let the person who is saying that come to me." He wants to cover and not expose. *Awlīyāullāh* hide their followers, they don't expose them or it might cause enmity. So they leave them and slowly, slowly fix them.

Someone told me here in America, in political events they keep the beast around them because if they let the beast loose, he might make too many problems. They keep petting the lion, not to let him loose. *Awlīyāullāh* pet us, and that is how they can catch us. Grandshaykh ق used to say, "I follow my *murīd* ninety-nine steps; I go according to what he or she likes.

When they are feeling they can trust me completely, I catch them. We go with them ninety-nine steps and then one step, they go with me."

Furthermore, the character of the shaykh must be rich in good manners and he must not be angry, except when you break Allāh's law. It is okay to get angry for Allāh's law, no problem. But for *dunyā* issues, the shaykh always forgives.

What is the duty of the *murshid* to his *murīd*? They are three. First, he has to put him on the right track to seek his journey. There are too many tracks, like a maze, and the *murīd* is not knowing where to begin or end. The *murshid* has to put him at the beginning of the maze. Second, he must inform the *murīd* when he has reached his goal; that is his duty. The *murīd* will be a guide for others and will be dressed with the Dress of Guidance. And third, the *murshid* will protect him when he is taking care of different followers around the world. The shaykh sends his senior *murīd* around the world to bring others to the shaykh.

And what are the duties of the *murīd* to his shaykh? First, he has to listen to whatever the shaykh says to him without question. Allāh said in Holy Qur'an:

Atiʿ ūllāh wa atiʿū 'r-Rasūl wa ūli 'l-amri minkum.
Obey Allāh, obey the Prophet, and obey those in authority among you.
(Sūrat an-Nisā, 4:59)

Here, "authority" means the shaykh. That is Allāh's order, and you cannot say no. You say, *samiʿna wa ataʿna,* "I hear and I obey." Can you do that? No, it is difficult. Even if you do it you still have doubts, thinking, "This doesn't work in my mind, it is not acceptable!" So he first has to listen to what the shaykh says. If the shaykh says "eat," then eat, "drink," then drink, "pray," then pray, "do this or don't do this." The second duty is, *kitmān sirr ash-shaykh.* If the *murīd* saw a secret of the shaykh, he must not expose it, even if it is something he doesn't like as he doesn't know the wisdom behind it.

Grandshaykh ق said, "One time I was in my seclusion under the order of Shaykh Sharafuddīn ق. During my seclusion he came to me." Your shaykh can come anytime during seclusion, but others cannot comer to you or it will interrupt the seclusion. He said, "ʿAbdAllāh Effendi," meaning "respected ʿAbdAllāh," "Prepare yourself tomorrow. I will pass by you and take you somewhere." Grandshaykh ق was thinking, "O, I am coming out of seclusion to go somewhere." He had no doubt; his belief was straight forward, and he was that way since he was a boy. When he was young, he had to walk up a hill to reach his shaykh.

One day Shaykh Sharafuddīn ق was sitting with *'ulamā* who said, "O Shaykh Sharafuddīn ق! You always give importance to that boy." Shaykh Sharafuddīn ق said, "He is there at the bottom of the hill now. If I send someone to him saying, 'Your shaykh is telling you to go to Mecca,' then without coming to me to confirm, he will direct himself to Mecca and begin walking."

So now look at us and look at how strong his belief is, not like some people today who say they are representatives. Look at the belief. Can you tell someone now, "Close your store and take a one-month vacation." They will say, "How will I make my payments?"

Shaykh Sharafuddīn ق said, "Prepare yourself tomorrow, I am taking you."

When Mawlana Shaykh Nazim ordered me into seclusion in 2005 in Damascus, he said, "Every Friday I want you to visit two *awlīyā,* Sayyīdinā Khālid al-Baghdādī ق and Sayyīdinā Muḥīyyidīn Ibn 'Arabī ق." I did my seclusion in Damascus, up on the mountain (in the home of Mawlana Shaykh Nazim on Jabal Qasiyoun). If the shaykh orders you to go out of seclusion, you do it; you go visit and come back. If you do that by their order it is alright, but you cannot do that on your own, or that breaks the seclusion.

Shaykh Sharafuddīn ق said, "Wait, I am coming." He came and took Grandshaykh ق to the big bazaar area in Istanbul, Kapalı Çarsa. It is a huge shopping area with a door at the beginning and a door at the end. You enter and you are inside, then they close the door in the evening and open it again in the morning. All kinds of people come there. When they reached the door, he said, "Let us hold each others' hand," and they stretched their arms. Although the door was bigger, but you could see that their hands were touching the door on both sides. Also, Allāh gave them above-average height, and everyone was able to pass under their arms.

Awlīyāullāh are not like us. Everyone coming in or going out had to go under their arms. Grandshaykh ق didn't ask Shaykh Sharafuddīn ق, "What is the wisdom?" There is no question in *ṭarīqah*. You do this, you don't change your mind. They stood all day until the noon prayer, then they prayed and came back. Time for 'Aṣr came, they prayed and came back. There are many mosques there and they went around. Then they stood there until the closing time, which was Maghrib, and then they left.

Shaykh Sharafuddīn ق was waiting to see if Grandshaykh ق will ask the wisdom. He didn't ask. That is his duty, *imtithāl al-amr,* to obey his order, and *kitmān sirrih,* what he sees, he has to hide (keep secret). He saw many things when people came and passed under their arms, as it is an open, public place.

The next duty of *murīd* to *murshid* is *t'aẓīm qadr ash-shaykh,* to raise higher the respect of the shaykh or his order. Some people might disrespect the shaykh if he orders them to go and open their hands at Kapali Çarşı (market) all day. They will say, "Why do I have to go there and raise my hand like that? People will say I am crazy and take me to the mental hospital." Grandshaykh ق kept quiet and did *t'aẓīm amr ash-shaykh;* it is not to exalt, exaltation is for Allāh ﷻ; it is to elevate and honor whatever the shaykh does.

Grandshaykh ق never asked. At the end of the seclusion, Shaykh Sharafuddīn ق said, "'AbdAllāh Effendi! Do you know why I asked you to do that? I was ordered to hold these two doors so that anyone who passes will see us, and from seeing us, if Allāh likes, He will guide them to Islam," Because the light coming from *awlīyāullāh* can reach their hearts.

Grandshaykh ق said, "If a person looks at a *walī* with love, it means that *walī* is responsible for that person in *dunyā* and *in ākhirah.* When someone loves you, it is because they feel that familiarity with you and light on you. That is how people feel with Mawlana Shaykh Nazim ق; they see his humility and love, and they are attracted. When people are attracted, then *awlīyāullāh* can work on their hearts.

So there are three things; obey the shaykh, keep his secret, and honor the respect given to him. That is one part. The second part for the *murīd* is: first, to have *adab* with Allāh; second, to have *adab* with Prophet, to respect and praise the Prophet ﷺ; and third, to have discipline with the shaykh and pious people. If you keep that, then you will reach the level of *dhikr* in the heart and you will be ready to be accepted. Then you are on the right track.

When a train comes, there are computers that put it on the right track. When pilots fly the plane, the computer guides the plane, even though the pilot might be sleeping. *Awlīyā's* hearts are responsible for their *murīds* and all of them are connected to his "auto pilot". Every *murīd's* wire is connected to the server of the shaykh.

But there is a question here. Sayyīdinā Muhyidīn ibn 'Arabi ق wrote Futūhāt al-Makkīyah (12 volumes). Western people and Muslims alike are drowning in what he wrote, and that was 1,000 years ago! Look how high he was. What about *awlīyāullāh* today? If they open those oceans, people will drown in them.

Yajib ʿalā shaykhun idhā ra'ā shaykhun ākhir, "It is an obligation of the shaykh that if he saw a shaykh higher than him in knowledge, to advise himself, and keep the service of the higher shaykh. This applies to him and his students. *Fa innahu ṣalāḥun wa ḥaqqihi wa ḥaqq aṣḥābih,* "This will be righteousness and happiness for him and his followers." This means he is not cheating; he is not saying to his *murīds,* "I am the shaykh."

Those who consider themselves shaykhs, if they see another one higher, they have to drop their shaykh-hood and follow that shaykh who is higher, in order to reach happiness for him and his students. *Wa mattā lam yafʿal hadha laysa bi munṣafin li nafsihi wa ṣāḥbih,* "If he doesn't do that, he is not fair to himself. He is falling in a valley or well, and failed his *himmah,* what he was ordered."

In other words, if someone has a shaykh and he finds another shaykh who is higher, he has to follow him. If a *murīd* finds a *murīd* who is higher, he has to follow the one higher. If that senior *murīd* finds a senior *murīd* who is higher, he has to follow the one higher. If he doesn't do that, he is failing and he might be falling in love with the chair he is sitting on. *Ḥubban li 'r-riyāsah,* "in love with leadership," wanting that people follow him.

What was the character we mentioned in the beginning? He has to know all kinds of *fiqh* and all kinds of *ʿaqā'id.* If your belief is not correct, what is the benefit? You cannot say, "I am a Muslim," and you don't know what kind of faith you have.

> The Prophet ﷺ said:
>
> *walladhī nafsī bi-yadihi law an Mūsā kāna ḥayyan mā wasiʿahu illa an tabaʿnī.*
>
> *By the One in Whose Hand is my soul, if Mūsā was alive in my time among you, he would have no choice but to follow me.*
>
> (Aḥmad, Abū Yaʿala, al-Bazār)

So according to this *hadīth,* a shaykh must follow a shaykh that is higher than him. That is why Shaykh Ḥusayn Zakarīya in Ghana didn't take the Tijaniyya Ṭarīqah, which is spread throughout Ghana. Because at 14 years of age, he dreamt that a shaykh of the Naqshbandi Order gave him initiation. We sent someone to find him, who spent six months in Accra, but he could not find Shaykh Ḥusayn Zakarīya. When I landed, he was there at the airport waiting for me. Do you think he came there by himself? No! He had a dream in which Prophet ﷺ told him to go there and meet me. And that is how he got connected to the Naqshbandi Ṭarīqah. He was a shaykh, but he went to a higher shaykh. He has followers himself. Prophet said, "If Mūsā was alive in my time, he would have to follow me, and even Ilyas and ʿĪsā (would have to follow me)."

This also applies to the inheritors of the Prophet in this time; they must follow the one who is higher. That means you must take your followers to the right fountain. If not, it means you love leadership.

In Islam, there is a pyramid. Leadership is not accepted in Islam except in a hierarchy. You must go from down to up. You must show humbleness. The shaykh is showing humbleness. Who is showing humbleness now? These kings and presidents? They are not showing humbleness, they are stubborn, saying, "I am better!" Then what happens in the end, they fight each other. But if they sit together and say, "We have to work together and open the borders," at least the Muslim countries (would benefit). Now to visit those countries, they require a visa and a background check, and in those countries, they are blowing people up! If you want to go to Afghanistan, they have to check your background. Why? Go check the people living there!

Where did the current flood come in Pakistan? In Swat. What did they do there two months ago? They blew up the tomb of Data Ghanj Bakhsh, ʿAlī Hujwairi's ق *maqām*. *Awlīyāullāh* don't like that. Therefore, look what happened! They are punished. When punishment comes, it hits those who are good and those who are bad. So don't come against a *walīullāh,* living or dead. When they are dead, they are stronger, more powerful.

All prophets are under Sayyīdinā Muḥammad ﷺ. This must be an example for *shuyūkh* of *ṭarīqah;* all of them have to be under one. That is why you have to see who is under:

wa fawqa kulli dhi ʿilmin ʿalīm.
Above every knower is a (higher) knower. (Sūrat Yūsuf, 12:76)

You have to find the highest *walī* and follow him or else you are not on the right way. This is important; it shows us principles of *ṭarīqah* and where we stand in regards to them. It is becoming a nice book for keeping discipline in *ṭarīqah,* which is important for all of us to learn. May Allāh bless this meeting and every meeting that calls people to Allāh ﷻ. May Allāh give long life to Mawlana Shaykh Nazim ق, and may all of us live to see Imām Mahdī ؑ!

Wa min Allāhi 't-tawfīq, bi ḥurmati 'l-ḥabīb, bi ḥurmati 'l-Fātiḥah.
And with Allāh is success. For the sake of the Beloved, for his sake we recite the opening chapter of Holy Qur'an.

Types of Baya¿, Their Conditions and Status

Aʿūdhu billāhi min ash-Shayṭān ir-rajīm. Bismillāhi' r-Raḥmāni 'r-Raḥīm. Nawaytu 'l-arbāʿīn, nawaytu 'l-ʿitikāf, nawaytu'l-khalwah, nawaytu 'l-ʿuzlah, nawaytu 'r-riyāḍa, nawaytu 's-sulūk, lillāhi Taʿalā fī hādhā 'l-masjid. Atiʿ ūllāh wa atiʿū 'r-Rasūl wa ūli 'l-amri minkum. (4:59)

Prophet ﷺ said, "If Mūsā was living, he would not be able except to follow me," because you have to follow the one higher than you. Also in Sharīʿah, you have to follow the one who is more knowledgeable than you. And also in *Ḥaqīqat*, you have to follow the one that Allāh ﷻ guided to the right path and whose knowledge is more than yours.

Imām ʿAbd al-Wahhāb ash-Shaʿrānī ق (d. Cairo 973 AH), one of the big scholars in Islam, said, *idhā rā'itu 'aḥadun aʿarafu minnī bi 't-tarīq lamadhtu ʿalayhi wa law kuntu maʿdhūnan min qabli li-shaykhin ākhir,* "If I see in my way, my journey, that journey never ends, and whatever you do is continuous and difficult. You have to face all these difficulties until you are able to reach the highest level of peacefulness and relaxation."

As it happened with Prophet Muḥammad ﷺ, he was tested and all his life was with obstacles, although he was the Seal of Messengers. Allāh ﷻ made him perfect, made him Insān al-Kāmil, "the Perfect Human Being." Allāh completed him, which means He is perfect and Allāh made him to reach perfection. When you reach perfection, it means you are not here; you are in the Divine Presence. The Divine Presence cannot accept anything except perfection. In *ākhirah,* when Allah ﷻ sends believers to Jannah, He makes believers reach perfection or else they cannot see Him in Paradise as Prophet said, "Allāh will be seen in Paradise." And that highest Paradise cannot allow anything except perfection.

There are lower levels of Paradise where there are all kinds of people who reached different levels, but the highest Paradise does not accept anyone except those who reach the highest level. The Prophet ﷺ reached perfection in *dunyā* when he was taken in 'Isrā' wal-Miʿrāj to *qāba qawsayni aw adnā,* "within two bows' length". He reached the highest perfection while he was alive in *dunyā,* so he is the one that has to be followed. That is why *awlīyāullāh* say, "This journey is long and you cannot reach perfection."

Allāh ﷻ said:

wa fawqa kulli dhī ʿilmin ʿalīm.
Above every knower is a (higher) knower. (Sūrat Yūsuf, 12:76)

It means there is something above everything; there is no limit, there is an infinite number of levels above and there is no limit to the levels of stations. As you move to one there is another, and another above that, so there are always higher levels. So for the Prophet, all his life there were difficulties and he said, *lā rāḥat fi 'd-dīn,* "There is no relaxation in religion." You have to keep struggling. He struggled until he reached perfection.

idhā jā naṣrullāhi wal-fatḥ, wa ra'āit an-nāsa yadkhulūna fī dīni llāhi afwājā.
When Allāh's support comes you will see people entering the Path of Allāh in big numbers. (Sūrat an-Nasr, 110:1)

So Allāh ﷻ gave Prophet ﷺ that nasr, victory, He also made the inheritors of Prophet ﷺ capable of giving victory to their followers, to enter into their *ḥaẓīra,* garden. They will enter inside their garden to be taken care of and to be safe, and they will be guided to that road to reach the presence of Prophet!

That is why Shaykh ʿAbd al-Wahhāb ash-Shaʿrānī ق said, *idhā rā'itu aḥadun aʿarafu minnī bi 'ṭ-ṭarīq lamadhtu ʿalayhi wa law kuntu mā'dhūnan min qabl li-shaykhin ākhir.* "If I find someone more knowledgeable than me in the path, I will become his student." So don't say, "No, I don't want to be a student." You always follow and listen to someone who knows more than you; go and sit in his association. Don't say, "I have no permission." No, especially if someone is in the same order you are, listen to each other and don't argue; you might get wisdom.

He said, "Even if I am given authority to conduct teachings or lead *dhikrūllāh* and I find someone in that *ṭarīqah* who knows more than I do, I will listen to what he says. Even if there is one *mā'dhūn* in the east and one in the west, and one in the north and one in the south, one should go and listen to the one with more knowledge. Don't say, 'I am the shaykh.' No, you are not the shaykh. That is why I went to listen to one shaykh after another."

Levels have no limits at which the servant will stop; there is always ascension, so go to the higher level. *Alḥamdulillāh* that Allāh ﷻ guided us to the highest! But when you are in an association and you are not in the presence of Sulṭān al-Awlīyā, if there is another *mā'dhūn* who is higher than you, go and listen and learn. Not everything has been given to you. So try to humble yourself. *fa idhan luzūm khidmat ash-shaykh al-akmal minhu.* "It is obligatory for a shaykh who knows himself to be lower than the other shaykh to sit and listen to that shaykh." As it is mentioned and happened in Holy Qur'an. Today they say, "Where is it?" They are authorized to give lectures and lead *dhikr*, and they think they are so high that they prevent those who follow them from listening to someone else. That is a sickness in them. They tell them, "That one doesn't know anything and we know everything!" If that is the case, why did Allāh ﷻ send Sayyīdinā Mūsā to Sayyīdinā Khiḍr? Mūsā was at a higher level than him, but there was a knowledge given to Khiḍr that Sayyīdinā Mūsā did not have. Allāh ﷻ told him, "Go and seek him in a journey." So he went with his servant to seek him in that journey

With everyone there is a taste that the other doesn't carry, and that is the case with Sayyīdinā Khiḍr ؏ and Sayyīdinā Mūsā ؏. So that is a sign to us, that if we are not near our perfect teacher, Sulṭān al-Awlīyā Mawlana Shaykh Nazim al-Haqqani ق, if there is someone of higher level than us coming to our area, he will be the one to conduct the ṣuḥbah and we will go and listen to him. But today the apples and oranges are together in one basket, so what can you do? The one who doesn't humble himself and listen to those higher than him will never smell the smell of *ṭarīqah*, because refused to go to a higher paradise. That is because one paradise leads to another. You sit in one paradise and that opens to the second, then the second opens to the third, and so on. You cannot open from the first to the fourth, it is impossible.

Today even children know more than us, with children's video games. Sometimes I see children playing them, especially in Cyprus, not here. They are playing these games in which you finish one part successfully and it opens to another level, and it goes like a gate, and you move through it to open another level. It is as if the people who made these games, *subḥānAllāh*, were inspired in their hearts! You don't jump from one level to a higher level; no, you go in a sequence and you have to go through all the levels. So the one who tries to jump through levels will stay in the first level and never reach his destiny, his goal.

Awlīyāullāh in previous times never gave *bayaʿ* before the student reached a certain level. It was not like today, when the *bayaʿ* is being spread quickly by Mawlana Shaykh, in his wisdom, since time is short and ignorance is filling *dunyā*. But in the past, the seeker had to reach a certain level before the shaykh would give *baya'*, and only after he had a dream or vision of Prophet authorizing him to give *baya'* to that one. *Baya'* was extremely difficult to get. As I said many times, Grandshaykh ق never gave *baya'* to anyone. We know of only two that have *baya'*, and of all those who came to him he never gave his hand and recited Āyatul-Baya', the Verse of Initiation. They used to sit with him and say, "You are our shaykh."

Previously they used to give *baya'* in the way of the narration of Sayyīdinā 'Umar ؓ, where Jibrīl came in the form of a man wearing very shining white clothes, which was impossible in that area and time, since it was dust and desert, but he didn't have any sign of travel. He entered the form of a man and sat on his knees with the Prophet ﷺ sitting in front of him on his knees, and their knees were touching and their hands were on their thighs. So in *ṭarīqah*, the way of dissemination or transmission of *baya'* has to be in such way, as Sayyīdinā Jibrīl ؑ was in the presence of Prophet ﷺ, putting his hands on his thighs. Then the shaykh has to make association with and receive authority from Prophet in the night, in *istikhara*.

And the Prophet ﷺ said:

mā khāba man istikhār wa lā nadm man istashār.

No one failed who made the guidance prayer, and no one regretted who consults.

That answer comes from a high level. And one incident, the only incident we know that happened in this way, was with Shaykh al-Lasūnī ق in Istanbul, when Mawlana Shaykh ق was young and went to him to follow and take *baya'*. He said, "O my son, your amanat is not with me." He didn't quickly give him *baya'* to "win" one more follower; they knew their limits. He said, "Your *amānat* is with someone in Damascus. Go and find him, Shaykh 'AbdAllāh al-Fa'iz ad-Daghestani." How did he know? They had no relationship. There was a world war, a big war, and to make a long story short, Mawlana Shaykh went moving from one place to another, one place to another, to go to Damascus to take *baya'* from Grandshaykh ق.

This was narrated by Grandshaykh. Mawlana Shaykh Nazim by Aleppo, Hama, and Homs. The war was very fierce where the French and English were fighting each other inside Damascus. And Mawlana landed in Homs and stayed one year in Khalid ibn Walīd's *maqām*; he is buried there. He was not going out, he was studying Sharī'ah. It was like *khalwah* in one room. Then slowly he was moving to Damascus, but he didn't know where to go. He ended up in a place called Mīdān, which still exists, and he asked people there, "Does anyone know a Daghestani shaykh?"

They said, "Yes, there."

Why did he go to that area, not to Marja for example, or to Rukn ad-Dīn or Romana? Because Allāh ﷻ guided him. He reached the door of that house and Grandshaykh ق opened the door and said, "Come."

He said, "*Sayyīdī*, I am on my way and they sent me to you. I am on the way for Hijra to Madīnatu 'l-Munawarra."

Grandshaykh said, "Stay here tonight and I will make *istikhara*."

That is the formal way, *mā khāba man istikhār*, and you will not be disappointed if you make a request to see Prophet in a dream. So he said, "You rest and spend the night, I will make you food." And they didn't talk more. The next morning after Fajr he said to him, "*Yā waladī!* There is no permission to go to Madīnatu 'l-Munawarra. There is more need for you to be in your country." And he sat as Sayyīdinā Jibrīl ؑ did with Prophet ﷺ and he gave Mawlana Shaykh *baya'* and sent him to where there was war, back to Cyprus. Mawlana didn't say, "No." It was his first time meeting the shaykh and he gave Mawlana the order to go back. Look at how much belief he had, when he had that intention, and he was counting the days until he would go to Madīnatu 'l-Munawarra and be *mujāwar*, the neighbor of Prophet! It was as if Grandshaykh blew up all his expectations.

But Grandshaykh ق was teaching him, "No, it is not according to your expectations, but according to our decision." People might expect a lot, but *awlīyāullāh* will change it for you and cut it down. And then the shaykh passes that *baya'* to that *murīd* one-to-one, and passes to him what he needs to know from *ṭarīqah*. And then after he is sitting, he takes the right hand of the *murīd* as if shaking hands. After that, they both recite *istighfār*, then recite Āyat al-Baya':

> *Innal-ladhīna yubai'ūnak innamā yubai'yūnallāh. yadullāhi fawqa aydīyhim faman nakatha fa innamā yankuthu 'alā nafsihi wa man awfā bimā 'ahada 'alayhullāh fa-sayu'tīyhi ajran 'aẓīmā.*
> Behold, all who pledge their allegiance to you pledge their allegiance to God: the hand of God is over their hands. Hence, he who breaks his oath breaks it only to his own hurt, whereas he who remains true to what he has pledged unto God, on him will He bestow a reward supreme.   (Sūrat al-Fatḥ, 48:10)

Then they close their physical eyes, and by the power of the shaykh the eyes of the heart will open. That is real *baya'*! All of them are real with

Mawlana's *barakah*, but that is the formal, strong *baya*ʿ. As soon as they close their eyes, by the power of Prophet ﷺ, the shaykh opens the eyes of the *murīd's* heart. Then when he opens his eyes, he will see himself in a different level. That cannot be described; you feel goose bumps and your whole body is numb, receiving. You are able then, at that moment, to begin *dhikrūllāh bi ʿIsm adh-Dhāt.*

The shaykh will make *talqīn* as you make *talqīn* at the grave of the one who just passed, saying, *yā ʿAbdAllāh qul ash-hadu an lā ilāha illa-Llāh...* the tradition of reminding the deceased to recite Kalīmat ash-Shahadah. Today they throw the body in the grave and run for the inheritance, and those who came to be with the family run to eat the food served on behalf of the deceased! The loved ones give them food, since they came to the graveyard, and everyone is running to eat rice and meat (no *adab*)!

So that *talqīn ʿIsm adh-Dhāt,* which encompasses all the Names of Allāh, passes from the shaykh's tongue and heart to the *murīd's* tongue and heart; I am speaking here of the Naqshbandi Order. Then the shaykh will give *talqīn* on the heart of the *murīd* as if he is in the Divine Presence, visualizing what he was not able to see before. He is seeing something he was not able to see, and his heart is pumping and trembling, and he will say *ʿIsmullāh.* He says, *Allāh Hūuuuuuuu, Allāh Hūuuuuuuu, Allāh Hūuuuuuuu Ḥaqq,* three times. What the *murīd* receives from hidden treasures in these moments is only for him or her, and the *murīd* has no right to mention or disclose what the shaykh opens to his heart, and this will be a secret.

So that gives us an idea of the difference between what we understand of *baya*ʿ and what is the reality of *baya*ʿ. And you can compare now which one is stronger: what we are receiving today or what they were receiving before? Which is stronger? In reality, what you are receiving today is hhigher, but you cannot see it. It will be given without your knowledge. Before it will be given and you can know it, your body will know what it has been given and you can feel it daily, that contentment, and the level in which you have been put, and the level from which you are ascending.

You are not given that *baya*ʿ unless you went into the journey, and you have reached the level of *muḥibīn,* lovers, having passed through Darajāt al-Mubtadi'īn, "Rank of the Initiates"; and Darajāt al-Mustaʿid', "Rank of the Prepared;" and then you reach Darajāt al-Murīdīn, "Rank of the *Murīds*."

So the *murīd* in Naqshbandi Ṭarīqah is like a shaykh; he is not given until he is like a mountain, then he is given *baya*ʿ. In previous times you went to these three levels and then you became a *murīd,* then they gave you *baya*ʿ. Today they give the *baya*ʿ since there is too much ignorance. You are not allowed to see it, as children are not given diamonds since they don't know their value and cannot be trusted to protect them.

Awlīyāullāh say, "There is the box and we will keep it for you." But in previous times they gave you the box and you saw it, since you had already passed through the three levels. Today, if we stay in the level of *muḥibīn*, that is a great job you did. So the shaykh is giving *ʿIsm adh-Dhāt* on the follower's heart by saying, "*Allāh Hūuu, Hūuu Allāh.*" It means from the Beautiful Name "Allāh," you have to go further into the Absolute Unknown of the Reality of the Essence, as mentioned in Sūrat al-Ikhlāṣ, *Qul Hūwa*, "Say, the Unknown, that is Allāh!"

As a *murīd* you begin with the opposite; you begin with "Allāh," because Allāh ﷻ can be described by Ninety-nine Beautiful Names and Attributes: Allāh, ar-Raḥmān, al-Quddūs, as-Salām, and so on. Allāh ﷻ leads you through the Ninety-nine Beautiful Names so you can reach the reality that you will never know about, and it is in Allāh's Hands, Allāh's treasures.

"Say, *Yā* Muḥammad! The One Who cannot be known is 'Allāh'!" So we begin with Allāh, then *Huuuuu*; we don't begin with *Huuuuu*. In Holy Qur'an you begin with *Huuuuu*, then Allāh. So he will give you that and you will see the Divine Attributes and visions of the Divine Presence in different colors. You will make *istighfār* and read Ikhlāṣ and you will be put in the *silsilah*, the chain and *rābiṭah* of your shaykh and you will be connected in that chain.

You will not do that until you are sure. You cannot give *bayaʿ* and then one day you are strong and one day you are weak, as Allāh ﷻ says in Holy Qur'an"

> *thumma āmanū, thumma kafarū, Inna alladhīna āmanū thumma kafarū thumma āmanū thumma kafarū thumma izdādū kufran lam yakūnillāhu li-yaghfir' lahum walā li-yahdiyahum sabīl.*
> *Lo! Those who believe, then disbelieve and then (again) believe, then disbelieve, and then increase in disbelief, Allāh will never pardon them, nor will He guide them unto a way.* (Sūrat an-Nisā, 4:137)

So that is why they don't give the strong *bayaʿ* today; that cannot happen until it is known that you will not change, until you know that your shaykh *yunaba'u ʿanhu fi tarbīyyat al-khalq*, represents the knowledge given to him from the heart of Prophet, in order to raise up his *murīds* and those who come for guidance. So Prophet ﷺ said, "Mention that Allāh ﷻ is the cure for hearts." (Daylami in Musnad al-Firdaws) All that is by being connected to Insān al-Kamil, the Perfect Human Being, Prophet ﷺ! We will continue next time with that.

So the *baya*ʿ before has its own taste and with it you feel able to know things that you never knew, because the body is allowed to see what the soul is seeing. They give you a password for that, and allow your access, and you are a seeker in that journey. But today the *baya*ʿ is general and you are given more, but you are not allowed to see it as it is too much darkness all around. Before it was less and today is higher and that depends on the power of the shaykh. So try to reach the real *baya*ʿ, then you will experience the taste of real fruit, not only see the fruit but to taste them! That is what is the end-goal for *awlīyā* on their followers, a tasty garden, that you move from one to another and taste the honey and the fruits.

May Allāh ﷻ bless us and may Allāh forgive us.

Wa min Allāhi 't-tawfiq, bi ḥurmati 'l-ḥabīb, bi ḥurmati 'l-Fātiḥah.
And with Allāh is success. For the sake of the Beloved, for his sake we recite the opening chapter of Holy Qur'an.

The Status of Dhikrullah in Holy Qur'an and Tariqah

Aʿūdhu billāhi min ash-Shayṭān ir-rajīm. Bismillāhi' r-Raḥmāni 'r-Raḥīm. Nawaytu 'l-arbāʿīn, nawaytu 'l-ʿitikāf, nawaytu'l-khalwah, nawaytu 'l-ʿuzlah, nawaytu 'r-riyāḍa, nawaytu 's-sulūk, lillāhi Taʿalā fī hādhā 'l-masjid. Atiʿ ūllāh wa atiʿū 'r-Rasūl wa ūli 'l-amri minkum. (4:59)

We must ask support from *awlīyāullāh,* who in turn ask support from Prophet ﷺ. And we say, *Atiʿ ūllāh wa atiʿū 'r-Rasūl wa ūli 'l-amri minkum.* "Obey Allāh, obey the Prophet, and obey those in authority among you." (4:59)

Aʿūdhu billāhi min ash-Shayṭān ir-rajīm. Bismillāhi' r-Raḥmāni 'r-Raḥīm. We consider the recitation of, *Aʿūdhu billāhi min ash-Shayṭān ir-rajīm* is *dhikrūllāh.* When we say that, Shayṭān will be chained and stopped. And then we say *Bismillāhi' r-Raḥmāni 'r-Raḥīm.* By reciting this, you enter that garden of Allāh, Who created everything and made it appear by *Bismillāhi' r-Raḥmāni 'r-Raḥīm.* As He said, in the verse to Prophet:

Iqrā bismi rabbik alladhī khalaq.
Read in the Name of your Lord, Who created. (Sūrat al-Alaq, 96:1)

Creation has been given to Prophet and that is in the first revelation, "Read!" Prophet ﷺ said, "What am I going to read?" "Read in the name of Your Lord." *Bismillāhi' r-Raḥmāni 'r-Raḥīm* is the key to Paradise and the key to everything. Any *ʿamal* that doesn't begin with *bismillāh* is cut, *maqtuʿa;* it has leaks in its pipe and no water will come to its end. Therefore, when we dress we say *bismillāh,* when we eat we say *bismillāh,* when we drink, when we go out, when we do any work, we say *bismillāh.* That is the key to success. *Awlīyāullāh* know that *Bismillāhi' r-Raḥmāni 'r-Raḥīm* is *dhikrūllāh,* so they keep in their hearts remembrance of their Lord and are always doing *dhikrūllāh* in their hearts.

Prophet ﷺ said:

The remembrance of the prophets is considered worship, while the remembrance of the pious is expiation (of sins), and the remembrance of death is charity.

And the remembrance of pious people—for example, you or anyone who remembers Allāh is considered pious—*kafāratun,* takes away sins.

Prophets have no sins to take away, so *dhikr* for them is worship, and for pious ones it is a cleansing or waiving of sins.

The Prophet ﷺ said (continuing the *hadīth*):

wa dhikr al-mawtu ṣadaqatun.
To remember death is charity.

When you make *dhikr* with the intention of remembering your death, it will be considered *ṣadaqah,* like when you give a donation in the Way of Allāh. It will be written for you from beginning to end as if you are giving *ṣadaqah,* that you paid the *zakāt* of your entire life! That remembrance of death will protect you on the Day of Resurrection.

Wa dhikru 'l-qabr yuqarribukum mina 'l-jannah.
And when you remember the grave, that will take you nearer to Paradise.

What is after the grave? It is either Paradise or punishment. So if you remember you are leaving *dunyā,* you are giving *ṣadaqah* and to remember your grave makes you near Paradise.

As Prophet ﷺ said:

Those who are pious, Allāh will free their souls and turn their graves into a piece of Paradise. (Ad-Daylami in Musnad al-Firdaws)

Dhikr is better than ṣadaqah. (Abū Shuʿayb in Musnad al-Thawab)

In Ramadan, people run to give *ṣadaqah,* but after Ramadan they stop, as if there is nothing left, all engines are down. Your donation is limited, or you do it only one time. That is why *awlīyā* say put a box in your house and when you go in or out always put *ṣadaqah,* to keep it running. The same is with your *dhikr,* keep it running; then it is considered *ṣadaqah,* whether you are walking, standing, or moving. In every moment, you are doing *dhikrūllāh.*

There are many *aḥadīth* and verses of Holy Qur'an mentioning *dhikrūllāh.*

adh-dhikr al-ladhī la yasmaʿu al-ḥafaẓa khayrun min dhikr al-ladhī yasmaʿ al-ḥafaẓa bi sabaʿīn daʿf.
The (silent) dhikr the angels do not hear is better than the (loud) dhikr heard by angels by 70 times.

So *dhikr khafi,* (silent *dhikr*) by the heart, is 70 times better better than the loud *dhikr.*

Allāh ﷻ said:

Yā ayyuhalladhīna āmanū 'dhkurullāha dhikran kathīra.
O you who believe! Celebrate the praises of Allāh, and do this often.
(Sūrat al-'Aḥzāb, 33:41)

Fadhkurullāha ʿinda 'l-mashʿari 'l-ḥarām.
Celebrate the praises of Allāh at the sacred monument.
(Sūrat al-Baqarah, 2:198)

Wadhkurūḥu kamā hadākum.
And celebrate His praises as He has directed you. (Sūrat al-Baqarah, 2:198)

Al-ladhīna yadhkurūna Allāh qiyāman wa quʿūdan wa ʿalā junūbīhim.
Men who celebrate the praises of Allāh, standing, sitting, and lying down on their sides. (Sūrat 'Āli 'Imrān, 3:191)

Fa idhā qadaytum manāsikakum fadhkurūllāh ka-dhikrikum ābaūkum aw ashada dhikrā.
So when you have accomplished your holy rites, celebrate the praises of Allāh.
(Sūrat al-Baqarah, 2:200)

w 'adhkur rabbaka fī nafsika taḍaruʿan wa khufiyā wa dūn al-jahri min al-qawl wa lā takun mina 'l-ghāfilīn.
And bring your Lord to remembrance in your (very) soul, with humility and in reverence, without loudness in words, in the mornings and evenings, and be not of those who are unheedful. (Sūrat al-Aʿrāf, 7:205)

Wa la-dhikrullāhi akbar.
And remembrance of Allāh is the greatest (thing in life).
(Sūrat al-ʿAnkabūt, 29:45)

There are many verses in the Holy Qur'an about *dhikrūllāh* that show its importance. Just as the heart is mentioned approximately one-hundred times by name in Holy Qur'an, *dhikrūllāh* is mentioned many places as well, as it is the work of the heart. So keep *dhikrūllāh* on your tongue and you will be safe in this life and the Next Life.

Al-Fuḍayl ق said, "It has reached us that Allāh says, 'O My servant, remember Me one hour after Fajr.'" This is the saying of *awlīyā* and is why they keep *dhikrūllāh* for one hour after Fajr, as mentioned by Fuḍayl ق, who also said, "And after ʿAṣr prayer, remember Allāh for one hour." That is why if you want to follow this path, they will tell you, "Be sure to keep one hour after Fajr and one hour after ʿAṣr. Then that is enough for you to guarantee what is between them, that you will be safe." Those who cannot do that, as time now is changing, *awlīyāullāh* might reduce that to five minutes. So don't run away, sit and do five minutes after ʿAṣr time and five minutes after Fajr. Don't be lazy like us, and he is always sitting and doing *dhikrūllāh.*

> *Wa qāla ghanīmatuh majālis adh-dhikru al-jannah.*
> *And he said, "What you gain from associations of dhikrūllāh by yourself or with people is Paradise for sure."* (Aḥmad, at-Ṭabarānī)

If you want Paradise in *dunyā* and *ākhirah,* make *dhikrūllāh.* All of *taṣawwuf* is not only moral excellence, which doesn't come free; it works after your heart is pumping with *dhikrūllāh.* So what makes your heart in the Divine Presence will make you *yartāh fil al-jinān,* grazing and roaming in Paradise. In *dunyā,* you will always be in that *tajallī* of Paradise when you remember Allāh ﷻ.

The Prophet ﷺ said:

> *Law anna rajulayn aqbala āḥadahumā min as-sūq fī hijrihi danānīr yuʿṭīhā, wa'l-ākhir yadhkurallāh kāna dhākirullāhi afḍal.*
> *If there were two men, one a man with money in his lap and he is passing it to people, and there was one who is sitting remembering Allāh, that one who is remembering Allāh is better than the one distributing money.*

This is to encourage remembrance. *Taṣawwuf* is based on *dhikrūllāh.* If there is no *dhikr,* there is no *taṣawwuf.* Moral excellence comes with good behavior by remembering Allāh in different ways through his Beautiful Names and Attributes. When you remember Allāh by His Ninety-nine Names, the *tajallī* of these Beautiful Names takes you over. The *tajallī* will make you feel Goosebumps from the presence of angels that bring those Beautiful Names to dress you. That is what takes you from bad manners to good manners; without you trying to avoid the bad manners, it will carry and throw you to the good side!

This just came to me now, so I will share it. When I was young, I was ordered by Grandshaykh ق to put a cover when doing *dhikr.* He ordered me not to be open as we are here. It means to tighten your space or don't have huge space. Similarly, when doing seclusion, we do it in closed small spaces. In 1997, I was asked by Mawlana Shaykh Nazim ق to do seclusion in Istanbul. I went to that *masjid* and on the roof they had built a grave the size of this *minbar*, perhaps six feet long by four feet wide. When you sit in that, you have to bend down.

When I phoned Mawlana Shaykh Nazim ق, he said, "Where did they tell you to stay?"

I said, "They put me in a grave they built on the roof."

He said, "What will you do?"

I said, "I am going to enter it."

He was checking me. And that grave was scary; they close it when you go in and only let you out to do *wuḍū*. Then with Mawlana's mercy, he said, "You passed the test. Go and take a room." But in reality, years before, seclusion used to be done in a cemetery. You would sit in a closed grave between the deceased and listen to what goes on at night from different graves! It was not so easy. That is why you have to cover yourself. If you cover yourself you will know what we mean. If you want real *baya*ʿ, cover yourself, then you will be visualizing or seeing what cannot be seen at that moment.

So I was 22 years of age then, covering myself during *dhikr* and reciting, *lā ilāha illa-Llāh, lā ilāha illa-Llāh, lā ilāha illa-Llāh.* Naqshbandis recite *Allāh, Allāh*, but the *adab* is to recite, *lā ilāha illa-Llāh* and then go to *ʿIsm adh-Dhāt* (Name of the Holy Essence), which is *Allāh, Allāh.*

I was reciting loudly, in a melodious voice. At that moment I began to feel something unusual, and I was afraid. I was shaking and wanted to take the cover off, because it became heavy and difficult. As what happened today in Fajr, the first *rakaʿat* was silent. They didn't let me to say it out loud; it was not coming. But I was hearing Shaykh Sahib saying *Allāhu Akbar, Allāhu Akbar.* And then the second *rakaʿat* was in a loud voice. That is why I made *sajdat as-sahūw* at the end.

So, I felt like I could not take it anymore and at that moment, the presence of Prophet ﷺ came and entered from my head. As Prophet was entering slowly, slowly, I was shaking, but felt the beauty of that presence, which took me over completely. Then at that moment, what happened, happened. This is what I wanted to say, that when you cover yourself and do *dhikrūllāh,* cutting yourself entirely from *dunyā,* then *awlīyāullāh* and Prophet's ﷺ presence will reach you. That was Allāh's, Prophet's, and our shaykh's favor, that Prophet overtook my body completely and I was feeling myself enveloped in that beauty for many, many days after that.

Thus, if you disconnect yourself from *dunyā,* you will be able to take away your bad characters. Every Beautiful Name has its taste and remedy to cure you of your bad behaviors and forbiddens. There are 800 forbiddens that *awlīyā* count and their only remedy is *dhikrūllāh.* That is why every Friday, Thursday, or Saturday, you do *dhikr* with different Beautiful Names, because Āhlu 'l-Ṭarīqah do that and we do like them. The highest Name that is above all Beautiful Names and Attributes, *'Ismullāh al-jami'ī lil-'Asmā wa'ṣ-Ṣiffāt,* is "Allāh," it encompasses all Names and Attributes.

That is why on behalf of their followers, the shaykh of this *ṭāi'fa,* group, assigns them an *awrād* of reciting *Allāh, Allāh, Allāh, Allāh,* to clean them through their recitation of the Beautiful Names and Attributes and send them to that ocean of the Name "Allāh.". Some assign it for recitation 5,000 times a day and some 10,000 times. If you are a beginner in that Way, then it is 1,500 times a day. *Allāhumā ṣalli 'alā Sayyīdinā Muḥammad* ﷺ!

illa an yashā Allāhu wa 'dhkur rabbaka idhā nasīta wa qul 'asā an yahdīyanī rabbī li aqraba min hādhā rashada.
Except (with the saying), "If Allāh wills!" And remember your Lord when you forget and say, "It may be that my Lord guides me to a nearer way of truth than this." (Sūrat al-Kahf, 18:24)

Itba' as-sayīāt al-ḥasanat tamḥūhā.
Follow the bad deed with a good deed, as it erases it. (Tirmidhī)

When you commit a sin, immediately follow it with *"astaghfirullāh;"* that will erase the sin. Don't say, "I have too many sins," no, don't complain or it will be as if you are contradicting the verse of Holy Qur'an:

Wadhkur rabbaka idhā nasīta.
Remember Allāh when you forget. (Sūrat al-Kahf, 18:24)

When you commit a sin, follow it with goodness and that will erase it. We know when we do something wrong, then we say *astaghfirullāh'* that will erase everything.

Wa qāla man aḥaba liqā-allāh aḥab Allāhu liqāuh wa man kariha liqāuh karihallāhu liqāuh.
Who likes to meet Allāh, Allāh loves to meet him, and who hates to meet Allāh, Allāh hates to meet him. (Muslim, Aḥmad and Tirmidhī)

man āt'a'Allāh faqad dhakr-Allāh wa in qallat ṣalātahu wa sīyāmahu wa tilāwata 'l-qur'an. wa man 'asa 'Llāh faqad nasīy 'Llāh wa in kathurat ṣalātuhu wa ṣīyāmahu wa tilāwata 'l-qur'ān.
Whoever obeys Allāh remembers Allāh, even if he doesn't do extra prayers and extra fasting, and doesn't read Qur'an (and whoever disobeys Allāh has forgotten Allāh, even if he does much prayer and fasting and reading of Qur'an). (Bayhaqi, ibn Mundhir, Sa'īd ibn Mansūr, Ṭabarānī)

It means when you obey Allāh, you remember Him, and when you remember Him, you obey Him.

lā yaqu'd qawmun yadhkurūn Allāha Ta'alā illa ḥafathum al-malā'ikata wa ghashīyahum ar-raḥmata wa nazalat 'alayhim as-sakīnata wa dhakarahumullāha fīman 'indah.
Never do a group of people sit in circles remembering Allāh except that the angels will surround them and they will be covered with mercy and tranquility descends on them, and Allāh remembers them to those in His Presence. (Muslim)

When you go to a meeting with a king, you wear a nice dress with medallion from the king. Then the next day when you come to door, you are admitted immediately as you already have the medallion from the king. Likewise, can anyone stop you from entering Paradise when you come dressed with *dhikrūllāh?* Saying *lā ilāha illa-Llāh* one time will dress you with that mercy and you will be admitted to Paradise!

For example, military personnel have on their uniforms rows of ribbons that distinguish what they achieve, so the military people know them. On the Day of Judgment the believers will come with all these ornaments and the doors of Paradise will open for them. Depending on what ornaments you have, different doors will be opened to you. May Allāh give us high levels in Paradise! Don't follow those people whose hearts are heedless.

Waṣbir nafsak ma' alladhīna yada'ūna rabbahum bil-ghadāti wa 'l-'ashīyya yurīdūna wajhahu wa lā ta'daw 'aynayka 'anhum turīdu zīnat al-ḥayāt ad-

dunyā wa lā tuṭ'i man aghfalnā qalbahu 'an dhikrinā wa't-taba' hawāhu wa kāna amruhu furuṭā.

And keep your soul content with those who call on their Lord morning and evening, seeking His Face; and let not thine eyes pass beyond them, seeking the pomp and glitter of this Life; no obey any whose heart We have permitted to neglect the remembrance of Us, one who follows his own desires, whose case has gone beyond all bounds. (Sūrat al-Kahf, 18:28)

Stay with those whose hearts are in remembrance day and night. Those who are doing *dhikrullāh* are more important than anyone else. That is why you cannot leave weekly *dhikrūllāh* except for three circumstances: you are traveling, you have a guest, or you are sick. Don't leave it; you may even do it at home, with or without company. *Dhikrūllāh* is the most honored worship. It is the best, the greatest, and the most complete, perfect form of the aspect of purifying and cleaning the hearts.

So if you want to purify the heart from the sickness of *dunyā,* stay on *dhikrūllāh.* And it is not only to clean and purify the heart, but to sweeten it as well. It is as if you put sugar in tea, coffee, and juice. If you don't put sugar, it will not be sweet. It is said that if worshipers, *'abidīn*, spend their day and night in all kinds of worship, rarely will they get a purified heart. That is why you see scholars are arrogant, because they feel that they are different, and higher than others. *Awlīyāullāh* say that even if they are worshipping day and night, *qalama taḥṣala taṣfiyya qulūbihim*, rarely will they achieve to sift something. "Sifting" hearts keeps the good in the heart and removes the bad.

And those who remember Allāh ﷻ, when they finish their prayers and *'ibadāt,* they are busy with *dhikrūllāh,* and they don't say, "Pray your prayer and then wear your jeans and go to the mall," as today some famous *imāms* say. Also, *fa amma adh-dhākirūn lamā yashtaghil bi dhikrillāh 'alā ad-dawām lā yashudhu minhum aḥad illa ḥaṣal 'ala ḥaqīqatih,* "Those who remember Allāh all the time, will be dressed with lots of secrets and the connection to the Divine Presence," because *dhikrūllāh* is the only *'amal* the heart can do that contains all the different principles of remembering Allāh.

It will bring you nearer and nearer to Maqām al-Yaqīn, "the Station of Certainty," which includes 'Ilm al-Yaqīn, "Certainty of Knowledge," 'Ayn al-Yaqīn, "Certainty of Vision," and Ḥaqīqat al-Yaqīn, "Certainty of Reality." You enter these three oceans by *dhikrūllāh.* Don't ask how; Allāh will take you from blindness to vision, from deaf to hearing, from dumbness to speaking. When *ināyatullāh,* Allāh's Care comes, even if you are at the bottom of the valley, Allāh will take you to the top of the mountain; that is your recompense that can happen in a moment! It is not like going up a ladder step-by-step and that ladder is endless, so you will never reach; that happens in the blink of an eye!

Grandshaykh ق said, "If you do *dhikrūllāh* in *jamaʿah* or by yourself, you are dressed with one medallion and the next time, you are dressed with another medallion, regardless of what you have done." So when you do *dhikrūllāh* once a week, that cleans whatever you have done the previous week of and the second *dhikr* cleans you again for the next week. It is *nūr ʿalā nūr*, "light upon light." Prophet ﷺ said:

Lā ilāha illa-Llāh ḥuṣnī wa man dakhala ḥuṣnī āman min ʿadhābī.
Lā ilāha illa-Llāh is My fortress; whoever enters it, is safe from My punishment. (Ibn Najjār)

Let us say altogether, *lā ilāha illa-Llāh Muḥammadun Rasūlullāh*! *Lā ilāha illa-Llāh Muḥammadun Rasūlullāh*! *Lā ilāha illa-Llāh Muḥammadun Rasūlullāh*! We are sending that to our shaykhs to present to Prophet, and for Prophet in his holy grave to present on our behalf on the Day of Judgment.

Qul Allāh thumma dharhum fī khawdihim yalʿabūn.
Say, "Allāh," then leave them to play in their vain discussions.
(Sūrat al-'Anʿām, 6:91)

You can recite it (or pronounce it) as *qul Allāh*, "say 'Allāh'". How do they say there is no *dhikr bi 'Ism adh-Dhāt?* Wahabis say, "Don't do *dhikr* by Allāh's Name." Allāh is saying in Sūrat al-Anām, verse 91, "Leave them playing with what they are doing. You say, 'Allāh.'" We say "Allāh" because we are following the way of our *shuyūkh* and by the order of Allāh in Holy Qur'an. Say "Allāh," as we are ordered! Maybe they are saying, "Shayṭān, Shayṭān" (as their *dhikr*)! And they don't use beads. Allāh said in Holy Qur'an, "Say, 'Allāh.'" Therefore we are saying "Allāh," *dhikr* by *'Ism adh-Dhāt*. It is important in the Naqshbandi Way. May Allāh ﷻ forgive us.

Wa min Allāhi 't-tawfīq, bi ḥurmati 'l-ḥabīb, bi ḥurmati 'l-Fātiḥah.
And with Allāh is success. For the sake of the Beloved, for his sake we recite the opening chapter of Holy Qur'an.

The Oceans of Sayyidina Ali and Sayyidina Abu Bakr

Aʿūdhu billāhi min ash-Shayṭān ir-rajīm. Bismillāhi' r-Raḥmāni 'r-Raḥīm.
Nawaytu 'l-arbāʿīn, nawaytu 'l-ʿitikāf, nawaytu'l-khalwah, nawaytu 'l-ʿuzlah,
nawaytu 'r-riyāḍa, nawaytu 's-sulūk, lillāhi Taʿalā fī hādhā 'l-masjid.
Atiʿ ūllāh wa atiʿū 'r-Rasūl wa ūli 'l-amri minkum. (4:59)

The connection of the heart is very important, and that is why Allāh ﷻ said in Holy Qur'an, "Don't follow those whose hearts we made heedless from Our remembrance." (al-Kahf, 18:28) That means keep you heart always in remembrance of Allāh, keep that connection from when you took *bayaʿ*; the fitting in the pipe is there, but don't lose that connection, don't be heedless! You are forgetting there is a connection from you to the shaykh and from the shaykh to Prophet.

> *Afalā yatadabarūna al-qur'ān aw ʿalā qulūbihim aqfāluhā.*
> *Do they not then earnestly seek to understand the Qur'an, or are their hearts locked up by them?* (Sūrat Muḥammad, 47:24)

> *Inna naḥnu nazalnā 'dh-dhikri wa inna lahu la-ḥāfiẓūn.*
> *Verily, We sent down the dhikr and surely, We will guard it (from corruption).* (Sūrat al-Ḥijr, 15:9)

Or are there locks on their hearts? They don't want to remember Allāh. Keep remembering Allāh, as He has said in Sūrat al-Ikhlāṣ, *Qul Hūwa Allāhu Āḥad,* "Say, 'He is Allāh, *Āḥad*; no one is Creator except Him!'" Don't let them have locks on their hearts or be heedless. It is said *al-qulūb awwiʿatun wa idhā umlīyat imma al-ḥaqq wa imma al-bāṭil,* "Hearts are containers." The heart is a container that has to be filled; either you fill it with Ḥaqq, Truth, or you fill it with *bāṭil,* falsehood. Fill it with Truth and with Allāh's remembrance, as He said, "Don't let your heart have a lock; I am giving you *dhikrūllāh* to fill it."

And when it is overflowing as you fill it, when it reaches the top, what happens? It will overflow. When you fill the cup slowly, slowly, don't stop here and say, "I am not seeing anything," there is nothing need to see, you don't need to see because it is not for you to ask for something, it is for

Allāh, as Rābi'ah al-'Adawiyyah ق said, "I am not worshiping from the fear of Hellfire, and not for the love of Paradise, but I am worshipping for Your love, *yā* Allāh, so put me where You like!"

So don't stop filling, fill and keep going, keep going, and when you reach to the top, fill more. Then Shayṭān will come and say to you, "You are crazy, you wasted your time." If you don't listen, then keep going, then it overflows. At that time the light that was inside, when filling up, you can't see it, it is veiled, but when it overflows, it comes outside and that light of *dhikrūllāh's* light will overflow to all the parts of the body. And that happened in Lama in a moment, in one blink of an eye you will see that overflow of the heat and that is not easy to get. You have to struggle very hard against the ego. We are all struggling, as Grandshaykh ق said, *thumma āmanū thumma kafarū*, "One day up, one day down."

There are two ways to fill our containers: one is to fill it with *dhikrūllāh,* to not be heedless, and to not put a lock; and the other way is to do what Shayṭān wants and fill it with *dunyā,* and then all this darkness will come out of the heart and spread through the whole body. So our duty is not to let darkness fill our hearts, but rather to make that light of *dhikrūllāh* come out. Allāh is Merciful with *Ummat an-Nabī;* He said, "Remember Me, I remember you." *wa lā dhikrūllāhi akbar*, "And Allāh's remembrance of you is greater." It cannot be expressed or described; it is over limits.

Sahl ibn 'AbdAllāh ﵁ said, "It is forbidden, *ḥarām,* on a heart that the light of reality will enter in it." Because maybe that heart has in it something that Allāh ﷻ hates. What does Allāh hate? When you deny His mercy! Then Allāh is not happy, because He wants you to know He is All-Merciful and then He rewards you. And who is His mercy?

> *Wa ma arslanāka illa Raḥmatan lil-'Ālamīn.*
> *And We have sent you not (O Muḥammad) but as a mercy for 'Ālamīn (all the worlds).* (Sūrat al-Anbīyā, 21:107)

That is His Prophet! So you must be happy because you don't deny Allāh's mercy, His Prophet. But those who deny Sayyīdinā Muḥammad ﷺ must repent, as Allāh is not happy with them. We say, "*As-salām 'alayk, yā Rasūlullāh*! We love you and hope to be with you on Judgment Day. We love our *shuyūkh* and Mawlana Shaykh, and we love your family!"

And az-Zuhrī ﵁ said, *ṣalāḥ al-qulūb afḍal min 'ibādati 'th-thaqalayn*, "To remedy the heart for one hour is better than the worship of Sayyīdinā Adam

ﷺ to the Day of Judgment." That means sitting in *dhikrūllāh* for one hour is better than the worship of *ins* and *jinn* from day one to the end of *dunyā*!

That is one *walī* describing how much he is getting through his experiences through one hour. Imagine then in khalwah how much you are doing *dhikrūllāh*! They allow only two hours of sleep. When given permission for *khalwah,* you feel you don't need to eat or sleep as you have power. So you read Qur'an and mention Allāh's Beautiful Names and Attributes, and that is *dhikrūllāh*. That is worth more than all the combined worship of *ins* and *jinn*. When Allāh sees you devoting and doing that remembrance, He will give you from His mercy! That means He will give to you from Sayyīdinā Muḥammad ﷺ, and when that happens you see things and hear things that never occurred before!

It is said that in our way the only condition that the shaykh takes from the *murīd* is to leave forbiddens. That is why Grandshaykh ق said, "There are 800 forbiddens that we have to take away from ourselves, and to leave one forbidden is better than the worship of the *ins* and *jinn*." You will be rewarded more than that worship. It doesn't mean you have to leave your prayers, obligations are required; we are not talking about that. Beyond that Allāh gives you, *ma lā ʿaynun rā'at wa lā udhunun samiʿat wa lā khaṭar ʿalā qalbi bashar*, "What no eye saw and no ear heard and what no one can understand of what Allāh give of reward for leaving one forbidden."

That is more valuable, to leave one (of 800) forbiddens than to do all the 500 *māmurāt*, all the forms of worship. Why? Because you are letting your heart's container be filled with the lights that Allāh wants there and not letting Iblīs take it from you! What did Sayyīdinā ʿAlī ؓ say? We know this kind of knowledge is coming from two sources to the Prophet ﷺ, one is Sayyīdinā ʿAlī ؓ and one is through Abū Bakr aṣ-Ṣiddīq ق. Sayyīdinā ʿAlī came to the Prophet and this is not a *ḥadīth,* but it was mentioned by Sayyīdinā Ali, *dhu nafs ar-radiyya. Dullanī ʿalā aqrab aṭ-ṭuruq il-Allāh wa afḍaluhā*, "Guide me to easiest, nearest of ways to Allāh and the most easy one."

Because there is a *ḥadīth* that one *Ṣaḥābī* ؓ came to Prophet and said, *qad kathurat ʿalay sharīʿah al-Islām*, "I am a person who is weak. There are too many obligations in Islam and there are too many rules." That is why people today are so dipped in the oceans of liberalism and love of *dunyā* that they cannot accept more than the easy way. They don't want to be *awlīyā* and that relationship with Allāh is forgotten.

ʿalā inna awlīyāullāh la khawfan ʿalayhim wa lā hum yaḥzanūn.
Verily, on the friends of Allāh there is no fear, nor shall they grieve.

(Sūrat Yūnus, 10:62)

As one scholar said, "Wear jeans, pray your prayers and then go to the mall. That is enough for you." No, that is not enough! As we said, leaving a forbidden is better than the worship of *jinn* and *ins,* and that *Ṣaḥābī* ﷺ asked for something to make easy for him Islam. And Prophet ﷺ said, "Keep your tongue wet with *dhikrūllāh.*" And is that difficult or easy? It is easy!

w 'adhkur rabbaka fī nafsika taḍaruʿan wa khufiyā wa dūn al-jahri min al-qawl wa lā takun mina 'l-ghāfilīn.
And bring your Lord to remembrance in your (very) soul, with humility and in reverence, without loudness in words, in the mornings and evenings, and be not of those who are unheedful.

(Sūrat al-Aʿrāf, 7:205)

"Remember Allāh in yourself or in your heart, or don't make it loud." That means keep it in your heart. Don't let Shayṭān enter your heart, let Allāh enter your heart! Then, "I will let My lights and manifestations enter your heart." So that *Ṣaḥābī* ﷺ wanted something easy and so Prophet said, "Do *dhikrūllāh* through your tongue," as doing heart *dhikr* is more difficult. So Sayyīdinā 'Alī ﷺ said, "Guide me to a way to Allāh that is easiest." And the Prophet said, *ʿalayka bi dawāmati dhikrillāh fil-khalwah,* "Your duty is to remember Allāh ﷻ in your seclusion, when you are alone." It means keep Allāh's remembrance always; when you are able, do it. "In *khalwah*" means in secrecy, not like the *Ṣaḥābī* who asked the Prophet ﷺ and he said, "Keep your tongue busy with *dhikrullah.*" For Sayyīdinā ʿAlī it is higher, "Keep doing *dhikrūllāh* in hidden way to fill your heart with *dhikrūllāh.*"

That means your heart has to be with Allāh, but your face, *dhāhir,* has to be with the people, as the Prophet said, *lī saʿatun maʿ Allāh wa saʿatun maʿ al-khalq,* "I have one hour with Allāh and one hour with people." Or, "One face with Allāh and one face with people." And so you keep that secret. Where do you keep secrets? You lock them up in the heart. And how do you lock them after you do *dhikr*? It is as Mawlana Shaykh and Grandshaykh ق taught us to recite, *awdaʿna hādha adh-dhikr ʿindak, yā Rasūlullāh,* "We have placed this *dhikr* in your presence, O Messenger of Allāh!" to hand it off to Prophet for him to keep for us, or else we will lose it slowly, slowly to Shayṭān. "*Yā Rasūlullāh*! We immediately deposit that prayer or *duʿā* or *dhikr* in your bank, before we spend it!" You can easily spend it when Shayṭān comes. He says, "I give you this, I give you *dunyā,*" and you lose it.

And Sayyīdinā 'Alī ؇ asked, *kayfa adhkur, yā Rasūlullāh,* "How do I do that *dhikr;* what is the technique or way?" He said, *ghammi 'aynayk,* "Close your eyes and listen three times what I am going to say." Why did he say, "Close your eyes." That means, "Disconnect yourself completely from *dunyā.*"

Inna as-sama' wal-basar wal-fu'ād kullu ulaika kāna 'anha masūla.
And pursue not that of which thou hast no knowledge; for every act of hearing, or of seeing or of (feeling in) the heart will be enquired into (on the Day of Reckoning). (Sūrat al-'Isrā', 17:36)

May Allāh ؇ forgive us, by us saying, *"Yā Rasūlullāh,* we love you!" *Allāh, Allāh. 'alā kull man taghā wa tajabbar 'alā anfusinā.*

So the biggest connection to *dunyā* is what? It is the eyes. With ears you hear but you cannot see. So to see is through the eyes, and when *awlīyāullāh* want to attract *murīds* it is through their eyes. They attract people when they look into their eyes. When they look into their eyes then that shaykh will carry them. So that is what we mentioned about Shaykh Sharafuddīn ق and Grandshaykh ق. They went to a mall in Istanbul to make people to look at their eyes. As an ironic thing, seeing these two shaykh with their two turbans and seeing that and smiling and laughing, that is a joke. And they look into their eyes and as soon as they do that they carry them, attract them.

So eyes are very important for *awlīyā*. When you look into the eyes of people that attracts them and one day Allāh will guide them.

Inna ad-dīn 'indāllāh al-Islām.
The religion before Allāh is Islām. (Sūrat 'Āli 'Imrān, 3:19)

So he said, "Close your eyes and repeat three times." When you close your eyes, where are you? Away from *dunyā* and with the One you mention. And he said to him, "Say, *'lā ilāha illa-Llāh Muḥammadun Rasūlullāh.'"* And Sayyīdinā 'Alī was hearing. *Aghmid 'aynayk wa asma'.* So do both, disconnect from *dunyā* and close your eyes and enter the garden of the Divine Presence, and though you might not see anything, of course Sayyīdinā 'Alī was seeing, but we listen to *lā ilāha illa-Llāh.*

Fa'lam annahu lā ilāha illa-Llāh w'astaghfir li-dhanbik wa li 'l-mu'minīna wa 'l-mu'mināti w 'Allāhu ya'lamu muqallibukum wa mathwākum.
Know, therefore, that there is no god but Allāh, and ask forgiveness for your faults, and for the men and women who believe, for Allāh knows how you move about and how you dwell in your homes. (Sūrat Muḥammad, 47:19)

"Know that there is no Creator except Me. When you carry that power, I am giving that power," and then, *astaghfir li dhanbik wa li 'l-mu'minīna wa 'l-mu'mināti,* "Then ask forgiveness for believers." That is the biggest power that Allāh gave to *Ummat an-Nabī.* Allāh will be happy with that *lā ilāha illa-Llāh,* Maqām at-Tawḥīd. You are declaring there is none to be worshiped except Allāh!

That is the message of Islam, you have to know there is no Creator except Allāh ﷻ. And if you say *lā ilāha illa-Llāh,* that is the most powerful tool. And then Sayyīdinā 'Alī ؓ closed his eyes and repeated what the Prophet said. So at that moment when you say that *dhikr,* the Prophet is present and that is the *dhikr* that Prophet ﷺ taught Sayyīdinā 'Ali. So Sayyīdinā 'Alī is present, and that takes you to the Divine Presence and you might not see that but Allāh is witness that you are saying to Him, "There is none to worship except You!"

So that is the tool that was given to Sayyīdinā 'Alī and we are saying, "O Allāh! We are accepting that tool to remember You all the time in our life and if we are forgetting to do that, we ask You to send angels to do that on our behalf!!" And Prophet ﷺ is the city of knowledge and 'Alī is its door. So that is the loud *dhikr* given to Sayyīdinā 'Alī and that is through every *ṭarīqah* that comes from him, the door to it is that *dhikr*. So the other door to Prophet is Sayyīdinā Abū Bakr aṣ-Ṣiddīq and the method of Sayyīdinā Abū Bakr is a different way. Those coming through the Naqshbandi Way are combining the two ways from the prophet of Sayyīdinā Abū Bakr ق and Sayyīdinā 'Alī ؓ, and they combine in Sayyīdinā Jafar aṣ-Ṣadiq ق. He was one of the twelve *imāms* of Islam and they were coming from time to time, and Sayyīdinā Jafar combined in him those two sources, as mentioned in the Qur'an:

maraj al-baḥrayni yaltaqīyān.
He has let free the two bodies of flowing water, meeting together.
(Sūrat ar-Raḥmān, 55:19)

The word "merge" comes from Arabic, does it not? *SubḥānAllāh*, the English language takes from the Holy Qur'an; also in French, "merger," takes from the Holy Qur'an. So, *marraj al-baḥrayn yaltaqīyān*, "The two oceans are merging," the ocean of Sayyīdinā 'Alī ﷺ and the ocean of Sayyīdinā Abū Bakr ﷺ. That is the Golden Ocean whose value cannot be described!

That is why we say, *lā ilāha illa-Llāh, lā ilāha illa-Llāh, lā ilāha illa-Llāh.* That is why we said yesterday to people on the Internet who were typing, "*Allāh, Allāh, Allāh, Allāh...*" that is an electromagnetic voice that goes forever and you will be continuously rewarded! *Dhikr* of *lā ilāha illa-Llāh* leads to Allāh!

May Allāh ﷻ forgive us.

Wa min Allāhi 't-tawfiq, bi ḥurmati 'l-ḥabīb, bi ḥurmati 'l-Fātiḥah.
And with Allāh is success. For the sake of the Beloved, for his sake we recite the opening chapter of Holy Qur'an.

The Four Levels of Dhikr and the Heart of Sayyidina Ali

Aʿūdhu billāhi min ash-Shayṭān ir-rajīm. Bismillāhi' r-Raḥmāni 'r-Raḥīm. Nawaytu 'l-arbāʿīn, nawaytu 'l-ʿitikāf, nawaytu'l-khalwah, nawaytu 'l-ʿuzlah, nawaytu 'r-riyāḍa, nawaytu 's-sulūk, lillāhi Taʿalā fī hādhā 'l-masjid. Atiʿ ūllāh wa atiʿū 'r-Rasūl wa ūli 'l-amri minkum. (4:59)

We must always remember to ask *madad* from our shaykh, and he is taking *madad* from Prophet, whom Allāh made *khalīfah* of this Creation and a Mercy for all the Worlds, *Raḥmatan lil-ʿĀlamīn,* which can also be *Raḥmatan lil-ʿĀlamayn,* "Mercy for the Two Worlds," and sometimes scholars explain *ʿalamayn* as, "Mankind and *jinn*." So there is *mulk,* this world's Creation, and *malakūt*, Heavenly Creation. He is mercy for both. And no one knows when Allāh ﷻ created His Beloved Prophet ﷺ. From him *ʿUlūm al-Awwalīn wal-ʿĀkhirīn*, Knowledge of Before and After, is coming. So we cannot say other than that Prophet ﷺ is *khalīfah* on Earth and in Heavens.

May Allāh keep us always in Presence of Prophet. To him there are doors that you can enter, big or small, but there are doors. *Awlīyā* know the doors. We mentioned yesterday the importance of the door of Sayyīdinā ʿAli, *karam-Allāhu wajaha,* and how Prophet ﷺ taught him to make *dhikrūllāh* with *lā ilāha illa-Llāh.* It is also mentioned in many books of previous *awlīyāullāh* and by Grandshaykh ق and Mawlana Shaykh Nazim, may Allāh give him long life, that *dhikrūllāh* is of different kinds and has different levels.

One of them is *dhikr al-lisān, "dhikr* of the tongue", to keep your tongue always in remembrance of Allāh ﷻ and always mentioning His Beautiful Names and Attributes, which allows you to enter that Reality. By always doing that *dhikr* of *lā ilāha illa-Llāh,* it is the sword against our bad *ʿamal,* deeds. Ego always likes to be something. That *dhikr* is telling us, "Don't listen to or believe your ego, as Shayṭān can play with it."

So before going to Abū Bakr aṣ-Ṣiddīq's door, we say one of the types of *dhikr* is *dhikr al-lisān, Dhikr* of the Tongue, which is considered the first step to enter the Ocean of Heavens. That is why *awlīyā* can understand that from the verse:

maraja al-baḥrayni yaltaqīyāni baynahumā barzakhun lā yabghiyān.
He has let loose the two seas meeting together. Between them is a barrier which none of them can transgress. (Sūrat ar-Raḥmān, 55:19-20)

That *barzakh* is an area of quarantine; it stops one ocean overtaking the other. If you want to pass from one ocean to another you have to enter that area, *barzakh,* and wait until they are ready to let you go to the other ocean. This happens among sea creatures. Scientists discovered that the Mediterranean and Atlantic Oceans don't mix, and between them is, to us, an imaginary line, but fish sense that line and stop at it to enter that quarantine. When they are ready, they move to the other ocean.

It means with those with *dhikr al-lisān* are in the ocean of Sayyīdinā ʿAli, and that is why we begin with *lā ilāha illa-Llāh,* and when we finish that, in the Naqshbandi Order, we go to *dhikr* of "Allāh". This is in *jamaʿat*, but when we do *dhikr* alone we begin with "Allāh". In *jamaʿat,* in a technical sense, we are all moving from one ocean to another ocean so we have to come with *lā ilāha illa-Llāh, lā ilāha illa-Llāh, lā ilāha illa-Llāh, lā ilāha illa-Llāh,* and we are approaching the area where we have to go, before entering the ocean of Abū Bakr aṣ-Ṣiddīq. So you stop there, and they check whether are you able to go on or whether you need quarantine. You enter the quarantine area and they will keep you there until you are ready to go into the other ocean by remembrance of *ʿIsm adh-Dhāt*, "Allāh".

That is why it is said, *falzam dhikr adh-Dhāt,* until you reach the other ocean, the *Dhikr* of Paradise, *dhikr ul-jinān* is through *ʿIsm adh-Dhāt*, "Allāh".

Dhikr of *lā ilāha illa-Llāh* takes you from *dunyā,* and it states Allāh's Oneness, to show humanity, "There is no god but Allāh." That is denial of the ego and Shayṭān, and denial of anyone who associates anything with Allāh. Allāh is The One Who saves you, from Hell and from punishment, and sends you to be with Sayyīdinā Muḥammad ﷺ! That takes you from *dunyā* to the remembrance of Allāh, so then you are entering Jannah, Paradise. That is why it is called *dhikrūllāh: Allāh, Allāh, Allāh,* is *dhikr* of the heart, which is *dhikr* of Paradise!

So that is why in the Naqshbandi Order the first step they take, the shaykh will carry you with his power and lead you by your hand, and you will that through quarantine in the blink of an eye! Then he puts you in that ocean of *ʿIsm adh-Dhāt*. And that is why the Naqshbandi begin with *dhikr* of *ʿIsm adh-Dhāt,* sitting by themselves quietly, going from 1500 times daily recitation to 5,000 to 10,000 times, as much as you can.

Grandshaykh ق said, "O *'IbādAllāh,* Servants of Allāh! *Faqsud hum washtanshiqhum... arwāḥi 'ṭ-ṭayyib.* Run to these Naqshbandi shaykhs and smell their beauty and smell their sweat, as their sweat is the sweat of love in the Divine Presence! You are never going to smell such a fragrance and you can never imagine how nice it is! Through that smell, *fatafūz 'alā hadhal-jawhar an-nafīs,* you are going to be able to attain that beautiful diamond that takes away all obstacles on your way. And their way, the Naqshbandi Way, is the easiest way. They don't let the *murīd* go hungry, and don't make the *murīd* stay awake all night. Moderation is their way. They are always moderate and they don't put you under too much pressure, as Allāh ﷻ said:

> *lā yukallifullāh nafsan illā wus'aha.*
> *On no soul does Allāh place a burden greater than it can bear.*
> (Sūrat al-Baqarah, 2:286)

So they prepare you according to your capacity in a moderate way so that you go quickly. And every *masjid* is a *zāwīya* for them; they can do their *dhikr* anywhere and no one can asks them what they you doing, as they are doing silent, *khafī, dhikr*. And their hearts are always with their Lord.

> *Wa man dakhalahu kāna āminan w 'alā an-nāsi hajj al-bayt man istaṭa'a ilayhi sabīlā.*
> *Whoever enters the House of Allāh is safe, and pilgrimage to the House of Allāh is a duty on Mankind (who are able).* (Sūrat 'Āli 'Imrān, 3:97)

Safety is there as you enter His House, so whoever enters it is in safety. Allāh ﷻ said to Prophet ﷺ directly in Ḥadīth Qudsī:

> *Ma wasi'anī ardī wa lā samā'ī wa lākin wasi'anī qalbī 'abdī al-mu'min.*
> *My Earth did not contain Me, nor My Heavens, but the heart of My believing servant contained Me.*

So that means if you let your soul enter the heart, and the ego has been cut down, at that time your soul and spirit can enter your heart, and then you find safety. That is why *awlīyā* found safety, because their ego has been prevented from entering their hearts. But by listening and obeying, and through love and respect, Allāh cut their ego down and made an easy way for them to enter their hearts and then when they enter they are safe.

> *Wa man dakhalahu kāna āminan w 'alā an-nāsi hajj al-bayt man istaṭa'a ilayhi sabīlā.*

And there is an obligation to visit the House of Allāh, and as a believer, like visiting the House of Allāh in Meccatu 'l-Mukarrama, you have to visit the "House of the Heart". And when you circumambulate the heart, you circumambulate the Light that Allāh ﷻ is sending to your heart.

Allāh wants His servants to visit His House; those who are able, *istitaʿa 'ilayh sabīla,* are in reality those who step on their ego, not those who are happy in *dunyā* doing what they like, who say, "It is enough that we pray." Okay, you have to pray, but you cannot open the door of the house to those lights without stepping on your ego. *Dhikrūllāh* is the key to that door of that house with that light! Who entered is in safety, and Allāh ﷻ wants you to circumambulate that House, in that kind of movement that expresses your ecstasy.

That is like in *ḥaḍrah,* expressing yourself in that movement, which is similar to circumambulating the House, which is expressing your love. That is not dancing, but going around the House. And at that time, you go around your own House that Allāh made ready for you. And this moves on to why they said that remembrance is of four types in every level.

There are four types of *dhikr* in every level you go to. On the level of *dhikr* of *lā ilāha illa-Llāh* and *dhikr* of *Allāh, Allāh,* there are four types. First is the *dhikr* that you mention. You may mention a Beautiful Name or make *ṣalawāt* or whatever you want. Second is *dhikrun tadhkuru bih, dhikr* in which you mention Allāh; it might be through His Beautiful Names. Third is *dhikru tadhkuruk,* the *dhikr* that mentions you. Fourth is *dhikr yadhkuru bika, dhikr* in which you will be mentioned.

The first one is *dhikrun tadhkuruhu, dhikr tatrud al-ghaflah,* the *dhikr* that throws away heedlessness. You are doing something good to throw away your heedlessness. The second is *tadhkur madhdkūrun imma al-ʿadhāb aw imma al-qurb,* the *dhikr* that brings you near and saves you from punishment. The third is *wa dhikrun yadhkuruka.* "Remember Me and will I remember you," so when you mention Him through His Beautiful Names, Allāh mentions you in return. The fourth is, *hūw dhikrūllāhi li ʿabdihi wa laysa li ʿabdihi mutaʿallaq,* "Allāh mentions His servant without His servant having done anything."

Without His servant mentioning His Names, His love, punishment or reward, there is a *dhikr* that remembers you! Who is "you"?

> *inna Allāh wa malā'ikatahu yūṣallūn ʿalā an-nabī yā ayyuhalladhīna āmanū ṣallū ʿalayhi wa sallimū taslīmā.*
>
> *Allāh and His angels send blessings on the Prophet: O you that believe! Send blessings on him, and salute him with all respect.* (Sūrat al-'Aḥzāb, 33:56)

That is the one that without him mentioning Allāh, He mentioned him. That is *wahbana,* a grant from Allāh. Nothing is a cause of what He does, or what the Prophet did, it is a direct grant from Allāh. That is why *awlīyāullāh* say that representatives of Prophet have been chosen without them doing anything; he takes one and says, "You are Prophet's representative." Allāh mentioned him. Who can dispute this? That is the highest *dhikrūllāh,* that He mentioned them.

And *awlīyā* are lucky, as because of Prophet they are mentioned. *Inna Allāh wa malā'ikatahu yuṣallūn ʿalā an-nabī.* It means, "Follow My Way by doing as I do, and send *ṣalawāt* on Prophet. Then you are following what I ordered in Holy Qur'an:

> *Qul in kuntum tuḥibbūn-Allāha fattabiʿūnī yuḥbibkumu Allāhu wa yaghfir lakum dhunūbakum w'Allāhu Ghafūrun Raḥīm.*
> *Say, "If you love Allāh, follow me (Muḥammad). Allāh will love you and forgive you your sins, for Allāh is Oft-Forgiving, Most Merciful."*
> (Sūrat 'Āli ʿImrān, 3:31)

"Say to them, O Muḥammad, 'If you really love Allāh, then follow and love me, and then I will love you."

And the Prophet ﷺ said, "When I love you, then Allāh loves you." That is why Prophet made it easy for us by saying, "Follow my son-in-law and cousin. I am the city of knowledge and ʿAlī is its door; open the door and enter through that way. If you want the other way, the hidden way, I am giving you Abū Bakr aṣ-Ṣiddīq." That is why it is said by many different *awlīyā* and scholars, it is certain that when Allāh mentioned Abū Bakr aṣ-Ṣiddīq in Holy Qur'an, when they were in the cave, Prophet ﷺ said, 'O Abū Bakr! Don't be sad.'"

> *Illa tanṣu Rūḥu faqad naṣarahu Allāhu idh akhrajahu alladhīna kafarū thanīyy ithnayni idh humā fi 'l-ghāri idh yaqūlu li-ṣāḥibihi lā taḥzan inna allāha maʿanā fa-anzalā Allāhu sakīnatahu ʿalayhi wa ayyadahu bi-junūdin lam tarawhā wa jaʿalā kalimata 'Lladhīna kafarū 's-sufla wa kalimatullāhi hīya al-ʿulyā wa 'Llāhu ʿAzīzun Ḥakīm.*
> *The second of two, when they (Prophet and Abū Bakr) were in the cave, and he said to his companion, "Be not sad (or afraid), for surely Allāh is with us." Then Allāh sent down His sakīnah (calmness, tranquility, peace) upon him, and strengthened him with forces which you saw not.* (at-Tawbah, 9:40)

Which cave? Yes, we know it was Ghāri Thawr, when they were migrating from Mecca to Medina, hiding. Hiding? For what? Does Prophet need to hide? He went for Mi'rāj, who can touch him? But he entered there for a certain reason: to pass that authority to Sayyīdinā Abū Bakr aṣ-Ṣiddīq, that knowledge Allāh is sending, *anzalā Allāhu sakīnatahu 'alayh,* He manifest His tranquility, peacefulness, love, mercy on them. It means when they entered the Cave of Sayyīdinā Muḥammad ﷺ, it is like *as-hāb al-Kahf,* the "Companions of the Cave." Where did they enter?

> *Fa awū il al-kahf yanshur lakum rabbukum min raḥmatih wa yuhayyi lakum min amrikum mirfaqā.*
> Betake yourselves to the Cave: Your Lord will shower His mercies on you and disposes of your affair towards comfort and ease."   (Sūrat al-Kahf, 18:62)

"Run to the cave, O People of the Cave!" Who is in that cave? That is Sayyīdinā Muḥammad ﷺ! It's also like when He ordered them to enter the *fulk al-mashhūn:*

> *wa khalaqnā lahum min mithlihi mā yarkabūn.*
> And We have created for them similar (vessels) on which they ride.
>   (YāSīn, 36:42)

Sayyīdinā Nūḥ put everyone in that ark, *fulk al-mashhūn,* the boat of Sayyīdinā Nūḥ ؑ is like the heart of Sayyīdinā Muḥammad ﷺ. Literally it is the boat of Sayyīdinā Nūḥ but it is also an indication that if you run to that boat, you will be in safety. "And We have created something similar to it in which you can ride." And what is similar to that boat? Where that boat is Sayyīdinā Muḥammad ﷺ, the ones similar is Sayyīdinā Abū Bakr aṣ-Ṣiddīq and Sayyīdinā 'Ali, and *awlīyā,* according to their levels, to take *Ummat an-Nabī* to safety.

So that is why Sayyīdinā Abū Bakr ؓ entered the boat and the cave, and Allāh sent that *sakīnah* on them, that peacefulness, and He defeated their enemies for them, meaning, the enemy that attacks and whispers in ears of people, Shayṭān. So those who entered with Sayyīdinā Abū Bakr aṣ-Ṣiddīq are going to be with him in that cave and they were present, and generation after generation and century after century, those receiving their sainthood from Abū Bakr aṣ-Ṣiddīq have authority to bring people to safety. Through their power and their spotlight they attract people to safety.

About Sayyīdinā 'Ali ؓ, Prophet ﷺ said, "I am the city of knowledge and 'Alī is its door." So what did Sayyīdinā 'Alī do? He was the door of safety, they were not able to enter the city except through Sayyīdinā 'Ali. He was the guardian for the Prophet ﷺ, although Prophet doesn't need this, but he put these *Ṣaḥābah* ؓ, about whom he said:

Aṣ-ḥābī ka 'n-nujūm bi ayyihim iqtaḍaytum, ihtadaytum. My Companions are like stars. Whichever of them you use as a guide, you will be rightly guided.

So Sayyīdinā ʿAlī ؓ was in Prophet's bed when the Quraysh made their conspiracy to kill the Prophet ﷺ. Who went in that bed? Is that a normal bed or something special? That is the bed of prophecy, and he received the secrets of prophecy! When they opened the door and found Sayyīdinā ʿAlī there, they were blocked. That means that no Shayṭān can go through that door! So Sayyīdinā ʿAlī is at the heart of every believer, meaning, "I am the ocean of knowledge in the heart of every believer and ʿAlī is there at the door." That means when you enter the door, you enter the cave, and the door is Sayyīdinā ʿAlī ؓ and inside is Sayyīdinā Abū Bakr ؓ!

That doesn't mean Abū Bakr is higher than Sayyīdinā ʿAli, or that Sayyīdinā ʿAlī is higher than Sayyīdinā Abū Bakr, nor that they are higher than Sayyīdinā ʿUmar. The Prophet ﷺ loves and guides all of them the same, but he might have more family love toward Sayyīdinā ʿAli, as he was his son-in-law and cousin and the first young person to accept Islam.

So that heart of the believer is where Prophet's city is ready, and if you are able to go through Sayyīdinā ʿAlī to that city, you receive what *awlīyā* receive. May Allāh open that city for us! Whoever enters it is safe. That means saftety is in that city, and in that heart which Allāh ﷻ gave you. Every heart is different; in some hearts that city will expand and be huge, and in some it will be smaller, depending on the capacity of each one. Next time we will go into what Prophet put in Sayyīdinā Abū Bakr's heart.

Wa min Allāhi 't-tawfiq, bi ḥurmati 'l-ḥabīb, bi ḥurmati 'l-Fātiḥah.
And with Allāh is success. For the sake of the Beloved, for his sake we recite the opening chapter of Holy Qur'an.

Enter Through the Door and Dwell in the City

Aʿūdhu billāhi min ash-Shayṭān ir-rajīm. Bismillāhi' r-Raḥmāni 'r-Raḥīm. Nawaytu 'l-arbāʿīn, nawaytu 'l-ʿitikāf, nawaytu'l-khalwah, nawaytu 'l-ʿuzlah, nawaytu 'r-riyāḍa, nawaytu 's-sulūk, lillāhi Taʿalā fī hādhā 'l-masjid. Atiʿ ūllāh wa atiʿū 'r-Rasūl wa ūli 'l-amri minkum. (4:59)

Those who are on authority have the key for the door of Prophet ﷺ. To reach the main door, you must go through many doors until you reach the door of that city. Every door has people who are attracted to it, and these are *awlīyāullāh* who receive from Prophet ﷺ, to whom they came through one door, as Prophet ﷺ described:

> *'ana madinatu 'l-ʿilmi wa ʿAliyyun babuha.*
> *I am the city of knowledge and ʿAlī is its door.* (al-Ḥākim, Tirmidhī)

They enter through that main door and inside they find the one who is with Prophet ﷺ always, who migrated with him from Mecca to Madinah, Sayyīdinā Abu Bakr as-Siddiq ؓ! That means if you want to reach that city it is easy: first use the *dhikrullah* that Prophet ﷺ showed to Sayyīdinā ʿAlī ؓ, described as *"lā ilāha illa-Llāh."* Prophet ﷺ said to ʿAlī, "Close your eyes and listen to what I say," and he ﷺ said, *"lā ilāha illa-Llāh,"* three times.

Why three times and not four, or four times and not two? *li-anna Allāhu witrun wa yuhib al-witr.* "Allāh is 'One' and He loves everything to be with odd numbers."

Regarding the recitation of *lā ilāha illa-Llāh* three times, the first recitation is to negate, deny and throw out of the heart everything from *dunya*. You are saying, "*Yā Rabbī*! I am directing myself to You by throwing away *dunya* and coming to You!" The second recitation of *lā ilāha illa-Llāh* means, "I am coming through your beloved, Sayyīdinā Muḥammad ﷺ!" The third recitation of *lā ilāha illa-Llāh* is to come through the door where Sayyīdinā ʿAlī is standing. These are the three parts of the key and the code of, "I am the city of knowledge and ʿAlī is its door."

When that door opens, that is something else. Like on Hajj, on the day of Arafat before everyone comes, they open Kaʿaba to wash it and what is inside? That door is the Kaʿaba that is in everyone's heart, where there are guardians: Sayyīdinā ʿAlī ؓ, Sayyīdinā Abu Bakr as-Siddiq ؓ, and

Sayyīdinā Muḥammad ﷺ! When you open the first lock, you enter there by the way that Prophet showed Abu Bakr as-Siddiq to come to Allāh ﷻ and to him. When you use that word, the door of Prophet opens and from there you begin to see all these manifestations that are inside the Kaʿaba. Prophet ﷺ said to the *Sahabah* ؓ and to Sayyīdinā ʿAlī ؓ and to all Prophet's *khalīfahs*:

> *ma fadalakum abu bakr bi shay'in min ṣalāt wa sawam wa lakin hajattan fī qalbih.*
> *Abu Bakr did not surpass you by offering excessive prayers and fasting, but by 'shay'in waqara fī qalbihi,' something (unique) that entered his deepest, innermost heart.*

That is something unique that Abu Bakr ؓ used to approach Prophet ﷺ and Allāh ﷻ, and it distinguished him from others. (Mawlana sneezes.) That sneeze is confirmation of what we are saying, and that Sayyīdinā Abu Bakr as-Siddiq ؓ is looking at us from his place!

So as we said, the Prophet ﷺ taught Sayyīdinā ʿAlī ؓ Dhikr al-Lisān, "Dhikr of the Tongue," by saying *"lā ilāha illa-Llāh,"* and he showed Sayyīdinā Abu Bakr ؓ Dhikr al-Jinān, "the Hidden (silent) Dhikr." This hidden *dhikr* is not by tongue, as the tongue is the main door to enter. Then when you enter, you do *dhikrullah* of *ʿIsm adh-Dhāt*, Allāh's Most Beautiful Name that encompasses all Names, *lafdhatul-Jalālah*, "Allāh."

That is why Allāh ﷻ said in Holy Qur'an:

> *Qul Allāh thumma dharhum fī khawdihim yalʿabūn.*
> *Say, "Allāh," then leave them to play in their vain discussions.*
> (Sūrat al-'Anʿām, 6:91)

SubḥānAllāh! This is a prediction of today's situation and something new coming with Mawlana Shaykh Nazim's *madad*. It was mentioned in the Holy Qur'an 1,400 years ago that there will be people who deny making *dhikr* by *ʿism al-Jalālah*. Just as ignorant people from the time of Prophet ﷺ denied the existence of Allāh, there are people today who deny the mention of Allāh in the heart by reciting Allāh's Name; they say it is *bidʿa, kufr, shirk,* and *harām*. Allāh ﷻ said to Prophet ﷺ, "Don't listen to them, but instead say *'Allāh, Allāh,'* as it has been mentioned in Holy Qur'an; say it and don't listen to them."

Why does He want the mention of "Allāh;" why not "ar-Raḥmān", "ar-Raḥīm," "al-Mālik," "al-Quddūs," "al-Mu'min," or "al-Muhaymin"? Because Allāh ﷻ manifested upon every prophet one of His Beautiful Names; what

He gives to that prophet is under that Divine Name, which He can manifest on many of the 124,000 prophets. But Prophet Muḥammad ﷺ is highest among all prophets, so Allāh gave him the highest Name and manifested Himself to Prophet by that Name. Therefore, all prophets have to be under him and under that Name, "Allāh, The One, Unique." They cannot all be under the same various Divine Names.

Awlīyāullāh are inheritors from prophets, and which prophet they inherit from is based on the manifestations of the Beautiful Names they are under. As long as there are *awlīyā,* there will always be one on top, the Sultan al-Awliya, as Sayyīdinā Muhyidīn ibn ʿArabi ؓ mentioned. Similarly, for *anbīyā* there is the only one with the station Khatam al-Anbiya, "Seal of Prophets," and Sultan al-Anbiya, "King of Prophets." Prophet ﷺ gets something special in addition to what he has, and he also shares everything he receives with all prophets. Other prophets don't share; each of them is under a private Beautiful Name, but Prophet ﷺ is under *ʿism al-jamiʿ lil-ʿasma wa'ṣ-ṣiffāt.* Allāh ﷻ is manifesting Himself to Prophet ﷺ through His Beautiful Name that encompasses all Beautiful Names and Attributes, "Allāh".

So He said, "Say, *'Allāh'*." Why not say "ar-Raḥmān"? Because ar-Raḥmān is a description, an adjective; "Allāh" is the main Name. He ﷻ said, "Come to Me directly through the Name "Allāh" as there is no obstacle for you, *yā* Muḥammad! All My doors are open to you and I brought you in Miʿrāj to dress you with that Name!" The proof that Prophet ﷺ is under that Name is in Holy Qur'an:

> *Wa annahū lamma qāma ʿabdAllāh, yadʿūhū kādū yakūnū ʿalayhi libada. Yet when the devotee of Allāh stands forth to invoke Him, they just make a dense crowd around him.* (Sūrat al-Jinn, 72:19)

Is there anywhere else where Allāh mentioned Prophet directly as "*ʿabdAllāh*"? That is exclusively for Prophet ﷺ and it means he is the one under the *tajalli* of that Name. As he is under that *tajalli,* how he is going to be called? ʿAbdAllāh, "Servant of Allāh"; that is the real *ʿabd,* the rest are imitations. What is he called, other than *Raḥmatan lil-ʿĀlamīn*, "Mercy to all the Worlds"? Every scholar you ask will say Prophet ﷺ is al-Insān al-Kāmil, "the Perfect Human Being." There is no other, there is only one: the Prophet ﷺ *Allāhuma sallī ʿalā Sayyīdinā Muḥammad* ﷺ!

That Beautiful Name has been described in Sūrat al-Ikhlās:

Qul Huw Allāhu Ahad.
Say (O Muḥammad), "He is 'Allāh', The One, Who has no partner."
(Sūrat al-Ikhlās, 112:1)

Say "Allāh," *qul Huwa,* "The One Who Is completely unknown," Whose reality of that Essence cannot be known, except under the Name, Allāh. All the descriptions from the Beautiful Names and Attributes come under that. But in reality, His Essence, the Absolute Unknown, the Hidden, is "Allāh," and He is "Ahad". "Allāh" is higher than "Ahad," the description. Say, "Allāh, the One with no partner, no child, no description of Him." That is "Allāh".

Wa annahū lamma qāma ʿabdAllāh, yadʿūhū kādū yakūnū ʿalayhi libaḍa, "the One Who is also Unknown," as no one knows the Prophet's ﷺ rank or what Allāh ﷻ gave him. He is known as "The Only (real) ʿAbdAllāh," because the Name "Allāh" means, "The One Who is Absolutely Unknown," so the one who is under that Name is Muḥammad ﷺ, al-Insān al-Kamil.

That Holy Name was put to give The Essence a name, which is "Allāh." But to understand that Name is impossible, so you understand through the other holy descriptions. "Allāh" is described through all the Godly Attributes, *ʿAsma ar-Rubūbiyya,* the Names of Lordship, al-Jalāl, "The Majestic," al-Jamāl, "The Beauty," and al-Kamāl, "The Perfection"; these are descriptions of Allāh ﷻ.

Wa huwa ʿIsmun lidh-Dhāt al-Buht is the Name given to the Secret, the Essence. As close as you zoom in, it is the Name for that Absolute Unknown, *al-ʿAma al-Mutlaq*. No one can see it as it is veiled. Even the Prophet ﷺ cannot see that Essence, although He is under the manifestation of that Name we just described, "Allāh." So the Name "Allāh" is higher than all the Divine Beautiful Names.

That is why Prophet ﷺ is higher than all prophets, as he is carrying the manifestation of that Name, and he is *Raḥmatan lil-ʿĀlamīn.* He was dressed with that Name, and that is why all prophets will come with their nations asking for Prophet's ﷺ mercy, *shafāʿa,* and blessing, because he is under the manifestation of that highest Name which all other Names are under. It is considered in the Islamic Schools of Thought, especially in the Hanafi *madhhab,* that *ʿIsmullāh al-ʿĀzham* is the Name that Allāh manifested on His Prophet ﷺ.

Sayyīdinā Musa ﷺ asked, "*Yā Rabbī*! Tell me, what is Your Greatest Name? Let me see you. Let me know Your Greatest Name," and all prophets asked that. But Allāh ﷻ said, "O Musa! That is not for you, that is only for My Beloved, Sayyīdinā Muḥammad. So what is for you? Look at the mountain." He sent His manifestation on the mountain and Sayyīdinā Musa fainted, because he had trespassed his limit. In Miʿrāj, Sayyīdinā Jibrīl ﷺ said to Prophet ﷺ, "I cannot go further or cross this limit, but you can go further." Sayyīdinā Musa asked to cross the limits, and Allāh taught him a lesson.

> *He said, "O my Lord! Show Yourself to me, that I may look upon You." Allāh said, "By no means can you see Me (directly), but look upon the mountain; if it abides in its place then you shall see Me." When his Lord manifested His glory on the mount, He made it as dust and Moses fell down in a swoon. When he recovered his senses, he said, "Glory be to You! To You I return in repentance, and I am the first to believe."* (Sūrat al-Aʿrāf, 7:143)

That is when he realized that what he requested from Allāh ﷻ is reserved exclusively for Muḥammad ﷺ!

In his *tafsīr,* Ibn ʿAbbas ؓ said, "When Musa fainted, he saw all the prophets in *sajdah,* except for the 313 who were standing in prayer." So it is not a sin for them, but it is a limit not to transgress. Allāh ﷻ is teaching them, "That is reserved for My beloved one, Sayyīdinā Muḥammad!"

According to Sayyīdinā Abu Hanifa an-Nuʿman's ؓ *madhhab,* that Name is the exclusive manifestation for Prophet only; no one can share it. That is why he was able to go on Miʿrāj. If he was not carrying *ʿIsmullāh al-ʿĀzam,* he would have fainted, but because he was carrying that he was able to go through.

So what is our luck? In Naqshbandi Ṭarīqah, our *dhikr* is "Allāh". With that, they take you there directly. As soon as they give you initiation, if that shaykh is real and connected, as soon as you put your hand you enter in that unique area and you are inside. You pass through the door of Sayyīdinā ʿAlī ؓ, who says, "He is our guest, let him in." Like with Sayyīdinā Muḥammad ﷺ when he went in Miʿrāj with Jibrīl ﷺ, they knocked on the door at each Heaven, and the angels asked, "Who is with you, Jibrīl?" Sayyīdinā Jibrīl answered, "Muḥammad." Then they asked, "Is he invited?" "Yes," replied Jibrīl. Do you think that angels don't know he is invited? Of course they know, but this is to show more honor. When you take initiation, it means you are invited.

O People! Who are listening or not listening around the world, if you take *baya*ʿ on the Internet or through a representative, that means you have an invitation to enter that city. You then wear a name tag on your chest, a medallion that reads, "Come in, you are invited! *Allāhuma sallī ʿalā Sayyīdinā Muḥammad*!

We try to remind ourselves of the person upon whom Allāh manifested the *ʿIsm adh-Dhāt* by making *dhikr* with the Name "Allāh" as ordered by our shaykh. That Name represents, "The One Who created the perfect servant." When Adam ﷺ was between clay and water, or between body and soul, that is the "perfect human being" who accumulates from the Divine Name, "al-Jāmiʿi," which contains *kull al-marātib al-ilāhiyyah,* "all different divine levels."

That is the reality of that perfect human being: he contains the heavenly world, Malakūt, and worldly universes, Mulk, and carries all universes' secrets, as he is under the *tajallī* of *ʿIsmullāh al-ʿĀzham*. All minds, souls, and hearts of human beings are under his control, under his keyboard. He can see every one of them by their heavenly name. All universes, worldly and heavenly, are under him. They are created by Allāh ﷻ and are under the blessing of that Name. Prophet ﷺ is *khalīfatullāh fī 'l-mulkih,* "deputy of Allāh among His Creation." So he represents Allāh in every Creation, in Heaven and on Earth.

This might not be even one drop of the ocean of *awlīyāullāh*! We can see how great and strong *awlīyāullāh* are and how weak we are. This will show that we know nothing; the knowledge comes and goes, and we cannot repeat it. These cameras can repeat it, but we cannot. It is in our heart, downloaded, but it needs someone who has the key and is able to upload it.

The heart receives it, but because we are not awake it feels like a dream. Sometimes you remember the dream, sometimes you don't. If you remember, it is good, and if you don't, it is also good, because when they take you to higher levels they close dreams for you. That is good tidings in *ṭarīqah*. As much as you don't know, they keep giving to you in slow doses, but when it becomes a big dose, you might be finished. If they leave you, you might go crazy, then you would drop everything, and they allow that only for a few people. But for everyone else, if Mawlana Shaykh Nazim ق would open what you have in your heart, you could not bear it and you would run away. You would be in a heavenly coma, always staring at something invisible, no longer "here," so they give it to you slowly.

At the beginning of *ṭarīqah,* they show you so many dreams, then later they stop. What do you want to see dreams for, to grow the ego? They give you dreams in the beginning to attract you, but when you reach the other shore they destroy the boat.

As in Holy Qur'an, when Sayyīdinā Musa was with Khidr ؏ they went in a boat and he made a hole. When it reached the other side it was sinking and therefore the king didn't need it. They take you with your ego to the other side like that boat, but they make a hole and when it reaches the other side the boat begins to sink. That way, you cannot go back! Then they chain you and you become angry, but you have nowhere to run.

So what if the shaykh shouts at you? Keep quiet, don't show him anything now. There is no bridge to bring you back to where you were before. Now you are in the minefield and you have to be clever. They put you in a minefield and say, "Cross it." How will you cross? You need a plan. What is the plan? It is *dhikrullah;* that will make you cross the minefield! And all of that enters *baytullah,* where people are circumambulating. That *baytullah* in your heart is a duplicate of Ka'abatullāh in Mecca.

That is to make sure your home becomes *mazhar tajalliyāt min 'al-'asma wa'ṣ-ṣiffāt,* "the appearance of manifestations of Allāh's Beautiful Names and Attributes." When your heart is like that, it is safe. Allāh's houses are hearts of believers. "Neither Heaven nor Earth contains Me, but the heart of a believer contains Me." Enter your heart, your "inn," then you are safe. Say, "Allāh"! Say, "*lā ilāha illa-Llāh!*"

May Allāh bless you one by one, and may Mawlana Shaykh be happy with all of you.

Wa min Allāhi 't-tawfīq, bi ḥurmati 'l-ḥabīb, bi ḥurmati 'l-Fātiḥah.
And with Allāh is success. For the sake of the Beloved, for his sake we recite the opening chapter of Holy Qur'an.

Secrets of the Two Oceans

A'ūdhu billāhi min ash-Shayṭān ir-rajīm. Bismillāhi' r-Raḥmāni 'r-Raḥīm. Nawaytu 'l-arbā'īn, nawaytu 'l-'itikāf, nawaytu'l-khalwah, nawaytu 'l-'uzlah, nawaytu 'r-riyāḍa, nawaytu 's-sulūk, lillāhi Ta'alā fī hādhā 'l-masjid. Ati' ūllāh wa ati'ū 'r-Rasūl wa ūli 'l-amri minkum. (4:59)

Allāh ﷻ manifests Himself to all prophets through His Beautiful Names and gave every prophet a way to carry and dress in a different manifestation of His Beautiful Names. Allāh ﷻ manifests Himself on Prophet Muḥammad, the Seal of Messengers ﷺ, through the Name that encompasses all Beautiful Names and Attributes, "Allāh," which is *'Ism adh-Dhāt*. That carries a lot of knowledge to Prophet ﷺ, and under it comes all the different Beautiful Names and Attributes.

How many (Arabic) letters are in "Allāh"? *Alif, lām, lām, hā.* Four is where Allāh ﷻ gave the Prophet ﷺ authority to reach. The heart is of five different spiritual levels, but physically the heart is comprised of four chambers. Every chamber represents one of these letters. *"Alif"* is the first letter of "Allāh." It represents the secret of *"alif"* and goes in one chamber. The secret of the next letter, *"lam,"* goes in another chamber, then *"lam"* in another chamber, then *"ha"* in another chamber. That has been given.

The heart has five spiritual levels. The lowest is "Maqām al-Qalb," and the whole of *dunyā* affairs is there. The second level is "the Level of the Secret," given to all prophets and all *awlīyā* inherited from that *maqām*. That is why *awlīyāullāh* who inherited from different *ṭarīqahs* are in the second level, "the Secret". So the second and third levels merged together. Who wants to come to the Prophet ﷺ must come through that second level, which is the door of Sayyīdinā 'Alī ؓ. If you want to enter the Secret, pass by Sayyīdinā 'Alī ؓ, and there is no other way. And the third level is Sirr as-Sirr, "the Secret of the Secret." There you enter the Name, "Allāh". There are two kinds of *dhikr* of *lā ilāha illa-Llāh*: *ithbāt wa nafiy*, "to affirm and to deny." You affirm "There is no god save Allāh," and you deny everything that is other than Allāh.

Then you are ready to make *dhikr* with *'Ism adh-Dhāt*, the Name that encompasses all Names: "Allāh." That is the *dhikr* Prophet ﷺ taught Sayyīdinā Abū Bakr aṣ-Ṣiddīq ق, and those who took from him are people of the Naqshbandi Ṭarīqah. The two oceans of Sayyīdinā 'Alī and Sayyīdinā

Abū Bakr aṣ-Ṣiddīq ق merge, *maraj al-baḥryan*, in Sayyīdinā Jafar aṣ-Ṣiddīq ق. Then that takes you to the fourth level, Akhfā, "the Hidden," which is exclusively for Prophet ﷺ; no one else can enter there. *Lā sharīk lahu*, in that position there is no associate with Prophet ﷺ in his servanthood. The fifth level, Maqām al-Khafā, "the Absolute Hidden," is exclusively for Allāh. The *'Amā al-Kāmil* is completely veiled and no one can see anything in that level. So with these four letters of the Name "Allāh," the secret goes into the four chambers of the heart. And as you open it, chamber after chamber you will see what cannot be seen, you will hear what cannot be heard (the *ḥadīth* of Prophet about the Station of Moral Excellence).

When you say "Allāh," you are describing the Essence of Allāh. With the *alif*, you understand it means "the Creator." When you remove the *"alif,"* "Allāh" becomes *"lillāh," lām-lām-hā,* which means "what belongs to God." It is no longer His Name, but describes what belongs to Him; the Name is gone. What belongs to Him? Everything. But whatever belongs to Him, He gave to you; He is not in need of anything He created, and He gave it to Sayyīdinā Muḥammad ﷺ. Allāh ﷻ is not in need and He created what belongs to Him. So we are subject to Him, not only humans, but everything that is created. People's thinking is limited, so you cannot expand it to see what belongs to Him. This example will show us what belongs to Him, and this is one of the descriptions of al-Insān al-Kāmil, "the Perfect Man," (Prophet Muḥammad) who receives all kinds of manifestations.

To understand what belongs to Allāh, Sayyīdinā Jibrīl ﷺ asked, *"Yā Rabbī*! Can I see Your Kingdom?"

"Yes, why not? No problem." Allāh ﷻ loves His servants. "If you want, I will show you. I gave you 600 power engines, turbines, 600 wings."

When he came to Prophet ﷺ, Jibrīl ﷺ used two wings. He came from his place beyond the universe, a heavenly Kingdom, with two wings in less than one second. When Allāh ﷻ orders it, it appears. Don't be surprised; that is Allāh! Physicists have calculated the smallest fraction of a second; they found at 10^{-22} of a second, time disappears and only energy remains. So in that fraction of time, energy moves so fast. That is why he was there immediately in front of Prophet ﷺ.

So he said, *"Yā Rabbī*! Show me Your Kingdom."

"I will show you. Why? You don't believe?"

"It's not that, but it is to make my heart content."

Behold! Abraham said, "My Lord! Show me how You give life to the dead." He said, "Do you not believe?" He said, "Yes (I believe), but to satisfy My own understanding." He said, "Take four birds, tame them to turn to you, put a portion of them on every hill and call them. They will come to you (flying) with speed. Then know that Allāh is Exalted in Power, Wise." (Sūrat al-Baqarah, 2:260)

Sayyidinā Ibrāhīm ☤ said, "O Allāh! Show me how You create."

"Why do you want to know that?"

"How do You create?"

The *anbiyā* want to teach us, so they ask, but Prophet Muḥammad ﷺ never asked.

So Allāh ﷻ said, "You don't believe I can create?"

Sayyidinā Ibrāhīm ☤ was afraid then; how he had asked that question? But he could not take it back. It is like on a computer when you write a text message or email, you press "send" and after you send it, it is gone. In the past you would write a letter, but before you sent it, it would take time and you might change your mind about what you wrote. But on the computer you send it, and you cannot bring it back. So be careful what you write. And be careful with Facebook! It is the worst thing, teaching people bad character. Allāh ﷻ and Prophet ﷺ and *awliyā* are not happy with Facebook. Close your Facebook! (Mawlana Shaykh speaks to people in the assembly.) Do you have Facebook? (Of course.)

So Allāh ﷻ said, *awalam tu'min*, "Do you not believe?" Ibrāhīm answered, "No, it is not that, but I am asking so my heart will be content."

"What Ibrāhīm? Your heart is not content?"

He said, "Show me how You create, as I want my heart to be content."

Sayyidinā Muḥammad ﷺ never asked, because his heart is always content.

Allāh ﷻ said, "Okay, you are My *khalīfah* on Earth, so I will show you. Take a bird, cut it into pieces and put them on four hills and then call those pieces. They will come together and they will come running to you!"

Allāh ﷻ is the Creator. So when Jibrīl ☤ asked, "Can I see Your Kingdom, *yā Rabbī*?" Allāh ﷻ said, "Okay," since Jibrīl ☤ also wanted contentment, to see how big this universe is. And Allāh ﷻ ordered him to use his 600 wings, not to use two wings. Through this universe, he was appearing in less than a moment with two wings. What do you think about him using those 600 wings, or turbines? Allāh ﷻ knows what they are, these heavenly wings, or turbines, to move in space, able to see Allāh's Kingdom. By that order he was moving. Imagine how much he could move and see in one moment! Can we calculate that, to see how big is Allāh's Kingdom? No. Allāh's Kingdom is not this Earth, according to the *hadīth*:

Law kānati 'd-dunyā tazin ʿindallāhi janāḥa baʿūda mā saqā kāfir minhā shurbatu māi.

It means, "In Allāh's Sight, the value of this world is less than the wing of a mosquito." And Jibrīl moved, moved, moved by Allāh's order until he became exhausted. Do angels get exhausted? No. So why did he? Because this Kingdom was beyond his power, beyond his 600 wings.

He told Allāh, "This Kingdom is so big it is beyond me! Is there still more?"

"*Yā* Jibrīl, what do you mean, 'still more'? You didn't move around a corner yet!"

He moved non-stop for 70,000 years and he got tired. That is why human beings get tired after they grow old. If Jibrīl ﷺ didn't get tired, then human beings would not get tired and you would have long life; that reflection came on this Creation.

And he said, "Is there still more?"

"What you did is nothing, not even an epsilon."

He was so small and it was 70,000 years! And what he saw in that moving was indescribable, with no beginning and no end. It was straight and flat, and we can call it an ocean, full of very small white crystals. Like when you go to the beach and you see white sand, to us there is no beginning and no end and you cannot count how many crystals of sand there are.

Through his power, Sayyīdinā Jibrīl ﷺ was not moving around a corner after 70,000 years of flying, and he saw transparent white crystals without end. They cannot be described, and they were where he was. And in the middle of this was a tree and on it was one green bird that went down, took one crystal in his beak, went up the tree, slowly ate it and swallowed it. And then again went down, picked up another crystal, went up the tree, ate it, and swallowed it, and repeated that again and again.

Jibrīl said, "*Yā Rabbī.* I didn't see anything except this ocean of crystals."

And Allāh ﷻ said, "*Yā* Jibrīl, every *dharrah*, atom, of that crystal is a universe by itself." If Allāh ﷻ can make the Earth go through the eye of a needle without making the needle bigger or making the Earth smaller, can't Allāh then make each crystal a universe?

He said, "So what is that bird?"

"*Yā* Jibrīl, that bird is My beloved, who is ordered to go down and pick up one crystal and swallow it. As soon as it is swallowed, that is an indication that he is *khalīfatullāh* in that *mulk* and Malakūt, in Earth and Heaven. And as soon as he takes that crystal, that universe is created within him, not outside of him."

So that is why all prophets, from Adam ﷺ until the Day of Judgment, come to Prophet ﷺ for *shafāʿ* on Judgment Day. They are within him, so how will Allāh ﷻ send anyone to Hellfire when they are within Prophet ﷺ?

W ʿallamū anna fīkum rasūlullāh.
And know that Prophet is within you. (Sūrat al-Ḥujurāt, 49:7)

Since he is within you, you are within him. And every time he swallows one crystal, that is one Creation, and Prophet ﷺ is Allāh's representative for that Creation, as Muḥammad ﷺ is His Messenger. That is the Perfect Human Being, *al-insān al-kāmil.*

Wa laqad karamnā Banī Adam.
We have honored the Children of Adam. (Sūrat al-'Isrā', 17:70)

That means no Creation is honored more than human beings. Even angels are not honored as human beings are honored. All that is because of Sayyīdinā Muḥammad ﷺ, who is encompassing all the heavenly and Godly levels. And he is the one who overtakes all the souls of human beings in him. Allāh ﷻ gave him that authority to reach anyone. Previously, the idea of reaching anyone was not understood, but now it is easy to understand through technology. You can reach anyone, you can send an email to anyone. If a server can reach thousands and thousands through networking, can't Prophet ﷺ have a heavenly server to connect with all of humanity? But what do you need to do? You need to reply. If you don't reply, you are the loser. He is ready; his heart is open but you have to go there.

Hūwa al-Jāmiʿ lil marātib al-ilāhīyya min al-ʿuqūl wa 'n-nufūs al-kullīya wa 'l-juzī'yyah. He is "the One that Contains." "Al-Jāmiʿ" accumulates, collects, contains *marātib al-ilāhīyya,* all the Godly stations Allāh ﷻ gave him. He has already grasped or overtaken and encompassed every Godly station in the Heavens and the angelic world, and it is under his command; not only the Godly stations, but *kawnīyya* also. Whatever is in this universe is under him and, not only that, all brains, *min al-'uqūl*. That means in every brain there is a chip that is smaller than a lentil, filled with intelligence. It means that chip is connected to him, to that server. *Wa 'n-nufūs*, the selves, all people's selves are in his hands, *al-kullīya wa 'l-juzī'yyah*, all of it, even the smallest particle of it. That is why he is *khalīfatullāh*.

Innī ja'ilun fi 'l-arḍi khalīfah.
I will create a vicegerent on Earth. (Sūrat al-Baqarah, 2:30)

Under him is all Creation until there will be no more Creation. It is impossible, as creation is continuous, because Allāh is the Creator, "al-Khāliq." So every moment Creation is under the control of Prophet ﷺ. This level is called al-Martabat al-'Amīyya, "the Level of Blindness," not in the meaning of physical blindness, but meaning that the only one who can reach that level and see it is Prophet ﷺ; anyone else is blind and cannot see it. *Wa li-dhālika sār khalīfatullāh*. For that reason he became a *khalīfah*, representative, of Allāh ﷻ. That is why from the beginning Allāh ﷻ put his name with His Own, *Lā ilāha illa-Llāh Muḥammadun Rasūlullāh*.

There is no other who was raised as the Prophet ﷺ was, and that is why he has control over the heart. When we say "Allāh," *alif* represents the Name of the Essence which no one can know. *Qūl Hūw Allāh*. "Say, the One (Who was unknown) is Named 'Allāh'." If you take away the *alif*, it represents all that belongs to Him, *lillāh*. If you take the next *lam* it is *lahu*; that means no one can share anything with Him. You cannot say, "I am partner." Everything *lahu*, you cannot touch it. And if you take next *lam* it is *huw*, the Absolute Unknown. Those four letters have been given to Prophet ﷺ, who represents *'Ismullāh al-'Aẓam*.

And as Sayyīdinā Abū Ḥanīfa ؓ said, "That Name, "Allāh," is given to Prophet ﷺ and with it you can say to a thing, *kun fayakūn*, "'Be!' and it will be." (36:82)

According to Grandshaykh ق, that Name has been given to Prophet ﷺ in the beginning of every *sūrah*. So that is why he has given me this notebook of his shaykh, Shaykh Sharafuddīn ق, written in very beautiful calligraphy that I copied by hand, as there were no copying machines at that time. It contains the first verses of each *sūrah*, so if you read these first verses of each chapter, you are passing by Allāh's Greatest Name but you don't know what it is. That is why it is recommended to read it. We can write it and pass it to people. Sometimes it is one verse (*awail as-sūr*) and sometimes it is two. So that has been given to Prophet ﷺ.

Shaykh Aḥmad al-Fārūqī al-Sirhindī ق said that on the journey of seekers in our Way, the Naqshbandi Order, "When the seeker in our *ṭarīqah* is not busy with *dunyā* matters, we will make him busy with heavenly matters." It means stop running after *dunyā,* because *dunyā* makes you a slave to it and you must make *dunyā* a slave for you.

The *awlīyā* give everything to Allāh ﷻ; they have no privacy and their life is "hacked"; everyone can enter and see what they are doing. So Shaykh Aḥmad al-Faruqi said, "If they are not busy in *dunyā* work we will give them heavenly work by making them *nushghilahum bi wuqūf al-qalbi,* 'always alert in their heart,' preparing them to enter the Divine Presence through what we teach them, through *at-tawajjuh.*" This is how to prepare themselves, to direct themselves to enter the reality of the human soul's secret, *ar-Rūh al-insāni.* The human *Rūh* is not only the soul, but the inner soul of the soul. "We will show them how they can begin their journey within their own self."

Doctors today are mostly spies of the human body, where there is a sickness. They write what this one has and they make a big file about your health. *Awlīyā* are spies of the heart and doctors are spies of the body. This is especially true with the MRI today, when they put you in something like a coffin. You have to remember death, when you will be confined in a box. *Awlīyāullāh* have an MRI machine. Is there a more advanced machine? Not yet. *Awlīyāullāh* have a more advanced machine for what they detect, the *rūh al-insāni,* the soul of the soul. The doctors go through your whole body to eliminate all that is not needed, and similarly, to receive these beautiful manifestations of Allāh's Beautiful Names and Attributes, you have to go through the heart, *wuqūf qalbī.*

It is through that *wuqūf,* not through beads or anything. When they see you are not interested in *dunyā* life they put you directly on that journey. The *qalb* is the door of the inner soul, of the human soul. At the beginning, that inner soul of the human soul is inside the body. The *rūh* is in the prison of the body, the cage, but its life is connected through the heart. If the heart stops pumping, finished. So the heart is the controller of the inner soul, to keep it. When the heart is able to expand and the door is opened, it will set free your inner soul. When the inner soul of the soul is freed, then the soul is able to move everywhere within your self and it comes to know the inner self.

That is why Prophet ﷺ said:

Man ʿarafa nafsahu faqad ʿarafa Rabbahu.
Who knows his self knows his Lord.

So what do you know about yourself? Only your mistakes? No, Allāh ﷻ doesn't care about that! He wants to show you His mercy, and to show you Sayyīdinā Muḥammad ﷺ is in everyone's heart and body. He wants to show you His Light in you!

Allāhu Nūr as-samawāti wal-ʿarḍ.
Allāh is the Light of the Heavens and Earth. (Sūrat an-Nūr, 24:35)

Allāh ﷻ said to Prophet ﷺ directly in a Ḥadīth Qudsī:

Ma wasiʿanī arḍī wa lā samāʾī wa lākin wasiʿanī qalbi ʿabdī al-muʾmin.
My Earth did not contain Me, nor My Heavens, but the heart of My believing servant contained Me.

It means Allāh ﷻ is the heart of the *nūr* in every person. Allāh's Light shines in you! So you, O ignorant one, you dumb one! Do you think Allāh's Light is not in you? They are there, waiting for it to be given. Allāh ﷻ doesn't look at dirtiness, but He looks at everything *jamīlah,* beautiful. That is why He said:

wa laqad karamnā Banī Adam.
We have honored the sons of Adam. (Sūrat al-'Isrā', 17:70)

"We have honored human beings with *anwārullāh,* Allāh's Lights." Everyone has different lights and he is known by these lights to Prophet ﷺ, and not one resembles the other light, no way. So imagine what endless oceans of light have been dressed on human beings, the Perfect Creation. And at that time, Allāh ﷻ wants you to know, He will see that *'abd* and He will see the light of his soul and the perfection of his self, because this is the work that Prophet ﷺ is assigning, *man ʿarifa nafsahu faqad ʿarifa rabbah.*

That is why Allāh ﷻ is assigning helpers in your soul, to help you know yourself and your divine lights. The saying is not, "To know the badness of yourself, then you know your Lord." No, you must know the lights of your Lord inside you, then you know your reality in the Divine Presence. Everyone has a reality in the Divine Presence. You are connected with that reality, and this here is a copy of reality that is there. That came on the Day of Promises when Allāh ﷻ asked, "Am I not your Lord?" and everyone said, "Yes You are, *yā Rabbī*!" Even Iblīs knows his Lord, but he is cursed.

At that time you will know the reality and then you will be guided to *mā'rifatullāh* through these lights, to know about your Creator and what you can carry, what you can take. *Wa yukāshif asrārihi wa asmā'ihi Ta'alā*, "He will discover Allāh's Beautiful Names and Attributes in everything around him." He will know every secret of every tree, every herb and in everything that is created in humans or animal or nature, and will be able to know what every atom has been created for and what is its *taṣbīḥ*. That's why he says, *man kashafa 'anhu anwār nafsihi yankhashif 'anhu asrāra rabbih.* "Who discovers or uncovers the light of his self will uncover the light of his Lord's secret."

May Allāh ﷻ bless us.

Wa min Allāhi 't-tawfiq, bi ḥurmati 'l-ḥabīb, bi ḥurmati 'l-Fātiḥah.
And with Allāh is success. For the sake of the Beloved, for his sake we recite the opening chapter of Holy Qur'an.

Levels and Rewards of the Highest Character

Aʿūdhu billāhi min ash-Shayṭān ir-rajīm. Bismillāhi' r-Raḥmāni 'r-Raḥīm. Nawaytu 'l-arbāʿīn, nawaytu 'l-ʿitikāf, nawaytu'l-khalwah, nawaytu 'l-ʿuzlah, nawaytu 'r-riyāḍa, nawaytu 's-sulūk, lillāhi Taʿalā fī hādhā 'l-masjid. Atiʿ ūllāh wa atiʿū 'r-Rasūl wa ūli 'l-amri minkum. (4:59)

As we mentioned, the Prophet ﷺ is "the Perfect Human Being," al-Insān al-Kāmil, as it is mentioned in the Tawrāt that Allāh created human beings on *sūratih*, His Own Image. Okay, we understand that *(sūrah)* is more symbolic, but it means Allāh ﷻ reflected and manifested the continuous spring of His Beautiful Names and Attributes that have no end on the Prophet ﷺ.. Every moment a spring is coming; not just one spring, but springs are coming like fountains of water describing the reality of the Essence that cannot be understood, except through that one who is reflecting it to us, "al-Insān al-Kāmil."

He is the one receiving these blessings or manifestations and reflecting them to all Creation. The only one who can receive that is Prophet ﷺ, the Perfect Human Being. It is said that he is the mirror on which Allāh ﷻ reflects Himself. He sends those images or realities, and the mirror, Insān al-Kāmil, reflects them on anyone in the Heavens or Earth who needs them.

That is why Sayyīdinā Muhyiddīn ibn ʿArabi ؓ said, "The Prophet is the mirror of the Divine Presence." And he said more than that, he went so deep. "If Allāh wants to look at His Creation, he looks at His mirror, the Prophet ﷺ, who is the reflection of these appearances in this Universe." I hope we understood? That is why it is said the *ghawth* receives directly from the Prophet and then he sends on to those five *quṭbs* who are waiting for these manifestations. That is why it is said that one who has *qatratun,* one drop, is:

ʿaynun fīha tusamma salsabīlah.
A fountain there called, "Salsabīl." (Sūrat al-'Insān, 76:18)

That mirror reflects a spring mentioned in Sūrat al-Insān as *ʿaynun fīha tusamma salsabīlah,* "It is a spring called 'Salsabīl'." It is a knowledge that never ends, and who is able to drink even one drop from that spring will become a servant of Allāh. That is why Sayyīdinā al-Khiḍr was able to drink from that *mā' al-hayāt*, the "Fountain of Youth," but in reality, in Heavens it is called the "Spring of Salsabīl."

Salsabīl quenches the thirst of *ʿibādAllāh* whom Allāh dressed with that. It is said they understand the reality of al-Insān al-Kāmil through his best character as he must possess that.

> *Nūn wa al-qalami wa mā yasṭurūna mā anta biniʿmati rabbika bi-majnūnin wa inna laka la-ajran ghayra mamnūnin wa innaka la-ʿalā khuluqin ʿaẓīm.*
>
> *Nūn. By the Pen and what the (angels) write. You (O Muḥammad) are not, by the Grace of your Lord, a madman. And verily, for you will be an endless reward, and verily, you are on an exalted standard of character.*
>
> (Sūrat al-Qalam, 68:1-4)

Allāh gives an oath by the Arabic letter, "*nūn*," and what is *nūn*? Allāh knows best, but we will explain this once. "*Nūn*" is the ḥighest heavenly level by which Allāh gives an oath, that, "Yā Muḥammad! You are of the best character!" From it *ʿibādAllāh* are quenching their thirst, those who want to understand and become deeply involved in these fountains, and to reach *taḥaqquq*, Certainty. That is why it is said, *man taḥaqqaqa takhalaqa*, "Who reached (the Station of) Certainty, Allāh will dress with best character."

So if you wish to reach best character, you must reach the Stations of Certainty: ʿIlm al-Yaqīn, "Knowledge of Certainty," ʿAyn al-Yaqīn, "Vision of Certainty," and Ḥaqq al-Yaqīn, "Truth of Certainty."

Muhyidīn ibn ʿArabi ﷺ continues, "Whoever inherits from that will have perfect character. Any appearance from what Allāh creates can appear only through the mirror of the Prophet ﷺ." *Wa man takhalaqa taḥaqqaqa*, "Who inherits from the Prophet of good character will become certain of what he is hearing and seeing."

So if we want to reach the Station of Certainty, we need to reach good character. Do we have good character? (No.) Do you shout at your wife? (Sometimes.) So the best character is to be patient. Like the ocean, that never complains. If all the sewers go into the ocean, does it complain? No. And it is still clean, you can still make *wuḍū* in it. And if you put filth in any moving river you can still make *wuḍū* in it. So, who reaches the Station of Certainty, his character will be perfected. And whose character is perfected will be stamped, "He reached reality." *man takhalaqa tamazzaq*, "Who reached the best of character and these manifestations will be torn into pieces!"

The Prophet ﷺ is of the best character, and in *dunyā* the he said, "I am the one most abused," *tamazzaqa fil-ḥaqq,* "torn apart in truth." Who wants to reach the best character has to know that in front of him are torture and obstacles, because he knows the truth is there and he is not able to reach the Divine Presence easily. There are countless obstacles he or she has to overcome, *wa man takhalaqa tamazzaqa fil-ḥaqq.* Who has good character will be torn to pieces in the reality, the truth. And that is why *awlīyāullāh* suffered a lot to reach realities, and their life is filled with obstacles.

Al-Jilī ق, a big scholar and also a *walī,* said, *Istādhir dhi'nuka,* "Focus your mind on us; *mushattat al-afkār,* don't be distracted too much by your thoughts. Open your ears and bring your mind and your heart to focus."

Kullul-aʿrifīn al-muwajihīn min al-ḥaqq, "Gnostics crowned with the crown of *maʿrifah* never behaved in the perfect Heavenly Kingdom of Allāh ﷻ except with the best of their characters." So don't lose that. These are the levels of *aqṭāb,* the five *quṭbs,* who are in that level of perfection where they inherit from the Prophet ﷺ. That is why it is said that al-Insān al-Kāmil is always in connection with Allāh's Beautiful Names and Attributes that appear to him, and *awlīyā* cannot count how many Beautiful Names and Attributes appear in every moment.

Qul Allāh thumma dharhum fī khawdihim yalʿabūn.
Say, "Allāh," then leave them to play in their vain discussions.
(Sūrat al-'Anʿām, 6:91)

Allāhu Akbar! Say "Allāh," and don't mind about what they are playing; leave *khalq,* human beings/Creation and their affairs. Don't go to their level, as you are in that high level, saying, "Allāh," which is the highest Beautiful Name, that all other Names are under! Mention His Name! That is the source of all Beautiful Names and Attributes sent to Muḥammad ﷺ! So, *inna Allāh wa malā'ikatahu yuṣsallūn,* means Allāh is ordering His angels to carry the manifestations of these Beautiful Names and Attributes that are appearing in every moment, and to dress them on the Prophet. And according to *awlīyā* there is no limit to the Beautiful Names and Attributes manifested on him! It is continuous *khalq,* Creation manifested on the Prophet ﷺ!

It is also said that everyone is dressed with the *tajallī* of one of the Beautiful Names, and Prophet sees you under that *tajallī* and he gives you a name according to that Name, which he knows from the light appears in the divine mirror. As we said but didn't discuss, there is "ʿAbdur-Raḥmān, ʿAbdur-Raḥīm, ʿAbdul-Ghaffar." Whoever has those names are under the *tajallī* and servanthood of those Beautiful Names. There can be many people having the same name, but each is in a different light, because one Beautiful Name has an infinite number of *tajallīyat*. That is why we appear with that *tajallī*, our appearance is with the blessing of that light, and when *awlīyā* look at their followers they look at them under that light. They know their rank in the Divine Presence based on the light coming on them. And that is why Prophet is always in connection with the Beautiful Names and Attributes that can be envisioned and seen, and they are the real appearances of Allāh ﷻ on His Prophet ﷺ.

To understand that, you have to carry the best of characters. It is said that the best characters are an infinite number, but what some *awlīyā* counted are about one-thousand good characters. One *walī* who counted around one-thousand good characters said, "Allāh knows best how many there are, and Prophet said, *Anna aḥabakum ilayya wa aqrabakum majlisan akramakum akhlāqan*, 'The one who will sit beside me on Judgment Day is the one with the best manners.'"

And we lack these good manners. Muhyidīn ibn ʿArabi ق continues, "Some of these are *al-hilm*, forbearance, *ʿilm*, knowledge, to have humility and compassion, and *bashasha*, to be always smiling and friendly in companionship, and *al-ʿafūw*, to forgive, and *al-iḥsān*, to be generous to the one who harmed you, and to connect to the one who left you, *wa raḥmāh li 'd-duʿāfa*, to have mercy on weak people, and *tawqīr mashaykh*, to respect shaykhs." Who respects shaykhs anymore? They don't call themselves shaykhs any more, they call themselves 'doctors.' "And *al-ikhwān*, brotherhood, *wa 's-sabr*, patience, *wa 'z-zuhd*, asceticism, *qana'a, ridā, shukr*, to be thankful..." and it goes on.

Fa lā bud min as-sālik ḥattā yatakhalaq bi-hadhihi 'l-akhlāq, "For the seeker it is essential to attain all these good characters in his journey and not to be tough, but to be a real seeker." Today they say, "We are in *ṭarīqah*," any *ṭarīqah*, but are they really doing what *ṭarīqah* calls for? Any *ṭarīqah* calls for good character, that is why *mujahad* is not easy. That's why they send you to seclusion, for forty days, six months, one year, one after another, until they crush you completely, until you have good characteristics. When you enter seclusion it is not simple and you are always thinking about when are you coming out, counting the days.

They say, *ṣāḥib ḥusn al-khuluq la-wusil ṣāḥib aṣ-ṣawmi wa 'ṣ-ṣalāt*, "That one who has good character will be raised to the level of the one who is praying and fasting all the time."

Khudh il-ʿawfu w'amr bi'l-ʿurfi wʿarid ʿan il-jāhilīn.

Hold to forgiveness, command what is right, but turn away from the ignorant.

(Sūrat al-Aʿrāf, 7:199)

Be a forgiving person. Don't be like one who cursed you; say, "*Alḥamdulillāh,* he saved me.'" If someone cursed you, especially on the Internet, the least they do for you is to carry your sins! So what should you do? Forgive them, because they made something good for you, they took away all your sins. So what do you have to do? Pray for them, "Yā *Rabbī,* forgive them!" Be happy when they curse you, and don't be happy when they pet you. When they curse you Allāh and Prophet are looking at how are you going to react. Yesterday we had an example: there were two big *murīds* going to the food, and one blocked the way for the other. I was looking to see what he is going to do, as he was blocking the way of the other, who was patient and passed the test.

So, it is said, *al-khuluq afḍal manāqib al-ʿubūdīyya,* "The best character is the best of worship. It will take you to the highest level of Certainty," and realities that we mentioned before. That is why in Holy Qurʿan, Allāh mentioned him as of the best character:

wa 'innaka laʿalā khuluqin ʿaẓīm.

Indeed you are of a tremendous character! (Sūrat al-Qalam, 68:4)

The Prophet ﷺ passed through all of the earthly kingdoms and all the heavenly kingdoms, and reached *fa kāna qāba qawsayni aw adnā,* "within two bows' length or nearer," (an-Najm, 53:9) where no one can reach except a perfect one! And they are pure like angels, but even Jibrīl stopped, saying, "I cannot go further, you go!" With this Allāh showed the angels the high level of Sayyīdinā Muḥammad ﷺ. That is why Allāh said:

Yā ayyuha 'l-mudaththir qum fa andhir wa thīyābaka fa-ṭāhhir.

O you (Yā Muḥammad), who covers himself with blankets! Arise and warn, and magnify your Lord, and purify your garments!

(Sūrat al-Mudaththir, 74:1-4)

Prophet ﷺ was sick and covering himself, and here Allāh ﷻ was telling him, "No, in My Kingdom, shivering or not, someone has to keep moving, *qum fa andhir wa rabbuka fa-kabbir, so* wake up and warn people to say, '*Allāhu Akbar, Allāhu Akbar, Allāhu Akbar*! Allāh is Greatest and there is no resemblance to His Greatness.' Tell them to leave their bad characters. Warn them that there is a measure and a balance."

Wa 's-samā raf'ahā wa wada' al-mīzān.
He raised high the Heavens and put a balance. (Sūrat ar-Raḥmān, 55:7)

Allāh ﷻ raised Heavens and put the balance, so don't try to transgress it by being a tyrant: balance your *'amal*, your ego, your selfishness, and your sins well. That is why He said, *qum fa andhur*, "stand and warn them," then tell them, *Allāhu Akbar, wa rabbuka fa-kabbir*. "Say, '*Allāhu Akbar*,'" one hundred times daily. At that time comes: *wa thīyābak fa-ṭāhhir* , "clean your clothes." Not the normal clothes, but the clothes of the self, as it takes away the bad characters and puts the best characters. There are a thousand good characteristics that we cannot mention them all here, but let them carry these characteristics, *war-rujza fahjur*. "Leave the bad behind, migrate away from it, be an immigrant in Allāh's Way and don't look back at this worldly life, look at the heavenly life." Those are four verses from Sūrat al-Mudaththir.

And the Prophet ﷺ said:

Wa inna al-'abdu yablugha bi ḥusni khuluqihi darajāt aṣ-ṣā'im al-qā'im.
The servant of Allāh will reach with his good character and behaviors.
(Tirmidhī)

Even if he is making sins, if he can give one good character, Allāh will reward him like He rewards the one who is fasting and standing in prayer excessively, doing *nawāfil*, supererogatory, fasts and prayers. That doesn't mean that you can then leave fasting; you have to fast Ramadan, but it means Allāh will reward the one of good character like them. Look how easy it is. You cannot have the good character to smile in the face of others? Like this *murīd*, the other one was blocking him from food last night and he smiled; he showed good character, and that was enough for Allāh to accept all his fasts. And the other one Allāh accepted his fast as He used him to try this one!

Prophet ﷺ said:

Afdal al-mu'minīna imānan ahsanahum khuluqan.
The believers with the best faith are those with the best character.
(Bayhaqi, Ṭabarānī)

So let us see how much we have to balance. *Wa wadaʿ al-mīzān.* Balance yourself now. We find ourselves a complete failure. Allāh ﷻ said in Holy Qur'an:

> *Qālati 'l-ʿarābū āmanā. Qul lam tu'uminū wa lākin qūlū aslamnā wa lammā yadkhuli 'l-īmānu fī qulūbikum.*
> *The desert Arabs say, "We believe." Say, "You have no faith, but say, 'We have submitted our wills to Allāh,' for not yet has faith entered your hearts."*
> (Sūrat al-Ḥujurāt, 49:14)

Don't say, "We are *muʿmin,*" but say, "We are Muslim," because *imān* did not yet enter the heart.

Prophet ﷺ said:

> *Wa qāla khuṣlatān la yajtamiʿān fī mu'min: al-bukhl wa sūw al-khuluq.*
> *There are two things that cannot be found in a believer: stinginess, and al-khuluq as-sayyīʿāt, to carry bad character.*

Especially today, people are not concerned with anything. They are carrying bad characteristics; they get angry and they never smile in your face all your life. It is finished, as if mercy disappeared from their hearts. *Wa qāla dhun-nūn, akthar an-nāsu hamman aswāhum khuluqun,* Dhul-Nun said, "Those with the most problems are the ones with bad characteristics." Because of their bad characteristics they always go into problems, and their bad characteristics are reflected in their children. If their parents have good character you see the children are raised nicely, with good discipline. And we ask Allāh to give us good character and to take away our bad dresses!

> *Wa min Allāhi 't-tawfīq, bi ḥurmati 'l-ḥabīb, bi ḥurmati 'l-Fātiḥah.*
> *And with Allāh is success. For the sake of the Beloved, for his sake we recite the opening chapter of Holy Qur'an.*

Examples of the High Character and Forbearance of Awliyaullah

A'ūdhu billāhi min ash-Shayṭān ir-rajīm. Bismillāhi' r-Raḥmāni 'r-Raḥīm. Nawaytu 'l-arbā'īn, nawaytu 'l-'itikāf, nawaytu'l-khalwah, nawaytu 'l-'uzlah, nawaytu 'r-riyāḍa, nawaytu 's-sulūk, lillāhi Ta'alā fī hādhā 'l-masjid. Ati' ūllāh wa ati'ū 'r-Rasūl wa ūli 'l-amri minkum. (4:59)

We have discussed the good character, *al-khuluq al-hasan* and the *ayāt,* "O you, wrapped up (in the mantle)! Arise and deliver your warning! And magnify your Lord! And purify your garments!" (74:1-4) Allāh ﷻ is instructing Prophet ﷺ, "*Yā* Muḥammad! Leave the bed." That means, "Leave *dunyā,* and what makes you feel good."

When people want to feel good and relax, they go to bed to lay down, saying, "I am tired." *Ḥusn al-khuluq,* good character, is when you are tired, you must drop your *nafs* that wants to relax and do something for the benefit of all humanity. So Allāh ﷻ is saying to Prophet ﷺ, "*Yā* Muḥammad, leave the bed. *Qum,* wake up and warn, *andhir.*" Warn who? For Prophet, it means warn the *ummah.* But for us there is another interpretation, as Sufism is a taste and *awlīyāullāh* find ways to interpret Holy Qur'an's verses.

> *wa mā ya'lamū tāwīlahu ill 'Llāh war-rāsikhūna fil-'ilmi yaqūlūna āmana bihi kullun min 'indi rabbinā wa mā yadhadhakkarū illa ūlūl-albāb.*
> *But no one knows its hidden meanings except Allāh. And those who are firmly grounded in knowledge say, "We believe in the Book; the whole of it is from our Lord." And none will grasp the Message except men of understanding.*
> (Sūrat 'Āli 'Imrān, 3:7)

No one knows its interpretation except Allāh. *wa 'r-rāsikhūna fil 'ilmi yaqūlūna āmāna.* Those who are like mountains are strong; even a huge tornado cannot do anything to a mountain. It might take the forest, the trees, but the mountain is *rāsikh,* well established on Earth. He didn't say *'ulamā.* So those who are like a mountain of knowledge in religion, not Sharī'ah, say *āmanā,* "we believe," *sami'nā wa at'anā.* We believe that no one knows the interpretation except for Allāh ﷻ, but He gave Prophet ﷺ the Knowledge of Firsts and Lasts (before and after), which means He didn't hide that interpretation from the Prophet ﷺ. That is why Grandshaykh ق

told us that Sayyīdinā Mahdī ﷺ will bring the interpretation of every verse and every letter.

"Those who are well established in knowledge, say, 'We believe, everything is from Allāh ﷻ'". But if we read the verse in a different way, *wa mā yaʿlamūna tāwīlahu ill'Llāh wa 'r-rāsikhūn fi 'l-ʿilm,* in this reading, "No one knows its interpretation except Allāh and those whom Allāh made like mountains, well established." It is *waw ʿataf* from the first part of the word to the second word. *Wa ar-rāsikhūn,* Allāh and those who are well established in knowledge of the Holy Qur'an.

> *Yā ayyuha 'l-mudaththir qum fa andhir wa thīyābaka fa-ṭāhhir.*
> *O you (Yā Muḥammad), who covers himself with blankets! Arise and warn, and magnify your Lord, and purify your garments!*
> (Sūrat al-Muddaththir, 74:1-4)

Yā ayyuha 'l-mudaththir, "Stand up and be ready to warn the *ummah,"* and everyone must warn themselves, their ego. Get up to warn people and for people to warn their egos. How did *awlīyā* become perfected? By warning their egos. *Wa thīyābak fa-ṭāhhir,* "And make your character the best." Tell them to be of best character. If they can be of best character, then they have achieved a lot. Because a best character is to perfect oneself.

At the beginning of Ramadan, we spoke about the five *quṭbs* (poles): Quṭb, Quṭbu'l Bilād, Quṭbu'l Irshad, Quṭbu'l Aqtab, and Quṭbu'l Mutaṣarrif. We also spoke about the five different groups of *awlīyā:* Budalā, Nujabā, Nuqabā, Awtād, and Akhyār. Above all of them is the *ghawth,* and under them, 124,000 saints. All of them have *khuluq al-hasan.* All that we were discussing from the beginning of Ramadan was to show that *awlīyāullāh* have achieved these high characters and became *rāsikhūn fil-ʿilm,* "well established in high levels." Everyone, according to their group and level, has become well established in the Divine Presence. We didn't yet go into their names and what Allāh manifested on them, or what they represent!

So the best of us is the one with the best character. Allāh said to Prophet ﷺ, *wa thīyābak fa-ṭāhhir* , "Purify that dress." That is a *khitāb* to all humanity to purify your clothes, your character. *War-rujzu fahjur,* "Migrate and come out the bad characters." That is why in Arabic, every word in the Holy Qur'an has many meanings. *Fahjurhuna fil-madajiaʿ,* "Let them get a way to come out for men and women." *Fahjur* means "get out of it," don't be completely dipped in the well of Shayṭān.

They asked one person with good character and behavior, "From whom did you learned *hilm,* forbearance?"

He said, "I learned from Qays Ibn al-ʿAṣim ق. One day I was sitting in his presence, and a maidservant came to him with a container that had hot charcoal and on it was some hot food. *Wa saqat min yaddiha,* as soon as she came, all this charcoal and the hot container fell down from her hand onto his young son The child died immediately. The servant was afraid, she didn't know what to do. Qays Ibn al-ʿAṣim ق said, *la rawaʿa ʿalayk antī ḥur fillāh,* ' 'Don't be afraid, I am freeing you for Allāh's sake.' She harmed him and he freed her. Although he felt the pain in his heart for his son, he freed her to suppress his ego."

Today, cough suppressants control your cough, but we need tablets to suppress our egos! You can find that in a store that has that medicine: that is *awlīyāullāh.* If you want, they can give you the tablet and in forty days you will be finished from your ego. If they don't give you the tablets they are playing with you, as they know you are not yet ready yet.

Therefore, in order to suppress his ego, Qays Ibn al-ʿAṣim freed her, because his ego was saying, "She killed your boy, so kill her." From that pious actions, that person learned forbearance from Qays ibn al-ʿAsim. It is not easy. If someone kills your child, will you say, "No problem." If you killed someone's child, they will sue you for millions! There was insurance at that time also, heavenly insurance. You will get it in Paradise or in your grave, or you might even get it in *dunyā.*

Ibrāhīm ibn al-Adham was a king. He is buried in Damascus. Every night, he drank (alcohol) until he fell down. All of his engines would be down, he would vomit and get sick. One night he was sitting in his house looking at the stars through a big glass dome he had built, when he heard someone walking on that dome. He looked and saw a man. Who can come to Ibrāhīm ibn al-Ādham, the famous king?

He asked, "What are you doing?"

The man replied, "I am searching for my camel."

"How are you are searching for your camel on my dome?"

We look at others' mistakes and forget our own. He was looking at that one's mistake, but not at his own. We are dipped in our ego's arrogance. Struggle against it, and then Allāh will take you from the Shore of Ignorance to the Shore of Knowledge by *rīḥ aṣ-ṣibā,* the Heavenly Breeze. That is like a tornado, but you will sense the beautiful perfume in it and it will take you to the other shore in the blink of an eye! You don't need more than that. But you need to show continuity, that you are doing your work, your *awrād,* your *dawah,* and what is asked of you by your shaykh. Ibrāhīm ibn al-

Adham asked the man what he was doing and not looking at himself that he is drunk.

He said, "How can your camel be here on the third floor, on top of the dome?"

The man said, "There is a possibility to find my camel on your dome, but there is no possibility for you to find your Lord in your current state."

That was like an arrow shot through Ibrāhīm's heart! The people asked him, *hal farihta min ad-dunyā, yā Ibrāhīm,* "Did you enjoy your worldly life, Ibrāhīm?"

He said, "Yes, twice." These are examples that show us the good manners that *awlīyā* carry. He said, "One time I was sitting, *qaʿidan.*"

This is part of the story that Grandshaykh ق mentioned about Ibrāhīm ibn al-Adham ق, why he was sitting at that time; because he went to a mosque, as he was going in the way of Allāh. He was cold and bleeding. He entered the mosque, prayed ʿIsha, and layed down. The keeper of the *masjid* kicked him out.

Ibrāhīm ibn al-Adham ق said, "Leave me alone. I am an old man." The servant said, "Even if you were Ibrāhīm ibn al-Ādham, I would still throw you out! You are lying!" and he beat Ibrāhīm ibn al-Ādham, who left and went under a tree that had a tree house with three people inside. He explained to those who asked about his *dunyā,* "I was sitting there and one of them was drinking. He came out of the tree house and urinated on me. I was so happy and pleased, as he showed me what I deserved. That was one of the happiest things that happened to me in *dunyā,* because *that is dunyā*: to take poison out of the body. I understood it that He is giving me a signal to take out all the poison from my body."

Ibrāhīm continued, "The second time, I was sitting among a group of people and one of them came and slapped me on the face. When he slapped me, *ja'a āḥadahum wa ṣafaʿnī,* he woke me up to the remembrance of the Day of Judgment. Allāh ﷻ might send angels to slap me with no end. He made me aware of what might happen to me, both in the grave and on the Day of Judgment. These were the two times I was so happy from *dunyā,* because these incidents made me realize what *dunyā* is and what is represents."

Look at how much good character he has! One urinated on him and still he said, "No problem." The second one beat him up and he said, "No problem." If someone urinates on us, what will we do? If a baby in diapers urinates on you, you beat them!

It is said, once Ibrāhīm ibn al-Adham ق roamed a jungle in Allāh's love. A soldier passed by and asked, *ayna al-ʿimāra,* "Where is the city?" *ʿAmār* is where you build homes.

Ibrāhīm said, "There is the city."

The soldier took his stick and beat him on the head. He showed the soldier the city, so why did he beat him up? Because he showed him the cemetery, saying, "That is the city you are going to be sleeping in one day." The soldier thought Ibrāhīm was mocking him. He beat him severely, wounding his head.

When the soldier passed by the city, people asked him, "What have you done today?! You beat the most ascetic person in all Khorasan!"

Persia today is one of the main city of *awlīyā;* that is why it is going to be safe, and Mawlana Shaykh Nazim said no one can touch it.

The soldier came back to apologize. Ibrāhīm ibn al-Adham ق said, "When you beat me up, I asked Paradise for you from Allāh!" When someone beats you up, what do you do? Ask for Paradise by going to the police. You don't ask Paradise for him, but instead jail.

The soldier asked, "Why did you do that?"

He said, "Because you brought a reward for me when you beat me up. I didn't want that to be for me only, so I asked Paradise for you. And on the Day of Judgment, I didn't want you to be judged on my account, or to be the cause of your punishment, and I didn't want to be rewarded because you beat me. So I asked Allāh to give you Paradise."

Do you ask for Paradise for those who beat you? Look at how they teach children today, they teach them marital arts, to defend themselves. You don't need martial arts. When you surrender to Allāh's will, that is the real martial arts. Ibrāhīm ibn al-Adham ق was able to blow him far away with just one breath, but he didn't. Today they teach young children how to fight the enemy. Your enemy is Shayṭān! Be peaceful and there will be no fight.

It was said by Ḥātim al-Aṣam ق, *ḥusn al-khuluq an yaḥtamil kull wāḥid,* "The best character is to carry whatever they show to you, tolerate and accept them, except for one. Tolerate all else and you will be rewarded, but don't tolerate the one that will take you to Hellfire."

They asked, "Who is that?"

He replied, "That is your ego. Tolerate others for Allāh's sake, but beat your ego by not giving it what it likes."

Malik ibn Dinar ق was a famous *walī*, official, and judge. One lady came to him and said, *yā muraʾī,* "O hypocrite! The one who thinks he is something! He is nothing, and garbage in my eyes!" A lady said this to a big judge, and they say ladies have no rights (in Islam)!

He looked at her, not seeing a man or woman, and replied. "May Allāh bless you. I was looking for the name I lost. Today you came and gave it to me. *Wajadtu ʿismī al-ladhī adAllāhu ahlu 'l-basra,* I found the name that the people of Basra lost. *Alḥamdulillāh,* I am thankful to you."

He didn't tell his army or police to throw her in prison. So what is your name, *muraʾī*. Our name is to "show off" only; we are not dressing in the real dress as there is hypocrisy.

Sayyīdinā Luqmān ؑ advised his sons to have three characters: *Thalātha la tuʿraf illa ʿinda thalāth. al-ḥilm ʿindal-ghaḍab,* "Three things are only known through three others."

First is, to be patient when getting angry. All these emails that come to us are full of anger. "My wife did that, my neighbor did that." Every day there are hundreds of emails filled with complaints!

Prophet ﷺ said:
Man ʿarafa nafsahu faqad ʿarafa Rabbahu.
He who knows his self knows his Lord.

We interpret this *ḥadīth* as, "Who knows his bad characters knows his Lord." But *awlīyā* interpret it differently: "Who knows himself, what Allāh is showering on him of Beautiful Names and Attributes, to see the lights that Allāh is showering on us, that one knows his Lord."

Allāh doesn't look at the bad characters, but looks at the lights and manifestations of Allāh's Names. You cannot go to the Divine Presence without these lights as they are the code and password. That is why it is recommended on Jumuʿah to take a shower, *ghusl,* as it will clean you, to take you to these manifestations of Divine Lights, and to divine prayer in the Presence of Allāh. Surrender to Allāh's will, don't show anger and complain! Sayyīdinā Luqmān ؑ is telling his sons to have forbearance, as Prophet ﷺ said to Sayyīdinā Abū Bakr ؓ, *al-ghaḍabū kufrun,* "Anger is unbelief."

Second is, to have courage in war. Are we in war today? Yes, we are in the war against our ego. Not the war where they are blowing innocent people up, saying, "I am going to Paradise." You are going to Hellfire! So are we declaring war against our ego?

The third good character is, to give charity when you know someone is in need. That means to be generous with people and to help them. If someone is sick, help him; if someone is sad, smile at him. Prophet ﷺ said, "A smile is *ṣadaqah*." To visit a patient or to build a school, all of this is *ṣadaqah*. *Ṣadaqah* is when someone is in need, you help. That person will find you there. These are the three characters Sayyīdinā Luqmān ؏ advised his sons to keep.

One *walī* had a servant helping him. People asked, "Why are you keeping him? Set him free."

He said, "I can't set him free because I am learning forbearance from him. He does everything wrong. I am keeping him to learn patience."

One *murīd* invited his shaykh, ʿUthmān al-Hīlī ق, to his house. When he entered through the door, the *murīd* said, "I called you, but now I cannot accommodate you, so please go back." He is a *walī* and shaykh, coming to the house of his *murīd*. This means that when the shaykh comes with a stick, don't send him back as he comes with a stick against your ego.

Grandshaykh ق said, "*Awlīyā* look at their *murīds* at least three times a day, and they don't send candies, they send pain, to see how the *murīd* will react."

The *murīd* said, "I regret I called you to my house, you can go now," and the shaykh left.

A few days later, that *murīd* returned to the shaykh and said, "I regret I kicked you out. Please come back." The ego was telling him to fix that. So the shaykh went back. He didn't say, "I am not coming, you threw me one time, that is it," and he would never go. The shaykh went and at the door the host said, "No, sorry again, but I cannot accommodate you. Please go back." And the shaykh went back. The *murīd* did this to him four or five times and finally said to the shaykh, "I did that to try you."

SubḥānAllāh fa lillāh ḍarruk! That is a highly respected saying which means, "'Only Allāh knows how high you are,' (that I threw you out four or five times and you never said anything)."

The *murīd* asked, "What kind of *walī* are you and what kind of *khuluq* do you have? You kept on coming, not complaining. I called you back and you kept coming, then I kicked you out. What kind of high character you have? I don't understand!"

The shaykh said, *lā tamdaḥnī fī khuluqin tujid fī 'l-ḥaywān*, "Don't praise me, my son, for a character found in animals."

The *murīd* asked, "O *Sayyīdī*! What is that character that when you call, it will come, and when you kick it out, it goes?"

He said, "That is a dog's character. Don't praise me for that."

This is the first level in *ṭarīqah,* not to say a dog is better, but to learn that there are signs in everything around us. Nothing will stop a lion or a tiger in a jungle, but the goat is different, it eats anything. Or a donkey, which is patient; it carries any amount of load, no matter how heavy. So we have to learn from the characters of what Allāh created for the benefit of *Ummat an-Nabī,* not to be wild. "Don't praise me, because if the dog is invited, it will come, and if thrown, it will go."

It is said that one day that shaykh was passing by a house and someone threw ashes that came all over him, like ashes from a volcano. His *murīds* got upset and began to curse, "That is our shaykh! How dare you throw ashes!" The ones who threw it didn't know, they just threw it from their window. It was not like today, you will get a ticket for "littering."

The shaykh said to them, "Don't get angry. If the one who deserves Hellfire gets a substitute of ashes, he will take the ashes! I was feeling the Hellfire and was saved by ashes thrown on me."

These are examples of good character of *awlīyāullāh.* May Allāh guide us and teach us by means of these stories.

Wa min Allāhi 't-tawfiq, bi ḥurmati 'l-ḥabīb, bi ḥurmati 'l-Fātiḥah.
And with Allāh is success. For the sake of the Beloved, for his sake we recite the opening chapter of Holy Qur'an.

To Be Rightly Guided, Connect to Your True Fathers

Aʿūdhu billāhi min ash-Shayṭān ir-rajīm. Bismillāhi' r-Raḥmāni 'r-Raḥīm. Nawaytu 'l-arbāʿīn, nawaytu 'l-ʿitikāf, nawaytu'l-khalwah, nawaytu 'l-ʿuzlah, nawaytu 'r-riyāḍa, nawaytu 's-sulūk, lillāhi Taʿalā fī hādhā 'l-masjid. Atiʿ ūllāh wa atiʿū 'r-Rasūl wa ūli 'l-amri minkum. (4:59)

All of us must take examples from what is around us, of which there are many evidences that can give us signs of Allāh's Greatness. If you look at today's technology, you see just now on the Internet they say these programmers have programmed. Allāh gave them ability and logic, and the ability to put programs for people to express themselves. And these programs are based on a specific knowledge they studied, after which they made it possible for people to speak with each other and express themselves. This is what we see on the Internet; programmers put on the Internet a chat for people to say what is in their hearts.

Now, they might say on the Internet all kinds of good things, if they are on the way of Allāh ﷻ, which means they express themselves through sharing their love and inner beliefs with others. What do you think about the one who is in Sulṭān al-Awlīyā's associations? Their chat will be from east to west, not only the chat of *murīds,* but chats of *jinn* and *ins*. And what do you think about chatting on a heavenly Internet about the message of Prophet ﷺ? There will be an infinite number of angels and human beings, century after century, speaking of the greatness of the Prophet ﷺ!

O human beings! Allāh gave us a way to speak to the Prophet ﷺ, a program, to make *munajāt,* to seek his forgiveness through a heavenly chat, but on one condition: to follow that program. The program is set and every *walī* has his own program, and Sulṭān al-Awlīyā has combined all these programs reaching to Prophet ﷺ, who has his own program. That is why it is said, *ad-dunyā jīfatun wa ṭulābuhā kilābuhā,* "The *dunyā* is a carcass and those who seek it are wild animals." So that means, follow the program and don't follow *dunyā. Dunyā* will throw us in the Hellfire, and Allāh wants us to be saved through His program. As much as you are strong, as much more programs will open for you. As much as programs are opened, as much as strongly classified spiritual information is given to your heart. *Fa ʿalaykum bi ittibʿa an-nabī,* "Our duty is to follow the Prophet, w*a kāna khuluqahu al-*

qur'an, his character, his manners, were the Holy Qur'an." It means not one verse, not one *sūrah*, but the whole Qur'an! He is *al-Qur'an al-nātiq*, "the talking Qur'an."

Allāh gave the Prophet ﷺ the secret of the Holy Qur'an and from him these secrets, as mentioned in the previous session, *ma ya'lamu ta'wīlahu illa-Allāh war-rāsikhūna fil-'ilm*, no one knows its interpretation except Allāh and those well established in knowledge; they know and say, *amāna*, "We believe." So our duty is to believe and not to question those *awlīyā* that Allāh gave the ability to interpret knowledge; our duty to listen and follow.

Sami'nā wa ata'na ghufrānaka rabbanā wa 'ilayk al-masīr.
We hear and we obey. (We seek) Your forgiveness, our Lord, and to You is the return (of all, so forgive us.) (Sūrat al-Baqarah, 2:285)

If we disobey our *shuyūkh*, that will throw us away. So our duty is to learn to be of the best of character and Prophet ﷺ is the best of characters, and his *awlīyā* whom Allāh granted to carry the flag of Prophet until Judgment Day, until when Sayyīdinā Mahdī ؏ appears and *awlīyā* deliver their flags to Sayyīdinā Mahdī ؏. Then there are no more flags at that time except his flag, which is the secret of the Holy Qur'an!

I heard Grandshaykh ق say, in the time of Mahdī ؏, if you open a printed Qur'an of today you will not see any writings as it is printed with *dunyā* ink, and a heavenly Qur'an will come revealed in heavenly printing, and lights will come from every letter. When you look at the Holy Qur'an that was delivered to *Ṣaḥābah* ؓ, it is full with light, and the *Ṣaḥābah* were able to take from the lights of every letter, and it was opened for *awlīyāullāh*. Sayyīdinā Mahdī ؏ is waiting to come with those secrets! So our duty is to find our relationship and get the best characteristics, and to do that is to follow your teacher, as they are our spiritual fathers.

Allāh ﷻ said:
Ad'ūhum li-ābā'ihim Hūwa aqsaṭu.
Call them to their fathers; that is more just with Allāh.
(Sūrat al-'Aḥzāb, 33:5)

Ad'ūhum li-ābā'ihim, from the father to the mother, and then a child comes. So, "Call them to their fathers, to be known who is the father." It can be any father, you don't know. So a child has be named his father's name and even in western countries they put the wife's name following the husband's, and then her family name becomes like the husband's. You have to know your fathers all the way to Prophet ﷺ. If you don't know, you make a mistake. Allāh will forgive you, but try.

Sayyīdinā ʿAbdu 'l-Wahhāb ash-Shaʿrānī ق, one of the big scholars and big saints of Islam, said, *man lā yaʿlamu abā'uhu wa ajdādud fa huw aʿam,* "Who doesn't know his father and grandfather in *ṭarīqah* is blind, like someone who doesn't see at all." And it might be by mistake he will go to another father, as he is blind and doesn't know, so he doesn't connect to his true father. You cannot connect to another one, as the Prophet said:

laʿnAllāhu man antasaba ila ghayra abīh.
Who connects to whom is not his real father will be cursed.

If you connect to another shaykh, it means you are not trying to research the real connection; then you will be cursed as one who connects to whom is not his real father. So in our creation, the soul is more connected to your reality, and Allāh ﷻ created the soul first. *Al-arwāhu junūdan mujanada,* "Souls are like battalion in groups." Allāh called all these souls on the Day of Promises and asked, "Am I not your Lord?" They replied, "Yes!"

Wa idh ākhadha rabbuka min banī ādama min ẓuhūrihim dhurriyyatahum wa ashhadahum ʿalā anfusihim alastu bi-rabbikum qalū balā shahidnā an taqūlu yawma 'l-qīyāmati innā kunnā ʿan hadha ghāfilīn.
When your Lord drew forth from the loins Children of Adam their descendants, and made them testify concerning themselves, (saying), "Am I not your Lord (Who cherishes and sustains you)?" They said, "Yes! We do testify!" (This), unless you will say on the Day of Judgment, "Of this we were never mindful." (Surat al-Aʿrāf, 7:172)

"Am I not your Lord?" They said, "Yes." Who was there? Our realities, connected with the soul there and we knew we were Allāh's servants there, we accepted. Can you say no when you are seeing the Truth? Those are good tidings that everyone was in the Divine Presence. So the soul was created first then the body.

That is why Prophet ﷺ said, "I was a prophet when Adam was *bayni 'r-rūḥi wa 'l-jasad,* between soul and body. I was a Prophet already in *ruh* and Adam was still between *ruh* and body."

And from And from ʿAbd ar-Razzāq's Mūṣannaf, we take the *ḥadīth* of Prophet ﷺ, "The first thing that Allāh created is my Light."

So we take the soul first and then *jasad*, body, as you take the spiritual father first and then the biological father. Good tidings to the one whose biological father is the same as his spiritual father! In the previous times, for a long time they taught the students and followers, *adab abā'ihim*, the best manners of their parents and to know *ansābihim*, their lineage. That is for the physical connection, so what do you think about the spiritual connection with the father of your soul?

It is said that Sayyīdinā Abū Bakr aṣ-Ṣiddīq ق is the spiritual father of all Naqshbandi followers. The one who doesn't know or who didn't find his spiritual father has no right to sit and teach! His teaching is disconnected unless he will humble himself and find his spiritual father, going back to Prophet ﷺ. *Alḥamdulillāh*, we are connected with *as-Silsilat adh-Dhabiyya*, the Golden Chain!

Many authors of spirituality have mentioned that is a golden chain, as it connects through Sayyīdinā Abū Bakr ؓ on one side and through Sayyīdinā 'Alī ؓ on the other side, through Sayyīdinā Jafar aṣ-Ṣadiq ق. Those who have been authorized to give lectures, who have guidance from their fathers all the way to Prophet ﷺ, there is light in their speeches. We are so lucky!

Grandshaykh, may Allāh bless his soul, I quote him and people might say, "Why do you quote him so much and not Mawlana Shaykh Nazim?" There is no reason, except people hear from many sources about Mawlana Shaykh Nazim, but few are hearing from Grandshaykh. So we quote from that, in order to have a taste of what our grandfather taught, and from him we learn a lot about his spiritual father, Shaykh Sharafuddīn ق and his lineage to Prophet ﷺ.

Grandshaykh ق said, "What is the wisdom of going to the Cave Thawr when going from Mecca to Madinah? Was not Prophet ﷺ able to go to Madinah without passing through that cave? He was able to do so."

We have mentioned it before, but when watching a video on your computer and it "buffers" you press "F5". Why F5, and not F4? I don't know. Why not F6? What does F5 mean and what does F6 mean? I don't know, but they press F5 and it refreshes the connection. To refresh our memory we press F5, and all the pictures come back. That means in every heart there is an F5 button, and if we press it, brings everything back.

As for Allāh ﷻ, there is no past and no future! Always there is that moment you are in, here, and in the grave, and in Paradise. Don't look at the moment that is coming; the *adab* is to always reflect, "Am I good now, or not?" Fix yourself.

So press F5 and then in a moment everything comes. That is why when *awlīyā* mention a story from the past, they are living it as if they are in it, hearing and seeing and being there; to them that is F5. So he was relating that story and it was as if he was living that story, and for you it becomes like a living scene and you are in it, because *awlīyāullāh* don't tell you a story with no wisdom. No, you must enter it and you feel you are there.

One time I was *bayḍ ṣuḥafu,* transcribing from raw notes of *ṣuḥbat* and rewriting in a notebook. I share this with you, nevermind, and suddenly I came across *baya*ʿ and as I came across that I felt myself not writing anymore but the whole scenery changed, and I saw Grandshaykh, may Allāh bless his soul, and Mawlana Shaykh standing there. Grandshaykh said, "Extend your hand." At that moment, I went to extend my hand and I saw Prophet's hand come in and then 124,000 prophets' hands came and Prophet's hand was on top, then Grandshaykh's hand and then 124,000 saints' hands.

Grandshaykh said, "Put your hand," and then I felt Allāh's ﷻ Hands come on top and then I heard recitation of Āyat al-Bayaʿ. I was in that kind of vision or whatever you want to call it, a living scene. So these things happen. *Awlīyāullāh* can push a button and bring everything, and it is not difficult for them.

So when he was mentioning about the migration of Prophet ﷺ to Madinatu 'l-Munawwara, he said the wisdom of passing through Ghāri Thawr is to transfer the secrets from Prophet's heart to Sayyīdinā Abū Bakr aṣ-Ṣiddīq's heart, and to put Kalīmat at-Tawḥīd, which is *dhikr* of *lā ilāha illa-Llāh,* and also to put the recitation of *ʿIsm adh-Dhāt,* "Allāh," on the tongues of the spiritual children of Abū Bakr aṣ-Ṣiddīq!

Qul Allāh thumma dharhum fī khawdihim yalʿabūn.
Say, "Allāh," then leave them to play in their vain discussions.
(Sūrat al-'Anʿām, 6:91)

So he ordered Sayyīdinā ʿAbdul Khāliq al-Ghujdawāni ق and it was put on the tongue of Sayyīdinā ʿAbdul Khāliq, *Allāhu, Allāhu, Allāhu Ḥaqq. Allāhu, Allāhu, Allāhu Ḥaqq. Allāhu, Allāhu, Allāhu Ḥaqq.* And Sayyīdinā ʿAbdul Khāliq was ordered to call all Naqshbandi *murīds* coming in the future to be the spiritual children of Abū Bakr aṣ-Ṣiddīq.

They were called to the presence of Prophet ﷺ to Ghāri Thawr, where they all appeared. Not only that, but anyone who comes to ask you a question during the *dhikr* will be among them, as they are those who, *lā yashqa jalīsahum,* "Will never see a bad end in his life." He said, "All of them," and that means us also, migrated with Sayyīdinā Muḥammad ﷺ from Mecca to Madinah in the spiritual dimension, and will be given the reward of immigrants from *dunyā* to *ākhirah*!

When he was speaking about that scene, it was as if they were living it; for them it was not a story. If our hearts were strong we felt every moment of that story, we had goosebumps! So it is a live scene, not like watching a movie. The actors in the movie are living the story, and you are watching, but in the Naqshbandi Order we press our "F5" refresh button to live the story, so that past becomes present.

> *Wa wadaʿ al-mīzān allā tatghaw fi 'l-mīzān. Wa aqim al-waznu bil-qisṭi wa lā tukhsiru 'l-mīzān.*
> *And He has set up the Balance, that you may not transgress (due) balance, but observe the measure with equity and do not fall short of it.*
> (Sūrat ar-Raḥmān, 55:7-9)

So establish the weight justly, don't transgress in the balance. Don't make one side heavier than the another, except for *ḥasanāt*. Are you going to refresh your F5? *Inshā'Allāh.*

> *Wa min Allāhi 't-tawfiq, bi ḥurmati 'l-ḥabīb, bi ḥurmati 'l-Fātiḥah.*
> *And with Allāh is success. For the sake of the Beloved, for his sake we recite the opening chapter of Holy Qur'an.*

The Secrets of Talqin

Aʿūdhu billāhi min ash-Shayṭān ir-rajīm. Bismillāhi' r-Raḥmāni 'r-Raḥīm. Nawaytu 'l-arbāʿīn, nawaytu 'l-ʿitikāf, nawaytu'l-khalwah, nawaytu 'l-ʿuzlah, nawaytu 'r-riyāḍa, nawaytu 's-sulūk, lillāhi Taʿalā fī hādhā 'l-masjid. Atiʿ ūllāh wa atiʿū 'r-Rasūl wa ūli 'l-amri minkum. (4:59)

Everyone must know their relationships, especially with their father. And you have to search well in order to reach a perfect teacher and perfect guide connected to Prophet ﷺ through a lineage of *awlīyāullāh* that take you there. That is why what you receive depends upon the level of that *silsilah*, chain. If that *silsilah* of *awlīyāullāh* that goes to Prophet ﷺ is a Golden Chain, then you are lucky. If the chain is lower than that, then you are still lucky, and even if is at the first level, still you are lucky. However, what you take depends on the strength of that chain.

That is why Muḥammad al-Busayrī ؓ knew the secret of that through his heart, which was always connected to the heart of Prophet, and he dropped *dunyā* completely from his heart. If we don't drop *dunyā* there will still be obstacles and veils. And Muḥammad al-Busayrī, who is connected to the heart of Prophet ﷺ, said in his famous verse of poetry, *wa kullun min rasūlullāhi multamisan,* "Everyone is seeking and trying to get something, requesting, sending a petition, 'Please, *yā Rasūlullāh*, give us something!'"

And when he says, *kullun min Rasūlullāhi multamisan, "kullun"* doesn't mean only you and me, or that one and that one, but it means everyone: every prophet, every *Ṣaḥābī*, and every creature Allāh created, and not only *dunyā* creatures, but *ākhirah* heavenly creatures, as well! And that means everyone and everything to whom Allāh gave life is moving with that life, and they are in need of a connection with Prophet ﷺ, which means anything that is moving, not one will be left out.

Even the Earth is moving and it needs to turn from Prophet ﷺ! Allāh ﷻ created Creation and raised the Prophet to a very high station, *qāba qawsayni aw adnā,* "Two bows length or nearer." Everyone must to acknowledge respect of Prophet ﷺ because, as we know, Allāh raised the name of Prophet and put it with His Name! A name without an appearance is not enough, so when that appearance appeared, it had a name, and that is why they appear, because of Prophet ﷺ!

What are they saying about the *ḥadīth* of Jabir ﷺ in the Muṣānnaf of ʿAbdu ʾr-Razzāq, although they say it is not mentioned or not found or not true, that is the limit of their *ʿilm* they did not reach. But in the understanding of *awlīyā,* they ask Prophet ﷺ directly for anything they need, or else what is the benefit of being *awlīyā,* if they are not able to reach and ask the Prophet ﷺ?

Everyone accepts that Allāh ﷻ raised Prophet's name with His Name, and that to raise the name without the appearance is nothing. The missing part (in their understanding) is, you must have the appearance that is living. So when Prophet ﷺ said, "The first thing Allāh created was my light," then Allāh created that appearance of Muḥammad and raised him to His Presence. And that is the missing part that *awlīyā* are exposing. I cannot say, "Your name is ʿAli," if you are not appearing; how can I give you a name? The name signifies the reality. So the name of Prophet that has been raised to *lā ilāha illa-Llāh Muḥammadun Rasūlullāh* means the name signifies that he is there.

That is missing in the *ḥadīth* of Prophet ﷺ that all scholars accept:

Kuntu nabīyyin wa adamu bayna ʾl-māʾi wa ʾt-tīn.

I was a prophet when Adam was between water and clay.

And two other *riwayats* are accepted, meaning that Sayyīdinā Muḥammad ﷺ was a prophet before Adam ﷺ, and Allāh raised his name, which means He raised the significance of "Muḥammad," where He created his Light before all Creation, or else how will he be a symbol of all Creation? He is the one who Allāh will speak to and that is the reality that Muḥammad al-Busayrī ﷺ knew. He said, *wa kullun min rasūlullāhi multamisan,* "Everyone is in need of Prophet to reach them." That means Prophet's Light was created before anything else, in order that, *mustamidūn min nur an-nabī,* "everything in movement receives support from the Light of Prophet." Everyone is taking from the heart of Prophet ﷺ!

And Muḥammad al-Busayrī ﷺ said, *gharfan min al-baḥr aw rashfan min ad-diyami,* "Taking a huge amount of water from the ocean of Prophet, in huge containers (*gharfan*)," and *rashfan,* "sipping." So even at that lower level, you are taking from Prophet ﷺ through *awlīyā,* who take you and up, up, up, to reach to the reality of that Golden Chain. And we ask Allāh to keep us with the Golden Chain that takes from both Sayyīdinā Abū Bakr ﷺ and Sayyīdinā ʿAlī ﷺ! So if you take from *shaykh al-kāmil,* a perfect master, a high-level guide that is known from that Order, that he dressed in the *khirqah*, cloak, and his shaykh dressed from his shaykh's cloak, all the way to Prophet ﷺ, it means that pipe open to your heart is a pipe of guidance.

And you must understand that a guide of *irshād* is completely different from a guide doing *dhikrūllāh*. There are many *muqaddims;* Mawlana Shaykh, may Allāh give him long life, said there might be hundreds, but not all are guides. The one who is a guide dresses in the *khirqah* that has a connection to Sayyīdinā Muḥammad ﷺ. That guide is given the permission and authority to guide and make *talqīn*, to put *dhikr* on your heart. An example of that authority is like on computers or TVs, when you press the "menu" button and there is a big list of options: installing, settings, tools, colors, and you check one-after-one.

Talqīn is from the shaykh being given authority from his shaykh, and from his shaykh up to Prophet ﷺ, to guide you, and his authority includes a menu. Some guides are given a menu for *dhikr*, they cannot go more, like some TVs have a limited menu, and others have a sophisticated, higher-level menu with many different functions. So the one who is authorized to put the secret of *talqīn* on tongues and hearts takes his menu from his shaykh, all the way to Prophet ﷺ. And whenever the *murīd* is in need, the shaykh presses that menu button and chooses what he needs for that *murīd*. The secret of *talqīn* is that menu which connects you to the heart of Prophet!

As today, in technology they say, "We need a network to reach everyone," and they have these servers that process millions of emails, and from there they can reach everyone through email. So *awlīyā* have that server to reach everyone who has a connection. So you have to know, the secret of the menu that the shaykh put in heart of *murīds* is networking. So just now our cameraman was late for the live broadcast, and what did they do? One person sent a direct "tweet" (on Twitter.com) from here and informed many people, "The live broadcast is delayed because our cameraman is sleeping."

In similitude, the cameraman is the one who can see the hearts of people. There is a cameraman for *awlīyā*. They are the ones who can reach the hearts of people and see what is there. So in one moment, if you become heedless, that connection is interrupted; it "buffers" and the connection is gone. So then people will say, "What happened? We can no longer see." Of course! You have to be careful from whom you are taking your knowledge, and that cameraman has to always be present.

Awlīyā are always present, not like the *dunyā* cameraman; they are always ready to give you what you need from Prophet ﷺ, that secret to connect the heart of the *murīd* with the shaykh, to Prophet ﷺ, and to the Divine Presence.

Whoever takes initiation (*baya'*), that menu and secret is put on the tongue and heart. Some might have fewer functions, like volume and color, and some might have more and higher functions as in a plasma TV with many different programs and even connection to the Internet. So if that *murīd* reached the level of *talqīn,* if he opens his mouth to talk or his heart to send to the hearts of others, *idhā ḥaraka as-silsilah,* if he moved in his menu to advise, the whole *silsilah* will begin to move to reach that person! That is for one; all who he reaches are ordered to move immediately, *tujawib arwāḥ al-awlīyā,* and if he only shakes his menu it will open to all.

The grandshaykh of that *ṭarīqah* will be moving to reach him, and all the souls of *awlīyā* will be moving to reach that person, and Prophet ﷺ will move immediately to bring that one, with authority to give *talqīn* on his tongue, to reach the Divine Presence, *al-ḥadarat al-ilāhī*. So all that chain will move, from that shaykh to all the shaykhs, to Prophet, to the Divine Presence.

That is why Mawlana Shaykh Nazim always says, "These knowledges are sent to me. I come empty and what they send, I speak." And I am surprised, it is now more than two years, every day, every day, and before also when we used to sit in the 60's and 70's, every day he speaks. It is not easy, not like a professor who sits to prepare notes, not like *dunyā* knowledge. Here, in these associations, there is no subject. Here there is a menu! They have heavenly servers and email and when they connect, it comes immediately.

Today some students decide to research Naqshbandi Ṭarīqah for their PhD thesis. They check the biography of every grandshaykh of the Golden Chain, but that *silsilah* will not move as they don't have the menu, not even if they mention their names, because they are "outsiders," and only "insiders" have the menu. Any one of Mawlana's *murīds,* according to the menu he has been given, can activate and move the *silsilah* by that power given to him, using his password with that menu. That is why *awlīyāullāh* have been given "the perfect *khilāfah,*" *al-khilāfat al-tāmmat al-muṭlaq*. They reach the perfect level; *al-muṭlaqa* means their menu has no restriction, it has full authority.

These are grandshaykhs; they are not normal like us. They give something to keep encouragement in the hearts of *murīds* to continue on the Way. That is why they say every *murīd* is a diplomat, as they carry the flag of the shaykh. *Murīd*-to-*murīd* they attract each other, and the *ḥusn al-khuluq,* best characteristics, will attract others to the shaykh, like a hunter has helpers to attract their prey. *Murīds* are always helping the hunter to get his prey by talking to and attracting people. That is why there is *majamʿa aṭ-ṭarāʾiq*, the compound where all *shuyūkh* of different *ṭarīqahs* meet, like a university campus with many buildings, where many different *ṭuruq* coming to Prophet come together, and don't think they don't come together. Grandshaykh ق gave authority to Mawlana Shaykh Nazim ق on 41 *ṭarīqahs*, not just one. That Golden Chain is one which can overlook all other chains. That is why the Naqshbandi Ṭarīqah is taking from the two doors, Sayyīdinā Abū Bakr ؄ and Sayyīdinā ʿAlī ؄.

And so all that is in the menu; what is in the hearts of *awlīyā* is to teach you to have *ḥusn al-khuluq* and obedience and modesty, and to carry all these kinds of behaviors. And beyond that, they put on your tongue two levels of *dhikr*: Maqām at-Tawḥīd, which is to deny and confirm, *nafiy wa ithbat*, that is the first step; and, *dhikr* of Allāh's Beautiful Name that encompasses all other Names, "Allāh."

> *Qul Allāh thumma dharhum fī khawḍihim yalʿabūn.*
> Say, "Allāh," then leave them to play in their vain discussions.
> (Sūrat al-ʾAnʿām, 6:91)

It means, "O Prophet! Don't listen to those who are not with you, just as there came to Mūsā light before you! Say "Allāh," and let them play and waste their time!" And that is what we are trying to explain in a symbolic way, that *lā ilāha illa-Llāh* shows us the path. When we reach the end by denying and confirming, deny and confirm more and more, until you deny completely everything from *dunyā* and affirm everything from *ākhirah*. Then you reach the Divine Presence and you recite ʿIsm adh-Dhāt, "Allāh".

That is what *awlīyāullāh* want their followers to do! ʿIsm at-Tawḥīd, *lā ilāha illa-Llāh*, is a Name that describes all that is possible and which has an appearance. So *dunyā* appearances want you to make *dhikr* of *lā ilāha illa-Llāh*, to deny and cancel appearances you desire through your heart. Recitations of *lā ilāha illa-Llāh* take away these appearances and leaves you clean.

So by denying and confirming, you are wiping clean all dust of human nature of this life. You are completely wiping all the dust of the appearances of everything in this human life that we are in from the face of the unique Maqām al-Āḥadīyyah, the Level of Uniqueness that takes you to Allāh's ʿIsm adh-Dhāt in the Divine Presence, described by the Unique Name of the

Essence that encompasses all Names and Attributes. So by denying human desires, you will confirm all these lights that the Divine Presence is carrying. That is why *awlīyā* say there are not only Ninety-nine Names, but the Absolute Unknown Reality of the Creator, Allāh's Divine Essence. They say even the Prophet ﷺ cannot know anything about the Divine Essence except what appears from these Beautiful Name and Attributes, an infinite number of which that can be taken from the heart of Prophet ﷺ!

When you deny the human life, slowly the dust that covers your heart begins to clear up, until it becomes a transparent vision, until you reach the divine fountain. That is *mā'rifatullāh*, not by *dhāt*, the Essence, but to know Allāh by His Beautiful Names and Attributes that is given to Prophet and now given to *awlīyā*.

Before you had TV that doesn't show except a fuzzy picture, not clear, in black and white; then came color TV, then came high-definition TV, and then plasma TV. So by that path of denial and confirmation and then reaching the Level of Uniqueness, it means you see everything in *dunyā* indicating a Creator. Maqām al-Āḥadīyyah is the "Level of Uniqueness" and at that level you can visualize things with a high-definition screen. Still you are looking on the screen, but when you go further you will be living what is on the screen as if it is part of your life. You will have three dimensions as they have today 3D movies and TV. You will see things moving up as if you are in that scene.

So *awlīyā* take their followers to Maqām at-Talqīn, by denying and confirming, and then to Maqām 'Ism adh-Dhāt and Maqām al-Āḥadīyyah, where you see the beauty coming from the Divine Presence and you will be dressed in that. As you continue, you will have *dawām al-ḥuḍūr*, "continuity of presence," which doesn't come until you love that presence.

That is why the first level is *maḥabatūllāh, maḥabbat al-ḥabīb, maḥabbat ash-shaykh*. You have that love as shown by gathering in the presence of the shaykh; if there is no love, you don't come. When you have that love then always you will be present; you have *ḥuḍūr*. In that state, you never forget you are a servant to Allāh; you always remember His Name through *dhikrūllāh* on the tongue and heart. So *dawām a-ḥuḍūr* is a miracle of *awlīyā.*

It is not a miracle to walk on water or fly in air or walk on coal or put knives in your body, no. *Karamāt* al-Awlīyā is *dawām at-tawfiq*, continuity of being present with Allāh and with His Prophet. That will lead to Maqām al-Āḥadīyyah, and we will discuss that next time. We thank our cameramen that came at the end. If the cameraman is not here that *ṣuḥbah* will not be taped, but even if he is not here and it is not taped physically, that *ṣuḥbah* will be taped on our hearts. When we have transparency we will be able to download that from our connection to our *mashaykh,* and that is coming to Sulṭān al-Awlīyā through his connection, and whatever he gets he is downloading to us. And may Allāh give us long life to see Sayyīdinā Mahdī ﷷ!

The importance is the missing link between *nūr an-Nabī,* to be created first when Allāh raised the name with His Name; there must be something there to get that appearance and name. And at the door of the Divine Presence no one can enter as written there is, *lā ilāha illa-Llāh,* which means Allāh ﷻ is saying, "I was a Hidden Treasure," and when Creation was created, you deny *dunyā* and all that is other than Allāh and confirm by looking only to that Hidden Treasure, which is still hidden.

Wa min Allāhi 't-tawfiq, bi ḥurmati 'l-ḥabīb, bi ḥurmati 'l-Fātiḥah.
And with Allāh is success. For the sake of the Beloved, for his sake we recite the opening chapter of Holy Qur'an.

The Divine Dress of Kalimat at-Tawhid

Aʿūdhu billāhi min ash-Shayṭān ir-rajīm. Bismillāhi' r-Raḥmāni 'r-Raḥīm. Nawaytu 'l-arbāʿīn, nawaytu 'l-ʿitikāf, nawaytu'l-khalwah, nawaytu 'l-ʿuzlah, nawaytu 'r-riyāḍa, nawaytu 's-sulūk, lillāhi Taʿalā fī hādhā 'l-masjid. Atiʿ ūllāh wa atiʿū 'r-Rasūl wa ūli 'l-amri minkum. (4:59)

There is no salvation except with the kings and sulṭāns of this life and the Next. *Allāhumā sallī ʿalā Sayyīdinā Muḥammad wa ʿalā ālihi Sayyīdinā Muḥammad.* With hi-tech capability you can see everywhere from where you are. Also you have to notice that Allāh ﷻ has created angels especially to observe through, if we can say this, their continuous heavenly cameras.

They are observing the *ʿamal* of Bani Adam. We are always under observation in whatever we do and try to progress. Those who are on the right path and the right track will find at the end what Allāh ﷻ promised them. Those who are one day on the right track, and one day on the wrong track, like us, they are struggling, but with Allāh's ﷻ mercy, one day with His *ināyat*, Divine Care, they will arrive there. And there are those who are never interested in the right track or wrong track, they go on their own way. We cannot judge them because we are not judges, so we leave them and Allāh ﷻ will judge them.

This is a beginning, and I would like to mention that tonight our Sulṭān al-Awlīyā, Shaykh Nazim al-Haqqani ق, opened something of hidden knowledge about what is going to be seen in these coming days or weeks or months, or more. This is to give a taste to his students, his followers, and to prepare them through their hearts for major events that might and will take place. We mentioned why we are explaining the importance of preparing a power in ourselves, in order to face these coming, major events, and he reminded us with the verse:

> *wa aʿidda lahum mastaṭāʿtum min quwattin wa min ribāṭi 'l-khayl turḥibūn bihi ʿadūwullāh wa ʿadūwakum, wa ākhirīn la tʿalamūnahum, Allāhu yaʿlamahum wa mā tunfiqū min shay'in fī sabīlillāh yuwaffa ilaykum wa antum lā tuẓlamūn.*
>
> *Against them make ready your strength to the utmost of your power, including steeds of war, to strike terror into (the hearts of) the enemies of Allāh*

and your enemies, and others whom you may not know but whom Allāh knows. Whatever you shall spend in the cause of Allāh shall be repaid to you, and you shall not be treated unjustly. (Sūrat al-'Anfāl, 8:60)

wa a'idda lahum mastatātum min quwattin, to prepare whatever possibility of power is necessary, *turhibūn bihi ʿadūwuallāh,* through which you frighten Allāh's and your enemy. That preparation means you need a weapon, not what we think of in the physical or *dunyā* meaning, as Allāh doesn't need that. Allāh doesn't need us to carry an M-16 or *dunyā* weapons. But He wants us to prepare a very sharp weapon that destroys the kingdom of Shayṭān, Allāh's enemy, the biggest enemy. Allāh is not an enemy to anyone, Allāh is merciful to everyone, but Iblīs and Shayṭān and his army and followers, *shayatīn,* are enemies to everyone, as Shayṭān disobeyed his Lord.

So the enemy is within ourselves. *Awlīyāullāh* are preparing those on the track, who are one day this way and one day the other way, *thumma āmanū, thumma kafarū,* "Those who believe, then disbelieve." (4:137), to give them a sharp spiritual sword against Shayṭān, and that door of the right track is open for all *awlīyā,* and that has never changed.

mina al-mu'uminīna rijālun ṣadaqū mā ʿahadūllāha ʿalayhi fa-minhum man qaḍā naḥbahu wa minhum man yantaẓiru wa mā baddalū tabdīlā.
Among the believers are men who have been true to their covenant with Allāh; of them some have fulfilled their obligations and some of them are still waiting, but they have never changed in the least (Sūrat al-'Aḥzāb, 33:23)

Rijālun, men who have reached the level of manhood—who always kept on the right track with their covenant to Allāh ﷻ and who never changed—they are preparing *Ummat an-Nabī.* They reached a different level of manhood and are preparing their followers. That door opened in the beginning of Ramadan, and today Mawlana said to mention that we are speaking of knowledge about the importance of *dhikrūllāh* through two levels: *lā ilāha illa-Llāh* and *Allāh. Lā ilāha illa-Llāh* is the sword Allāh ﷻ gave *Ummat an-Nabī* that is sharp enough to cut Shayṭān completely and prepare us for the appearance of Sayyīdinā Mahdī ؑ!

Many people are sleeping and do not know anything about Mahdī ؑ, while some people know and are not following, and others know and are waiting. You are of the group that knows and is waiting! The time is coming shortly. If you want to believe, you believe. If you don't want to believe, it is up to you. Things don't come suddenly without plans. We plan for ten to twenty years. From pre-Eternal, when there was no Creation, Allah's Will was already declared to the one that was a prophet when Adam ﷺ was still between soul and body! It was declared to him what is Allāh's will, and when Mahdī will appear in the Last Days.

They know, and we don't know as we are veiled; it is going to be surprise! Do we know when a tsunami will come? When it comes it takes everyone. Do we know when an earthquake will come? With all their technology and machines, they never anticipate accurately when there will be an earthquake. Does anyone know when a tornado or hurricane will come? Did they know when the eruption of a volcano in Scotland would be? They (*awlīyā*) don't tell you when you will die in order to keep you on the right track, so they hide, to see if we remain straight-forward or not. It's no problem if you go here and there, to either side of the track, as long as you are on the right track and as long as you are struggling.

There are some, however, who are not interested; they are *thumma āmanū, thumma kafarū.* I am sorry to say, some don't know where is *qiblah* (direction Muslims face in prayer, towards Mecca), and they call themselves "activists" for Muslims and for Islam. How are you an activist for Islam and you don't know where is *qiblah* even in your own home? We say, may Allāh save them and us, and guide them and us!

That power that we were speaking of from the beginning of Ramadan to today, they dressed us not only with the explanation, but as if you entered it, and they dressed you as if you have done it! Like that, we appear in their presence and from there to the presence of Prophet ﷺ, and he is taking us to the Divine Presence of Allāh ﷻ! And we only heard about Kalīmat at-Tawḥīd, *dhikr* of *lā ilāha illa-Llāh,* but we never manifested anything of that. But our spirit can see and it is dipped in that ocean of Kalīmat at-Tawḥīd, denying and confirming, as if we passed that level to the higher level of the *dhikr* by *ʿIsm adh-Dhāt*, "Allāh".

Mawlana said to mention that everyone of us has a spiritual sword, "And if their hand is not moving, our hand is moving that, and we are the ones holding and moving their hand against Shayṭān and their ego." And he said, "Say to them they have been dressed with not only that spiritual power, but they have been dressed in any meeting they attend, and anywhere they attended they, and all *murīds* (of Mawlana Shaykh), have been under every session with 70,000 different lights appearing on them, in the presence of the Prophet ﷺ."

In every session there are 70,000 lights, *shawariq al-anwār,* "the ascending lights." And to everyone Allāh gave different lights; all 70,000 lights are unique to each person! And that is a good tiding that Mawlana Shaykh gave on Laylat al-Jumuʿah, that he said to mention, as a reward, because that Laylat al-Qadr is coming and Ramadan is ending. We will see later what he says for Laylat al-Qadr, *insha'Allāh.*

What we said before, we have to know that the best example of Kalīmat at-Tawḥīd, *lā ilāha illa-Llāh,* is Miʿrāj. The first part of Miʿrāj was moving in *dunyā;* the 'Isrā' was when Prophet ﷺ moved from Mecca to Jerusalem, Masjid al-Ḥarām to Masjid al-Aqsa.

> *Subḥāna al-ladhī asrā bi ʿabdihi laylān mina 'l-masjidi 'l-ḥarāmi ilā al-masjidi'l-'aqsā 'l-ladhī bāraknā ḥawlahu linūrīyahu min ayātinā innahu Hūwa as-Samīʿu 'l-Baṣīr.*
>
> *Glory be to Him Who took His servant for a journey by night from Al-Masjid-al-Ḥarām (at Mecca) to the farthest mosque (in Jerusalem), the neighbourhood We have blessed, so We might show him Our ayāt (signs), for verily, He is the All-Hearer, the All-Seeing.* (Sūrat al-'Isrā', 17:1)

It means, praise be to Allāh ﷻ that He moved His perfect human being, Sayyīdinā Muḥammad ﷺ, from the *masjid* in which no sin can be committed, Masjid al-Ḥaram (*ḥarām* means "forbidden"); there is no sin there, and if anyone commits a sin there it will be immediately burned by the Divine Light descending there. So whoever enters there is going to be peaceful, in safety and peace. As Grandshaykh ق said, *lā yumkin an yatadanas,* "there, there is no possibility of becoming dirty from people's sin. Sin immediately disappears there, it is burned completely, it disintegrates. Whoever enters in it, finished! He is there, it is what we explained at the beginning, that the heart is also a place in which these lights appear. "Neither My Heaven nor My Earth contain Me, but the heart of the believer contains Me." So in Maqām al-Qalbi, "the Level of the Heart," you will be clean as there is no dirtiness there when you enter, but until you enter there is still a grey area. Kalīmat at-Tawḥīd takes you from these grey areas to the area of safety, peacefulness, and lights.

The best example of this is in 'Isrā', when Prophet was moved from Masjid al-Ḥarām where there is no sin, to the Masjid al-Aqsa, Masjid of the Dome in Jerusalem, where he began his Miʿrāj. 'Isrā' is a movement within Creation through recitation of *lā ilāha illa-Llāh,* followed by ascension.

Ascension is upward through the universe, going beyond the limits of this *dunyā* with all its universes, which has been created with all its galaxies. Prophet ﷺ moved and was able to reach the heavenly Creation, which is still under *lā ilāha illa-Llāh.*

In that Holy Ascension, Sayyīdinā Jibrīl knocked at the door of every Heaven.

They asked, "Who is with you?"

He replied, "With me is the Seal of Messengers."

"Has he been invited?"

"Yes."

Only after this exchange and answering correctly, the door opens, and it continued like that until after the Seventh Paradise, and Sayyīdinā Jibrīl said to Prophet ﷺ, "*Yā Rasūlullāh*! I cannot go forward, you go!" The Station of *tawḥīd* ends there. There was no one moving in that reality except Prophet. There is the manifestation of *ʿIsm adh-Dhāt*, under which comes all the Beautiful Names and Attributes. He entered that station alone, where those are the lights given to the heart of Prophet ﷺ.

> *mā wasiʿanī arḍī wa lā arḍī wa lākin wasiʿanī qalbi ʿabdī al-mu'min.*
> *Neither Earth nor Heavens contained Me, but the heart of the believer contained Me.*
> *Wa annahu lamā qāma ʿabdAllāh yadūʿhu kādū yakūna ʿalayhi libada.*
> *Yet when the Servant of Allāh stands forth to invoke Him, they just make round him a dense crowd.* (Sūrat al-Jinn, 72:19)

Who is "ʿAbdAllāh"? The only one mentioned in Qur'an as "ʿAbdAllāh" is Sayyīdinā Muḥammad ﷺ. When he stood up for His Lord, the people were not happy with that. He is the only one and the right one to carry that name, and no one can carry that name in *ākhirah* except Sayyīdinā Muḥammad ﷺ! You can be "ʿAbdur-Raḥmān," or "ʿAbdul-Ḥafīẓ," but "ʿAbdAllāh" is only for Sayyīdinā Muḥammad ﷺ! That is why Turkish people have such real belief in Prophet ﷺ that they don't name their children "Muḥammad," as they believe that name is exclusive for Prophet ﷺ; instead they use the name, "Mehmet" because "Muḥammad" is reserved for only one. You can go through all of Turkey, from the Ottoman time until today, and you cannot find anyone with the name "Muḥammad," only "Mehmet." Out of respect they use that name exclusively for Prophet ﷺ.

So he entered that reality, the understanding and knowledge of *māʿrifatullāh*. *Lā ilāha illa-Llāh* takes you from *awḥāl ad-dunyā*, from the mud and dirt of this world, all the way from the *ḥarām*, forbidden, to the *ḥalāl*, Masjid al-Aqṣā, where no sin can exist, as it is immediately burned. And that is why Hajj al-Bayt is important, because as soon as you go there you are cleaned. And it not only cleans you of past sins, but Allāh ﷻ, in His mercy, will clean your future sins also.

That is why He ordered one Hajj, as that *tajallī* with which He dresses you will not disappear; it is there and it takes you forward through all your life. That Kalīmat at-Tawḥīd, *lā ilāha illa-Llāh*, will take you, as Mawlana said, "All students who are making *dhikr* with *lā ilāha illa-Llāh* from one-hundred to a thousand times daily, even if they are not, will be dressed with that *tajallī* from the beginning of Ramadan, to be ready when Mahdī ؑ comes." So *lā ilāha illa-Llāh* takes us from the dirtiness of *dunyā* to begin our ascension into Heavens!

And when Prophet ﷺ went into Miʿrāj, where was his *ummah*? Did he leave it behind or they were with him? That is why in every level of Paradise he was asked, "Is he invited?" Of course when Paradise has been decorated, Allāh is inviting a guest! When they invite a president they fill the place with flags, ceremonies, and decorations. So when Allāh decorated Paradise, it means He invited a guest. Then why did the angels ask, "Has he been invited?" Because they saw the tail behind him! He brought behind him the *ummah*, those whom Allāh knows are of what kind; we are what we are!

Like children pleading with their father, "Don't leave us behind!" Prophet ﷺ brought the *ummah* behind him. Are they accepted? Yes, as whatever Prophet brings is accepted. In the first row are 124,000 *awlīyāullāh*, all of them with their sulṭān, may Allāh give him long life, and behind every *walī* are his *murīds*. So if you are president and take your son with you to meetings, can anyone say "no"? Today one Arab president brought his son with him to peace talks in Washington; can anyone say to him, "Don't bring your son!"

What about the Seal of Messengers ﷺ? Is he bringing one, or all of them? In *dunyā*, in his passing, and in his holy grave, he ﷺ said, "My *ummah*, my *ummah*!" On the Day of Judgment, he will say, "My *ummah*, my *ummah*!" And so Allāh is saying to him, "Don't go without taking them."

So Kalīmat at-Tawḥīd is an appearance of the Name that contains all possible existence. He didn't say what exists, but anything that you can imagine in your mind to exist in *dunyā*, all of it is under that Name. So when you say, *lā ilāha*, you are denying *dunyā*, to get away from it. Essentially, you are saying, "*Yā Rabbī*! We are not interested in these appearances of *dunyā*, as we used to run to it, and are wiping off the dust of human existence, *al-wujūd al-imkāni*, "the possible existence," as it is covering the Uniqueness of His Beautiful Name, "Allāh."

So *lā ilāha* denies everything of this dirty life and its dust, and affirms the existence of Allāh. So that is why it is two parts: *"lā ilāha"* and *"illa-Llāh."* So *awlīyā* like us to enter the reality of that Name and reveal the lights Allāh is revealing to the heart of the believer. The "House of Allāh" is the heart of the believer. "Heaven and Earth cannot contain Me, but the heart of the believer can contain Me." So if we clean the walls of the heart, take away the dust of *dunyā* by saying, *lā ilāha*, and confirm Allāh's Manifestation by saying, *illa-Llāh*, that is what *awlīyāullāh* are trying to achieve. Mawlana Shaykh says, "That achievement has already been accepted by *awlīyā*, and they trust us with *lā ilāha illa-Llāh*."

Sayyīdinā 'Abd al-Qādir al-Jilānī ق, the *ghawth* of his time, said, "My feet are on the neck of every *walī*." It has a meaning that we will not go into now. And we have to be careful, as Prophet ﷺ said, "Shayṭān never comes in my image." We have to believe fully what Prophet said, "Shayṭān can never cheat my servant by (disguising himself) using my image." Prophet is the only one who defeated his *shayṭān*, as he said in that *ḥadīth, ghalabtu shayṭānī*, when Jibrīl ؑ opened his heart and took out the small black flesh that is the house of Shayṭān in everyone's heart. If you slaughter a cow, sheep or goat and look in the heart, you will see a small black clot; that is the entrance and home for Shayṭān in the heart. So the only one who defeated his *shayṭān* is Prophet ﷺ, who said, "Whoever saw me in a dream is going to see me in reality."

And 'Abd al-Qādir al-Jilānī ق said, "O *qawm*! Exhaust your *shayṭān* by '*ikhlāṣ*, sincerity, and by reading Sūrat al-'Ikhlāṣ." Say, *lā ilāha illa-Llāh*, and also recite:

Qul Hūwa Allāhu Āḥad Allāhu 'ṣ-Ṣamad lam yalid wa lam yūlad wa lam yakun lāhu kufūwan Āḥad.
Say, "He is Allāh, the Unique One! The Self-Sufficient Master, Whom all creatures need. He neither eats nor drinks. He begets not, nor was He begotten, and there is no one comparable or equal to Him!

(Sūrat al-'Ikhlāṣ 112: 1-4)

Sayyīdinā ʿAbd al-Qādir al-Jilānī ق said, *Lā ilāha illa-Llāh lā bi mujarrad al-lafdh bal maʿna al-haqiqi,* "It is not only by saying, *lā ilāha illa-Llāh* on the tongue, but by the reality in the heart. That is why we have to recite one-hundred to a thousand times, and that will burn Shayṭān from among the *jinn* and *ins* who are doing everything without limits. *annahu nāran,* it is fire to *shayāṭīn* and a light for believers."

Fire can burn fire; a huge fire takes over the smaller fire, which will disappear. So *lā ilāha illa-Llāh* is a big fire that takes Shayṭān's fire away and also your sins, and it is a light for *muwāhidūn*. The sun is an example of that; the fire on the sun gives us life. *Nār* becomes *diyā,* shining light, and it is fire but it gives you life. Without the sun you cannot live. So that *lā ilāha illa-Llāh* will burn Shayṭān and become a light for believers.

Sayyīdinā ʿAbd al-Qādir al-Jilānī ق continues, "O my *ghulām,* my child! How dare you say, *lā ilāha illa-Llāh,* and in your heart there are too many *ilah* (gods)!" How do you say, "There is no god except Allāh," when your heart is full of gods and goddesses, and every sin is a god? Recite *lā ilāha illa-Llāh,* as that cleans the heart so well that you don't need any other cleaner. Anything that you depend on and trust other than Allāh is *sanamak,* your idol. Run away from the idols, and run to Allāh!"

Allāhumā sallī ʿalā Sayyīdinā Muḥammad ﷺ.

Wa min Allāhi ʿt-tawfiq, bi ḥurmati ʿl-ḥabīb, bi ḥurmati ʿl-Fātiḥah.
And with Allāh is success. For the sake of the Beloved, for his sake we recite the opening chapter of Holy Qur'an.

The Reality of Tawhid, Allah's Oneness

A'ūdhu billāhi min ash-Shayṭān ir-rajīm. Bismillāhi' r-Raḥmāni 'r-Raḥīm. Nawaytu 'l-arbā'īn, nawaytu 'l-'itikāf, nawaytu'l-khalwah, nawaytu 'l-'uzlah, nawaytu 'r-riyāḍa, nawaytu 's-sulūk, lillāhi Ta'alā fī hādhā 'l-masjid. Ati' ūllāh wa ati'ū 'r-Rasūl wa ūli 'l-amri minkum. (4:59)

Allāhumā sallī 'alā Sayyīdinā Muḥammad ḥattā yarda, Sayyīdinā Muḥammad. Allāhumā sallī 'alā Sayyīdinā Muḥammad. Lā ilāha illa-Llāh Muḥammadan Rasūlullāh. Qul "Allāh"!

Awlīyā have many means to make their followers move like a rocket on the right path. Their track is always straight and the engine is always on the track. It is the main engine of the train, the locomotive, and it is very powerful, so anyone who jumps on it will arrive fast. That is why they ordered that every time you are in a meeting, you should make the *niyyah,* intention, that this meeting is your last, as your soul might be taken before the next meeting, so you should be in that meeting like someone expecting death.

Be one whose deeds are completely disconnected from *dunyā* by saying, *a'ūdhu billāhi min ash-Shayṭān ir-rajīm. Bismillāhi' r-Raḥmāni 'r-Raḥīm. Nawaytu 'l-arba'īn, nawaytu 'l-'itikāf, nawaytu 'l-khalwah, nawaytu 'l-'uzlah, nawaytu 'r-riyādah, nawaytu 's-sulūk, and nawaytu as-siyām,* to keep our *jawarih,* outside and inside, disconnected from *dunyā;* then you will receive the benefit as if you did seclusion for forty days!

Every time you sit for prayer or sit to give guidance for people for *ākhirah,* then you will be written in the book. There is a book that everyone invents all kinds of ways to be mentioned in, The Guinness Book of World Records. Someone who ate 200 kilos of meat would be written in that book. And *awlīyā* have their heavenly book and give us hints what to say, so it will be written in that as if you did that *'amal.* So in every association you should intend, "We are making seclusion, or making disassociation with the world, to make movement to Allāh, and we are separating ourselves from talk of *dunyā.*" This way you cut Shayṭān to pieces!

It is said, "If you know Allāh, you know everything." If you have *mā'rifat* about your Lord, then that leads you to have *mā'rifat* of everything Allāh ﷻ wants you to know. And who knows himself knows his Lord, and who knows his limits stands by the limit of what Allāh orders him to do.

Allāh sent messengers to put us on the track, so that when we reach the destination, pulled by that big engine to reach the door of *mā'rifat,* when you come to the door and knock, they will open it for you, as we mentioned in a previous session.

Prophet said, "I was given knowledge of *awwalīn wa 'l-ākhirīn,* what was and what will be.

One *walī,* ash-Shiblī ق, said, "For me, the Knowledge of Before and After is the knowledge of *Tawḥīd,* 'Oneness', and the knowledge of *Āḥadīyyah,* 'Uniqueness'." It is the cream of what the Prophet ﷺ came with. Why? Because it is Maqām al-Hudūr, "the Station of Presence," and Maqām ash-Shuhūd, "the Station of Vision."

So that is why we say, *Ḥuḍūr Allāh, Ḥuḍūr al-Ḥabīb, fanā'un fi-Llāh, Fanāun fi'l-Ḥabīb al-Musṭafā.* That means when you are in the State of Presence and Vision, and you are reciting *lā ilāha illa-Llāh,* you are in Maqām at-Tawḥīd. In the level of Oneness, *Tawḥīd,* you see everything is One. When you enter the Maqām of Vision, you enter the reality of the Beautiful Names and Attributes describing the Essence through the *dhikr* that reminds us of Allāh, *lā ilāha illa-Llāh.* The One of Whom we see the signs in *dunyā* is the One Whose Greatness we have to know in *ākhirah,* Allāh. This *maqām* is *al-ḥuḍūr wa ash-shuhūd fī istighrāq fī nūrun rabbī.* You will be dipped in the Light of the Lord!

Allāhu nūru as-samāwāti wa al-arḍi mathalu nūrihi ka-mishkātin fīhā miṣbāḥun al-miṣbāḥu fī zujājatin az-zujājatu ka-'annahā kawkabun durrīyun yūqadu min shajaratin mubārakatin zaytūnatin lā sharqīyatin wa lā gharbīyatin yakādu zaytuhā yuḍī'u wa law lam tamsashu nār. Nūrun 'alā nūrin yahdīllāhu linūrihi man yashā'u wa yaḍribullāhu 'l-'amthāla li 'n-nāsi w 'Allāhu bi kulli shay'in 'Alīm.

Allāh is the Light of the Heavens and the Earth. The parable of His Light is as a niche and within it a lamp, the lamp is in glass, the glass as it were a brilliant star, lit from a blessed tree, an olive, neither of the east nor of the west, whose oil would almost glow forth (of itself) although no fire touched it. Light upon Light! Allāh guides to His Light whom He wills. And Allāh sets forth parables for Mankind, and Allāh is Knower of all Things!

(Sūrat an-Nūr, 24:35)

Allāh is the Light of the Heavens and Earth: that level is *al-hidāya al-'uẓmā,* "the greatest guidance," *wal-maqām al-asna,* "and the highest level," *wal-hāl al-ḥusnā,* "and the most excellent of states," and *sa'adāt al-kubrā,* "the greatest happiness." So to be on that level is very simple; don't make it complicated. So many *awlīyā* have written about these stations, but if we say, *lā ilāha illa-Llāh,* we will reach the high levels that *awlīyā* reached! Some people are saying they cannot understand anything the *awlīyā* say, but we are speaking something to allow people to realize that Greatness, to give them a taste. It is *al-maqsad al-aqsa,* "the highest attainment," or "the highest state of excellence." It takes you to *qāba qawsayni aw adna,* "two bows' length or nearer," to be with Prophet ﷺ as a member of his *ummah,* from which he will not leave anyone behind.

So what is Ḥaqīqat at-Tawḥīd, "the Reality of Tawḥīd"? For example, this element is one; it has no resemblance to anything else. That is unique in itself and in everything. No one resembles that: it is "one." That is why for Allāh to show you His Greatness and your uniqueness, He gave you a unique thumbprint that doesn't resemble anyone else's, to show that you don't resemble anyone. No one's heart resembles anyone else's, no kidney resembles another. Okay, there is some resemblance in organs; for example: when a doctor does a transplant, he has to make sure you have the right tissue type or the organ will be rejected.

So there are groupings of people, and they are not the same. He also makes groups to follow their own shaykh, not everyone follows one shaykh. Take *ḥikmah* from that, don't say, "My shaykh is higher than yours, my shaykh is the best." That is no *adab.* You have the same group, to be together, you have the same tissue type, but still that thumb doesn't resemble any other, not even if you are of the same tissue type. Also, Allāh created every leaf on a tree to not resemble any other leaf in size or composition or tissue type. Ask a scientist to do tests for you to prove this!

The word "*tawḥīd*" means that element has no resemblance. So when we understand that there is no resemblance and Who it is that has no resemblance: *qul Hūwa Allāhu Āḥad, Allāhu 'ṣ-Ṣamad.* Allāh is independent, and all Creation is dependent. Who is holding the universe together? If Allāh let it loose it will collapse, *bi ghayri ʿamadin tarawnahā,* "with no pillars holding everything in space." Who can do that? Only Allāh! Compared to heavenly power and Allāh's Greatness, all their weapons are like toys. Allāh ﷻ is saying, "Everything that human beings have, We control!" Smart bombs and aircraft are like children's toys; if Allāh wills, in one second they disappear. If He says to the ocean to swallow all submarines and all vessels, what happens? They can disappear in one moment! May Allāh ﷻ protect us.

Look what happened (with the massive floods) in Pakistan, Allāh ﷻ punished everyone, and not all Pakistanis deserve that punishment. Like

Sayyīdinā Mūsā, when he said, "*Yā Rabbī*! When You are angry with someone, why do You destroy the whole city. Why not just that one?" He spoke like that because He had familiarity with Allāh ﷻ. So Allāh said to him, "O Mūsā! Let me show you My Judgment. Go to that jungle and sit for a while." So he went there, waiting to see Allāh's Judgment. And he doesn't have patience, he is "Kalīmullāh," so among the *anbīyā* he feels some preference and higher distinction. So if he likes, like a child speaking to his father can say anything, it is accepted.

So Sayyīdinā Mūsā thinks he is better than anyone else, so he says as he likes, and he said, "How do you punish everyone who is innocent due to the acts of one person?" Allāh ﷻ left him waiting for three hours. He became impatient and said, "*Yā Rabbī*! What is this?" And as soon as he said that, many small ants crawled up his legs. Then Allāh ordered one ant to bite him and that ant was happy, as Allāh had ordered an ant to bite a prophet! That is love to Allāh and love to Sayyīdinā Mūsā.

Allāh commanded the ant, "Bite him very strongly!" As soon as he bit him, Sayyīdinā Mūsā pressed his leg and killed all the ants except a few. Then he heard a voice, "O Mūsā! What have you done?"

He said, "An ant bit me!"

"But you crushed all of them! That is My wisdom, one bad person among them causes all of them to be punished."

Those (flood victims in in Pakistan) who were innocent were given Paradise, and those who did wrong, the Hellfire is ready for them, but since they were punished they are sent to Paradise. Here is one message to Pakistanis from one of His *awlīyā:* "If you keep doing that, Allāh will continue to send like that." They blew up the *maqām* of one great *walī,* Sayyid 'Alī Hujwiri ق!

It is as Allāh said in Ḥadīth Qudsī:

man ādha lī walīyyan ādhantahu bil-harb.

Who declares war on a Friend of Mine, I declare war on him.

alā inna awlīyāullāh lā khawfan 'alayhim wa lā hum yahzanūn.
Verily, on the Friends of Allāh there is no fear, nor shall they grieve.
(Sūrat Yūnus, 10:62)

So when they blew up that *maqām*, Allāh defended him. Sayyid 'Alī Hujwirī didn't want to defend himself, so Allāh defended him: He brought that huge flood. Twenty-five million for one. When they came to Sayyīdinā

Lūt, the angels said, "We are coming by Allāh's order to destroy your people!" His people were gay. Anyone who protects gay people is going to get that punishment. We don't care about "freedom" or not, gay or not.

Allāh said to Sayyīdinā Lūt ﷺ, "Don't look behind you as you leave!" And in one strike He finished them, in one tornado or one hurricane; their homes were destroyed completely in one strike. So Allāh showed Sayyīdinā Mūsā, "For one, I take all!"

And that is Allāh's Uniqueness; no one can be like that. And how to save ourselves? By Kalīmat at-Tawḥīd, *lā ilāha illa-Llāh.* When we recite that we are saying, "There is no one to resemble You, *yā Rabbī*!" And that is Maqām al-Hudūr and Maqām ash-Shuhūd, the Station of Presence and the Station of Seeing. To those doing their *dhikr,* Allāh will open these veils, slowly, slowly, for them to see this beauty.

So the Maqām at-Tawḥīd is a level of beauty. Every year they have a beauty contest broadcast on different TV stations. One is chosen as the most beautiful and is crowned, and I don't know what else she gets of jewelry, watches, and that person becomes so highly respected, for nothing! What do you think about the One Who created beauty? When you enter yourself by saying, *lā ilāha illa-Llāh,* He will dress you with heavenly beauty. He will be happy to bring you to His Heavenly Creation and say to them, "Look! These are my beautiful ones that have separated themselves from Shayṭān!" even if you only say it once a day, or even once in your life. So one recitation of *lā ilāha illa-Llāh* is enough for one day, and for one moment. Say, "*lā ilāha illa-Llāh*"; it is describing The One Who has no resemblance!

> *Qul Hū Allāhu Āḥad, "Say (O Muḥammad), 'He is Allāh, (the) One!'" Allāhu 'ṣ-Ṣamad, "The Self-Sufficient Master, Whom all creatures need; He neither eats nor drinks." Lam yalid wa lam yūlad, "He begets not, nor was He begotten." walam yakun lāhu kufūwan Āḥad, "And there is none equal or comparable to Him."* (Sūrat al-'Ikhlāṣ, 112: 1-4)

And the meaning of "Allāh ﷻ is One" is, He is denying the division of His Essence. *Nafiy al-inqisam fī dhātihi,* "There is no partner with Me and no division in Me." That One has no partner other than Him, and He is the One that looks like no one. He is Creator, and we are His servants and His Creation.

Sayyīdinā Junayd al-Baghdādī ق said, *Idhā tanā 'uqūl al-'uqalā ila 't-tawḥīd intihā il al-ḥīrā.* "The brains of the most intelligent men who have brains..." as not everyone has brains, those who have '*dunyā* brains' are considered to have no brain, as to Allāh said *dunyā* is not valued the weight of a mosquito's wing. So why have a brain for it? That means when you add all such brains together they don't weigh the wing of a mosquito, if you still say, "I am here."

Sayyīdinā Junayd ق said, "The highest of brains that understand are the *awlīyā*'s; whatever heights *awlīyā* can reach, they have the greatest intelligence as they have left *dunyā.* If we add all the intelligence of *awlīyā* with all their heavenly knowledge, and we add together their farthest possible goal in understanding Divine Oneness, they will be stunned and in bewilderment. *Ḥīra* means "they are bewildered". They reached that level of astonishment where they cannot comprehend. With all the *tawḥīd* they have made, they reached the Ocean of Bewilderment and they cannot swim in it. They must reach their limits!" That means that anyone who says, *lā ilāha illa-Llāh* one day reaches the Level of Bewilderment, in which there is no way to understand anything except traces of that Reality.

Sayyīdinā Junayd also said, *Tandarisu fīhi al-ʿulūm wa yabqā 'Llāh ka lam yazal,* "*Tawḥīd* means in it are all the images of Creation, and in it all the images of Creation disappear! Say, *lā ilāha illa-Llāh,* and everything disappears, and you get the reward of that, as all of Creation recites *lā ilāha illa-Llāh,* and all of that is written for you! The recitation of all creatures, deserts, sands, and particles, saying *lā ilāha illa-Llāh,* is written for you! All Creation is disappearing in that ocean and all knowledge stops and we cannot understand anymore."

That is why you say, 'I am standing, *yā Rabb,* at my limits.' And that is why you know you can go no further. And Allāh's Essence stays as it is, unchanged. We cannot say anything about 'it'. We don't know what to say, in Arabic there is no word to express 'it.'

And they said that the best of what has been said about *tawḥīd* is what Abū Bakr aṣ-Ṣiddīq ق said, "*SubhānAllāh,* Praise be to Allāh that He did not create a way for His Creation to know Him."

You cannot stand beside the Divine Presence, and that is your limit of knowledge; you cannot go in. That is the limit of knowledge. You are a particle in an ocean, so what do you know about *tawḥīd*? "Praise be to the One who didn't provide a means for Creation to know Him!" How do you know Him? By realizing your *inability* to know Him! "I am coming with complete *ajaz,* inability. With that inability, I know my inability to know You." You have to declare that you cannot know or understand the level of *tawḥīd.* If you cannot understand *tawḥīd,* how can you understand Maqām adh-Dhāt, the "Station of the Name 'Allāh'"? If you cannot understand *lā ilāha illa-Llāh,* which is Maqām at-Tawḥīd, how you can understand "Allāh"? So we can only follow the way of Prophet ﷺ, then you will be there:

Qul in kuntum tuḥibbūn-Allāha fattabiʿūnī yuḥbibkumu Allāhu wa yaghfir lakum dhunūbakum w'Allāhu Ghafūrun Raḥīm.
Say, "If you love Allāh, follow me (Muḥammad). Allāh will love you and forgive you your sins, for Allāh is Oft-Forgiving, Most Merciful."
(Sūrat 'Āli ʿImrān, 3:31)

So our duty is to follow, and to know our limits and not to trespass them. Today they come to you with all kinds of ways of expressing themselves and say, "We are one, we are united." United with whom? With Shayṭān. How can you declare you are united with Allāh; that is *kufr*! You cannot even understand *tawḥīd.* Sayyīdinā Abū Bakr aṣ-Ṣiddīq ق said you cannot, or you will completely disappear. "Glory to the One who did not give a way to know about Him, except by our complete inability to know Him!" Declare that! Don't say "I"!

Wa qīla fit-tawḥīd, and it is said that *tawḥīd* means to deny three words ending with *"yā,"* the last letter of the Arabic alphabet. There are all kinds of knowledge between *"alif,"* the first letter of the Arabic alphabet, which declares Allāh's Oneness in its standing up, and *"yā"*. So that means all knowledge is between *"alif"* and *"yā."*

So if you want to understand Oneness, drop the *yā;* this leaves *alif,* and that is in three words. First is *"lī" (lam yā),* which in Arabic means, "belonging to Me," and yet, you don't own anything. You go to the grave and if you have a ring they take it, and they take everything from you, and wrap you in the shroud and throw you in, then the one who digs the grave comes and if you have any gold teeth, he steals them also, and they take your organs and sell them. You are gone and no one cares how you are cut into pieces.

First is, *lā taqul lī,* "Don't say, 'it belongs to me'." And second, don't say, *bī,* "through me". "You are something because of me!" Or don't say, "I am existing, I am president," "I am king!" What for? Kings don't die? Then what do you think you are? Nothing. Third, don't say, *minnī,* "from me". So *lī, bī* and *minnī,* don't say them. (Note: These three Arabic words all end in the suffix *yā,* in these cases pronounced *'ī'*.) Say, "It is from Him to Him," or, *minka wa ilayk,* "from You to You (Allāh); there is nothing in our hands!" Then you will be saved.

Wa min Allāhi 't-tawfīq, bi ḥurmati 'l-ḥabīb, bi ḥurmati 'l-Fātiḥah.
And with Allāh is success. For the sake of the Beloved, for his sake we recite the opening chapter of Holy Qur'an.

Five Principles of Maqam at-Tawhid

Aʿūdhu billāhi min ash-Shayṭān ir-rajīm. Bismillāhi' r-Raḥmāni 'r-Raḥīm. Nawaytu 'l-arbāʿīn, nawaytu 'l-ʿitikāf, nawaytu'l-khalwah, nawaytu 'l-ʿuzlah, nawaytu 'r-riyāḍa, nawaytu 's-sulūk, lillāhi Taʿalā fī hādhā 'l-masjid. Atiʿ ūllāh wa atiʿū 'r-Rasūl wa ūli 'l-amri minkum. (4:59)

When one says, *lā ilāha illa-Llāh,* he is denying everything in this *dunyā* and confirming *illa-Llāh,* the Greatness of the Creator. *Awlīyāullāh* say not only are they denying what is in *dunyā,* but also they are not even looking at what is in *ākhirah,* as what they like is only to be in the Divine Presence. To them there is nothing except Allāh's existence and nothing else for them exists, as Rābiʿah al-ʿAdawiyyah said, "O Allāh! I am not worshipping You for Paradise and not from fear of Hellfire, but I am worshipping You for You Only!"

Today they have taught them, not tasty Sufi speech on their tongues, but to say always "I," or "my students," "my this and that". It is better to say "our". People might say, "Why use plural?" That is because it avoids selfishness and egoism. When you say "we" it is many people, but "I" is one person. Today they put this in their heads with technology. Today there is the iPhone (ego phone) and the iPad. Why didn't they write "eyePhone"? That is Shayṭān always making us say, "I". As we said before, in Maqāmāt at-Tawḥīd, you have to drop the three *ya's*: *"lī, wa bī, wa minnī"*. *Lī* means, "for me," *bī* means, "by me" or "through me," and *minnī* means, "from me." That means everything, "from me" and "to me". No, it is "from You to You, *yā Rabbī*! My appearance in this *dunyā* is from You, and my bad *ʿamal* is from me, and my good *ʿamal* is from You!"

Don't say everything is "from me." Allāh ﷻ said in Holy Qur'an, 'Who cares for my wife and my children? Only myself.' Those are the traces that go with you all the way to Day of Judgment. Prophet ﷺ doesn't say "myself," but he says, "*ummati,* my nation," and *awlīyā* say "my students" to take to the presence of Prophet ﷺ.

> *yawm yafirru 'l-marru min akhīhi wa ummihi wa abīhi wa ṣāḥibatihi wa banīh. likull imrin yawmaydhin shānun yughnīh.*
> *On the Day when a man flees from his brother, and his mother, and his father, and his wife, and his children! Every man that Day will have concern enough to make him heedless (of others).* (Sūrat ʿAbasa, 80:34-37)

Likull imrin yawmaydhin shānun yughnīh. Everyone is fearful for himself, if he is going to be punished or not, and it is a fearful day! "On that Day everyone must follow My Prophet. Follow the Way I showed through My messengers." *Wa yawma yufirru min akhīhi wa ummihi wa abīhi wa ṣāḥibatihi, wa banīh.* "When you run away from your brother and father and mother and your wife and your children, also you run away from them in *dunyā* when you are busy with Your Lord!" You want to be cleaned in *dunyā* of everything but attachment to Allāh.

That is why they went to Rābi'ah al-'Adawiyyah ☙ and said, "Why don't you marry?" she said, "I don't have time." She ran away. Even though it is an Islamic obligation, after her husband died she ran from her family, saying, "I am busy repenting to my Lord. My *istighfār* needs another *istighfār* to be accepted." As she did 100 *istighfār*, it came to her heart that they were not accepted and she did another 100 *istighfār* to make the previous *istighfār* accepted.

So never say *lī*, "to me," and never say *bī*, "by me" and never say *minnī*, "from me." It is more respectful to speak in the third person; it is higher *adab*. *Man waqa' bi bihār at-tawḥīd ma yazdad fī ayāmin illa murūr 'atasha,* "Who falls or leaves everything and left the love of *dunyā* behind his back." These are *awlīyāullāh*; they jump into the sweet oceans of *tawḥīd*, unity, where you will never quench your thirst; you will always be thirsty, like someone who is taking salt and is always thirsty.

That is why of the five pillars of Islam—Shahadah, Ṣalāt, Zakāt, Hajj and fasting in Ramadan—in the last you get thirsty. Allāh ﷻ said, *ramadun lī wa 'anā ajzī bih,* "Ramadan is for Me; you are fasting for Me and getting thirsty for Me in Oneness Oceans. I will dip you in and dress you in oceans of *tawḥīd*." Allāh ﷻ, in His wisdom, made us feel that thirst in our day in order to be *sabab*. This causes anyone fasting Ramadan to be dipped in the Ocean of Oneness without feeling anything.

On the Day of Judgment he will come out dressed in that dress of a real *muwwāḥid*, not a fake *muwwāḥid* who professes by tongue only. You are a real one, as you were dipped in the Ocean of Oneness. That is big and not small; that is something you cannot understand. You are going to be dressed by Allāh ﷻ in the dress of *tawḥīd*. *Aynas-sāimūn,* "They will be called, 'Where are those who are fasting?' and they will enter a door to Paradise called 'ar-Rayyān,' which means, 'quenched thirst.'" *Awlīya* like to quench their thirst in the oceans of *tawḥīd*, to appear as a *walī* on the Day of Judgment. And you don't know you are a *walī*.

Shaykh al-Husayri ﷺ said there are five principles in *tawḥīd*: *Rafʿ al-ḥadath,* the same word used for the shower you take after you experience carnal desires, but it has a different meaning. It means that Allāh ﷻ does not increase or decrease. *Ḥadath* is something that happens daily. For example, you go to work, you meet a person, or you're given a higher rank. Your life is changing, you are becoming older day after day. *Rafʿ al-ḥadath* means "to keep in mind that Allāh ﷻ never changes." He is Allāh, not more and not less. The second principle is, *wa ifrād ul-qidam,* meaning, "There is only One that is post-Eternal, ancient, the only One that is today as He will be tomorrow, only One that never changes, without beginning or end." These two are very important: there are no changes for Allāh ﷻ, He is as He was before, now and forever; and, He is the only One like that.

The third principle is *hajur al-ikhwān,* to be away from everyone else, "Leave the *ikhwān* and come to My Door. Don't look behind you." An example is, Sayyīdinā Bayāzīd al-Bistāmi ق was walking with his followers when he saw a lady coming from the other side, and as soon as they approached he hugged her. They were near a house and he entered the house with the lady and closed the door. His followers fell into speculation, saying, "What happened? Is this the conduct of a *walī*? This is not a *walī,* he did something wrong." Except there was one person, who stood at the door waiting for his shaykh to come out.

Sayyīdinā Bayāzīd said, "What are you doing, my son?"

He said, "I am waiting to do *khidmah.*"

"Where are your brothers?"

He said, "My job is only to be waiting, ready to serve you, and it is not my job to know what my brothers are doing. My entire focus is on you, exclusively!"

Sayyīdinā Bayāzīd ق said, "Come inside, my son. The others had bad thoughts, but this is my sister. You are the only one that understood and you didn't mind whether this was my sister or not. You were only concerned about when I would open the door and when you could do *khidmah.* Bring two witnesses and marry my sister."

So that *murīd* became his *khalīfah.* This is a very important lesson: don't play with *awlīyā*! If that happened to us, we would only look backward (to find dirt), to backbite as much as we could. *Hajur al-ikhwān* is to be concerned with only yourself, not with others.

The fourth principle is *mufāraqat al-awṭān,* "to leave your birth country or what you inhabit"; leave your "inn," and to go to Maqām at-Tawḥīd, which is *lā ilāha illa-Llāh*. The Prophet ﷺ said, *ḥubb al-awṭān min al-īmān*. "Love of country is from faith," but you try to leave even that. You want no connection to the country to which you are going, so most of your connections are to the country from where you came. They ask, "What is your *waṭan* (nation)?" *Waṭṭin qahrabā al-manzil*, "Find a house to put your electricity or telephone bill." *Waṭṭin* means "find a bank" to pay your bills today. You don't have to go every month to pay, but you find a house to take that responsibility. Separate with all these connections to the *waṭan* you inhabit.

Also, your soul inhabits your body, so it means, "Leave your ego and free your soul from your connection to the desires of the body." Today people are so connected to their bodies and how beautiful they look, jogging, going to the gym, where there are too many *shayṭāns*! Why do they want to become healthy?

La yastākhirūna saʿatan wa lā yastaqdimūn, "For every nation there is a time to go," and every person is a *waṭan*, nation. Each cell in the body is like a huge factory, with its own defenses and production. Allāh ﷻ counted them and knows everything about every cell, and they are all coming to His Presence on the Day of Judgment. Don't jog and go to hell's gyms. As it says in the first verse we read, you are not going to be delayed one hour or moved forward one hour. If you run from here to Antarctica, you are not decreasing or increasing your life. Don't bother to run, but also don't judge those who are running because Allāh ﷻ made them run, to make them healthy. And if you don't run, then Allāh ﷻ made you like that, to be healthy in that way.

People are judging each other, and they are coming to me and complaining. Why? Allāh knows what is with you and what is not with you!

The fifth and last principle is, *wa nusyan mā ʿulim*, "to forget what is known". Whatever you have achieved in your *dunyā*, forget about it as it will not benefit you. That is why *awlīyā* forget about *dunyā*. They live in the moment and they don't mention what was before, like someone who lost their memory; *awlīyā* have heavenly Alzheimer's Syndrome! Don't bother with it, but bother yourself to say, *Lā ilāha illa-Llāh*. *Dunyā* keeps you from seeing *shawāriq al-anwār*, the sunrise of heavenly lights.

Sayyīdinā Abdul Qadir al-Jilani, the *ghawth* of his time, may Allāh sanctify his soul, said, "How dare you say, *lā ilāha illa-Llāh*, when your heart is full with many *'ilāhs*,' gods!"

For a *walī* to say that is big. *Kayfa taqūlulā ilāha illa-Llāh wa qalba mamlu*ʿ *bil aliha,* "How are you sanctifying and praising; how are you worshipping?" Because you are not saying, *lā ilāha illa-Llāh* in a real sense; it is blended with the idols within you! It is like you are really saying, "there is no *ilah*" except you, like the Quraysh before Islam worshipped their idols. Don't say to your idols, "There is no god except you, my idols!"

Sayyīdinā Abdul Qadir was saying, "Don't put any statues in your heart." Love of money and love of self are statues that block the real *tawḥīd. Lā yanfa*ʿ*uk tawḥīd al-lisān wa anta* ʿ*ala shirk,* "It is not only speaking of papers, but when *awlīyā* speak, they dress us with whatever they are speaking." Sayyīdinā Abdul Qadir al-Jilani ق said that, to dress anyone who reads that and to take out the statues of the heart and replace them with the real meaning of *lā ilāha illa-Llāh.*

Awlīyā are not playing! They remind you about your mistakes, but they also take away the wrong you are doing. The normal scholar will remind you, but will not take away that mistake of having idols in your heart. That will not give you benefit, but it is like making prayer on a dirty carpet; you must first clean it. So it will not benefit you to have a correct word with a dirty heart. For *awlīyā,* dirtiness is not love of *dunyā;* they already left that. For them, dirtiness is love of *ākhirah,* as Rābiʿah al- ʿAdawiyyah ﵁ said, "O Allāh! I am not worshipping You for love of Paradise nor from fear of Hell, but for love of You!"

That is the reality of love, not like the standard cliché, "Islam is peace and love." The reality of love is to go through the path to *mā*ʿ*rifatullāh,* and then you see what people cannot see and hear what people cannot hear.

An example is, even if you bring all the best singers and musicians in this world, they cannot be compared with the singing of one angel. When you begin to say truly, *lā ilāha illa-Llāh,* the *taṣbīḥ* of angels comes to your ears and you become drunk from it! It is said that if one *ḥūrī* of Paradise would show her finger, from the beauty of her finger and its beautiful perfume, all in *dunyā* would faint! What is perfume? Today they sell you tons of perfumes, but *awlīyā* give you real perfume: to say, *lā ilāha illa-Llāh Muḥammadun Rasūlullāh.* You cannot say *lā ilāha illa-Llāh* without saying *Muḥammadun Rasūlullāh.* That is our safety. Whoever wants to get upset about this, let them do so!

Sayyīdinā Abdul Qadir al-Jilani ق said, *Al-qalb al-muwwāḥid yudnī shayṭān,* "The heart that is always mentioning the Oneness of Allāh will exhaust his *shayṭān.*" The one whose heart is always in *tawḥīd,* always saying, *"lā ilāha illa-Llāh",* that one's *shayṭān* will become exhausted. That is killing him and it is a sword against him. The *mushrik yudnihi shayṭān*, the one who associates partners with Allāh ﷻ, that *shirk* will make his *shayṭān* exhausted. Don't say, "I am not *mushrik*." Yes, we are. "Of course we are not *mushrik*! We are Muslims!"

But that is not what Sayyīdinā Abdul Qadir ق is saying. He is saying that the heart that has no one other than Allāh ﷻ will harm his *shayṭān*. The heart that doesn't mention any except Allāh, and the full heart that is in that *tawḥīd* makes his *shayṭān* exhausted. But the one who makes his heart open for all kinds of worldly desires, and also heavenly desires, that heart is making partnership with Allāh ﷻ so his Shayṭān will exhaust him.

That is why Muslims are exhausted today: we are molding clay, which is *dunyā,* with pure heavenly Paradise elements, trying to mold a statue. That is why our prayers have to be only for Allāh ﷻ.

Qul innamā anā basharun mithlukum yūhā ilayya annamā ilāhukum ilāhun wāhidun faman kāna yarjū liqā rabbihi falyaʿmal ʿamalan sālihan wa lā yushrik bi-ʿibadati rabbihi 'aḥada.

Say (O Muḥammad), "I am only a man like you. It has been inspired to me that your God is One God (Allāh), so whoever hopes for the Meeting with his Lord, let him work righteousness and associate none as a partner in the worship of his Lord." (Sūratu 'l-Kahf, 18:110)

Prophet ﷺ is so humble! With all that Allāh ﷻ gave him, he said only, "But I am different in that it is revealed to me." What is different? That means a huge difference, someone who can receive *wahī.*

Prophet ﷺ is telling us, "Don't worship nicely and then run to your work and not keep worship in your heart." Deal with *dunyā* matters, yes, but don't leave worship from your heart. The one who likes to meet with His Lord on the Day of Judgment, let him do a good *ʿamal*. What is that? To put no partner with His Lord. Don't put yourself with your Lord, saying, "I am an engineer, I am a doctor, I am a carpenter." Do you do that? Your honor is not with what you do, nor from any degree, but only Allāh's honor is what counts! Can you go to Allāh ﷻ on Judgment Day and when you are called, you say, "O, my Lord! Wait one second, I have a Master's degree!"

What does it say in Holy Qur'an about those who refute *ʿIsm adh-Dhāt*?

Qul Allāh thumma dharhum fī khawdihim yalʿabūn.

Say, "Allāh," then leave them to play in their vain discussions.

(Sūrat al-'Anʿām, 6:91)

"Say 'Allāh' and leave them in their playing." They say, "Don't say, 'Allāh,'" so then what else is there to say, "Shayṭān"? What should you say when you have a problem? Do you say, "O Hollywood!"

wa mā Muḥammadun illa rasūl. qad khalat min qablihi 'r-rusūl. Afa in māta aw qutil anqalabtum ʿalā āʿaqābikum wa man yanqalib ʿalā ʿaqibayhi falan yadurra allāha shayān wa sayajzī'Llāhu 'sh-shākirīn.
Muḥammad is no more than a messenger; many messengers passed away before him. If he died or were slain, will you then turn back on your heels (as disbelievers)? And he who turns back on his heels, not the least harm will he do to Allāh, and Allāh will reward to those who are grateful.
(Sūrat 'Āli ʿImrān, 3:144)

At the Station of Qāba Qawsayn, Prophet ﷺ saw Allāh ﷻ. "We have not yet reached Maqām at-Tawḥīd; the only one to reach it is the Prophet ﷺ." He is the only one to reach the Divine Presence, the reality of reaching *qāba qawsayni aw adna*! And the *mushrik,* who puts partnership of *dunyā* with *ākhirah,* is not yet outside *awhāl ad-dunyā* and will be exhausted by Shayṭān. There is not one person outside that, even who has ten or one-hundred billion dollars, multiple luxury homes and cars. Everyone has a problem and no one can say, "I have no problem," because Allāh ﷻ is teaching you that when you have problems you should remember Him, but you don't.

When you have no problems, you reached Maqām at-Tawḥīd; like *awlīyāullāh* don't care about *dunyā,* who dies, dies. What is better, to be in *dunyā* or *ākhirah*? So if someone comes to a *walī* and says, "I am sick, I am in a problem. Make *du'ā.*" What *du'ā*? Go to *ākhirah,* it is better. But with their mercy they make *du'ā,* and their *du'ā* is strong.

May Allāh ﷻ cure us and take away the *shirk* from our hearts! Say, *lā ilāha illa-Llāh.* Say, *Bismillāhi' r-Raḥmāni 'r-Raḥīm.* Say, *Qul Hū Allāhu 'Āḥad* (Sūrat al-Ikhlāṣ). If you recite these daily you will be saved, despite whatever comes from difficulties and miseries. The *awlīyā* dress you with the reality of *tawḥīd.* They are not like you. They don't speak to give you advice. Even if no one says, "*lā ilāha illa-Llāh*" and no one says Sūrat al-Ikhlāṣ, they dress you. They already have the dress and they dress you one by one. Whether you do this or not, they have to dress you because you took their hands in *bayaʿ*, so they are under that responsibility. They have to dress you as they are responsible in presence of Prophet ﷺ.

Ghawth, Quṭb, Nujabā, Nuqabā, Awtād, and Akhyār are different types of *awlīyā* that support servants of an-Nabī. They cannot leave you without clothes. Can you walk naked in the street? Someone will come and dress you, since we are all naked in *dunya,* from making a partnership of *dunyā* and *ākhirah.* They dress you in prepared dresses.

According to the *walī's* level you get a dress, and the higher level has a higher dress, w*a fawqa kulli dhi ʿilmin ʿalīm,* "Above every knower is a (higher) knower," (Sūrah Yūsuf, 12:76) until you reach Sulṭān al-Awlīyā. When he dresses you, then Prophet ﷺ will dress you and that dress is far higher than what the Sultan dresses.

May Allāh ﷻ forgive us and bless us and we will continue at Fajr, *inshā'Allāh.* We remind everyone that we began that series to explain what we know in Islam. It is not, as they say, that there is no hierarchy. In fact there is a reality of a pyramid and a hierarchy and *awlīyāullāh* have different things they do and duties. As of today we have made 23 or 24 *suḥbahs,* all of them to describe what these *awlīyāullāh* do, to describe the *ghawth,* what he does and to describe these five groups of *awlīyāullāh.* And then we come to the senior Muslims in these communities, to shed a light on this knowledge that no one is touching today.

Today what are they discussing? Only politics, as if the only concern is *dunyā* and nothing else. Mosques are used to promote political agendas. You can rent a hall and speak about what you want, but speak about *ākhirah* in the mosque, not politics or *dunyā* matters. Why do you bring such subjects to the podium of the mosque?

al-masājidu lillah.
The mosques are for Allāh. (Sūrat al-Jinn 72:18)

In the mosque, don't speak about what the president or the cabinet did, or about foreign policy, or what is or is not our right. The *masjid* is for worship! There you read Qur'an and *ḥadīth,* pray, and do *dhikr.* Don't make *halaqa* circles under false pretenses, to recruit people for evil, saying, "I like *jihad* and want to save the *ummah.*" You are putting the *ummah* in difficulties and problems! Mosques are Allāh's Houses, so don't make partnership with Him by bringing something dirty there!

Wa min Allāhi ʿt-tawfiq, bi ḥurmati ʿl-ḥabīb, bi ḥurmati ʿl-Fātiḥah.
And with Allāh is success. For the sake of the Beloved, for his sake we recite the opening chapter of Holy Qur'an.

Maqam al-'Ikhlas, the Level of Sincerity

A'ūdhu billāhi min ash-Shayṭān ir-rajīm. Bismillāhi' r-Raḥmāni 'r-Raḥīm. Nawaytu 'l-arbā'īn, nawaytu 'l-'itikāf, nawaytu'l-khalwah, nawaytu 'l-'uzlah, nawaytu 'r-riyāḍa, nawaytu 's-sulūk, lillāhi Ta'alā fī hādhā 'l-masjid. Ati' ūllāh wa ati'ū 'r-Rasūl wa ūli 'l-amri minkum. (4:59)

As we said before, the heart that keeps declaring and manifesting the Oneness of Allāh ﷻ, Maqām at-Tawḥīd, that person and that heart will make his Shayṭān exhausted. And the one who is always associating himself with Allāh ﷻ, who whatever he does of good he says, "I did that, I gave money, I gave a donation for Pakistan."

It is as if Pakistan became a commercial for everything, for violence, for disasters. I don't know what is happening in Pakistan. It might be there are too many *mushriks* there, too many people calling others to themselves. There is too much black magic there! I didn't see a Pakistani that didn't say, "I have black magic." It is rare to find someone who doesn't have black magic, like in Kenya, Ghana, Indonesia, etc., all these countries have black magic. May Allāh take away that black magic!

It is worthless when they use it on human beings. Black magic is really Shayṭān preventing you from declaring *tawḥīd*. So the one who is prevented from *tawḥīd* will be exhausted by Shayṭān. So what do you need? You need sincerity. When we have sincerity then we are going to throw out Shayṭān from our hearts. And how you can achieve sincerity?

> *Yā ayyuhal-ladhīna āmanū ittaqūllāh wa kūnū ma' aṣ-ṣādiqīn.*
> *O you who believe! Fear Allāh and be with those who are pious (in word and deed).* (Sūrat at-Tawbah, 9:119)

Those who have *taqwā*, sincerity, what is Allāh telling them? You must have *taqwā*, otherwise it is a waste of time. When you have *taqwā,* He allows you to be with trustworthy people to take you forward. So be with these trustworthy people, who kept their covenant with Allāh and never changed. *Taqwā* is to be steadfast, and we are struggling with that.

How do we achieve *ikhlāṣ*? In the Holy Qur'an there is a chapter, "al-Ikhlāṣ" that begins with, *Qul Hūwa Allāhu 'Āḥad.* If you want to achieve sincerity, read Ikhlāṣ Sharīfah. That is why *awliyāullāh* order their followers to read Sūrat al-Ikhlāṣ 100 to 1,000 times daily. When someone has a problem and I say, "Read *'yā Fattah'* 100 times," they say, "daily?" What do you mean? Do you want it monthly or yearly? It is too much for them! We are busy. In what? Busy in business. So read Sūrat al-Ikhlāṣ; it will become manifest in you. When you are coming to Allāh reciting Sūrat al-Ikhlāṣ, do you think He will throw you out? If someone is knocking at your door and you say, "I am not answering," if that person is persistent, what will you do eventually? You open the door; either you shout at him or you welcome him. Allāh is not like us. His door is from east to west, and if you want to go out, there is no way. That 'exit' is like the eye of a needle! Then He will manifest on you the *barakah* of the holy chapter, Sūrat al-Ikhlāṣ.

But Shayṭān makes us unaware of Sūrat al-Ikhlāṣ. If you go to a rich man, or a president or king, they give you medallions, showing his generosity. You come a second time, he gives another medallion. You come a third time, he might not invite you again! When you make *salām* to Prophet ﷺ, he will answer you with a better *salām*. Whoever makes one *ṣalawāt* on Prophet ﷺ, Allāh makes ten *ṣalawāt* on that person. Allāh's *ṣalawāt* on that person is far greater, even there is no description of it!

The *Ṣaḥābah* used to pass by Prophet ﷺ and say, "*As-salāmu 'alayk, yā Rasūlullāh,*" and he replied, "*Wa 'alaykum as-salām wa raḥmatullāh, yā 'abdAllāh!*" And then that *Ṣaḥābī* would pass another time and get another *salām* from Prophet ﷺ. *Ṣaḥābah* showed that sincerity by sending *salām* on Prophet ﷺ. And we are sending *salām* on Prophet ﷺ from here, *as-salātu was-salām 'alayk, yā Rasūlullāh* ﷺ! Do you think Prophet ﷺ is not answering? Of course he is! There are about 100 people here. So ten multiplied by 100 equals 1,000. Each one will get 1,000 *ḥasanāt*. And if there are 5,000 people you will get 50,000 *ḥasanāt*. If you want to get that benefit, go to Indonesia, where there are at least 5,000 to 10,000 attendees at every mosque!

So whoever comes with sincerity, with *Qul Hūwa Allāhu 'Āḥad*, the door is open. Sincerity is the pulp of all sayings and actions, *af'al*. That is the secret and the main seed of sincerity. It is the fruit that has the *qushr*, shell, of your sayings and your actions. The indication of sincerity is what appears or manifests through your sayings, what you speak and how you act. If you speak well and are respectful to everyone, that indicates sincerity. Sincerity is to be patient with the one you don't like, with whom you can never meet eye to eye, and that is very difficult. There it shows sincerity, as he is Allāh's servant also. Allāh sent him as a test for you to see how you are going to take it.

To save the fruit you need the shell, and to save your sincerity you need a shell, which is the actions and sayings. Whatever is inside manifests in the shell. If the fruit inside is rotten, then the shell is finished as well. So the shell must not be rotten, meaning, your actions and saying must be of a higher level. How do you speak to someone important? Very nicely, so that you can attract them towards you. How do you speak to Allāh and then to Prophet ﷺ? It is important to stand when Prophet ﷺ is being mentioned. Here we would be standing and sitting without end, but people are not accustomed to it. Therefore, stand in your heart. People ask me, "Is there a problem? Why are these people standing and sitting?" What should I say? So, be normal.

Sincerity is the fruit, and if there is no sincerity, then what do you have inside? What do you do with a dry shell? You don't throw it; it is something important. What you do with it? You burn it. Burn your bad actions and your bad sayings. Punishment is to clean and Hellfire is to burn bad actions and to keep the pulp clean. Try to throw away your bad actions and bad sayings from yourself.

Listen, O Believer! O *Muwwāḥid*! *Allāh* said in the Holy Qur'an:

Rabbu 'l-māshriqi wa 'l-māghrib fattakhidh-hu wakīla.
(He is) Lord of the East and the West. There is no god but He. Take Him therefore (as your) Disposer of Affairs. (al-Muzzammil, 73:9)

Be careful, He is the Creator of East and West, but there is a meaning here. Yes, He is the Creator of the beginning of the sunrise, *shawāriq al-anwār*, the rising lights. He is the Creator of the rising lights and Creator of the setting lights. But it is immediately followed by *lā ilāha illa-Hūwa,* bringing your attention to what is much deeper. *Lā ilāha illa-Llāh* means, "There is no Creator except Allāh." *lā ilāha illā Hūwa* means, "There is no Creator except the Unknown Essence."

That is *'Ism adh-Dhāt,* which is *qul Hūwa,* before *"Allāh,"* meaning, "more Unknown." So if He is Lord of East and West, then He is the One that is Unknown. Even the light of east and west goes down, but His Essence is Unknown. And then He said:

Rabbu 'l-mashriqayn wa Rabbu 'l-maghribayn, fa bi ayyi 'ālāi rabbikumā tukadhdhibān. (He is) Lord of the two Easts and Lord of the two Wests. Then which of the favors of your Lord will you deny? (Sūrat ar-Raḥmān, 55:17-18)

"He is the Lord of the two Easts and the two Wests." Why are you lying about Allāh ﷻ? Is there more than one east, one west, and one sun? Yes, it must be, or else He would not say it in the Holy Qur'an! *Rabbul mashāriq wal-maghārib,* "He is the Lord of the Easts (plural) and Lord of the Wests (plural)." There is no end to easts; in every moment He is creating easts. There are infinite numbers of easts and wests! So to accept you, you have to say, *"lā ilāha illa-Hūwa." Awlīyāullāh* order those who are more in seniority, to recite 100 to1,000 times *lā ilaha illa -Hūwa* after *lā ilāha illa-Llāh.* And that is why in *baya*ʿ we recite *Allāhu, Allāhu, Allāhu Ḥaqq,* to enter that ocean of The Unknown.

When He said, *Rabbul mashriq wal-maghrib,* "Lord of the East and the West," what does it mean? Allāh is *Nūr-us-samawāti wal-ʿarḍ,* the rising sun that shines over everything. That is why we were explained in previous sessions about *shawāriq al-anwār,* when you throw away all these veils and the dust that prevents you from receiving the rising lights. Come to Him with nothing, then you will receive these rising lights and they will manifest in your heart!

Who is The One to Whom all the Lights of all the Names and Attributes are manifested? It is the Prophet ﷺ! He is *Mashriq* (east) and *Maghrib* (west) that is rising all the time and downloading all these Names and Attributes. One of his names is *al-Mashriq* and *al-Maghrib,* because Allāh said, *rabbul mashriq;* that is where all rising lights come from. That is because Allāh is his Lord and that is why He raised Prophet's name with His.

Then what about *rabbul mashriqayn wa rabbul maghribayn?* That has no *sharīk,* no associate to Allāh. He is the Lord of Prophet ﷺ, Sultan al-Anbīyā ﷺ, and Sulṭān al-Awlīyā. That is the indication of the one who receives directly from the Prophet ﷺ and gives guidance to the *ummah.* And that is also an indication that Allāh gives to the beloved Prophet ﷺ, one who is Sulṭān al-Awlīyā. *Fa bi ayyi ʿalā rabbikuma tukhadhbān,* so who gave you permission to say, no? He is *al-Mashriqayn* and *al-Maghribayn.*

Muhyidīn ibn ʿArabi ق said, "The presence of Sulṭān al-Awlīyā is always facing the Prophet ﷺ to receive directly from him." What about the Creator of Easts and Wests? That means He is the Lord of all *awlīyā* that He gave to Prophet ﷺ. They are *shawāriq al-anwār,* spotlights moving in this universe, bringing the kernel of sincerity, *lubb al-ikhlāṣ.* When they carry that sincerity, they become *ayah min ayātullāh,* a sign from Allāh's Signs.

One of Shaykh Sharafuddīn's ق names was *"ayātun min ayātullāh tamshi ʿalā al-ʿarḍ."* When you enter these oceans you find yourself saying, "What I am doing here?" That is why most *awlīyā* are waiting for the day when Allāh calls them to the Divine Presence. When we know that Allāh mentioned Prophet ﷺ as *mashriq* and *maghrib*, as *mashriqayn* and *maghribayn*, and as *mashāriq* and *maghārib*, then we know there is no way to be sincere except through him!

So we have to be always knocking on the door, calling, "*Yā Sayyīdī, yā Rasūlullāh*!" But don't come alone; bring someone with you. If you come alone, they will not open because there is no sincerity in you. You have to bring someone that is accepted, a means, *wasīlah*, vehicle. If you bring your shaykh with you, for sure he has more access than you. When he says, "*As-salāmu ʿalayk yā Sayyīdī, yā Rasūlullāh*!" it is different from when we say it. He says it with sincerity, so then they will open the door. For those with no sincerity, they will get rewarded, but the door might not open. You must keep saying it every day and you must not get tired; keep knocking.

"Enter houses through their proper doors." Who are the doors? They are *awlīyāullāh*. Prophet ﷺ said:

> *'ana madinatu 'l-ʿilmi wa ʿAliyyun babuha.*
> *I am the city of knowledge and ʿAlī is its door.* (al-Ḥākim, Tirmidhī)

Sayyīdinā ʿAlī ؓ is the door. In every time, there is an inheritor for Sayyīdinā ʿAlī ؓ. So come with him and then you see the city. Who did Prophet ﷺ take with him as a companion in his migration? He took Sayyīdinā Abū Bakr aṣ-Ṣiddīq ق. There was never a moment that he was away from Prophet ﷺ. Therefore, he is always inside the city not outside. Inside you will find another door for you to be sure you are in the presence of Prophet ﷺ.

That is why the Naqshbandi Order is called, "the Golden Chain"; it comes from two great humans that are with Prophet ﷺ. Sayyīdinā ʿUmar ؓ and Sayyīdinā ʿUthmān ؓ are also among the greatest *Ṣaḥābah* ؓ, but they have other assignments, other things to do. The Naqshbandi Ṭarīqah connects these two sources in Sayyīdinā Jafar aṣ-Ṣadiq ق. When we come with these two sources, then Shayṭān becomes exhausted. When that happens, *dunyā* comes to you. But right now, we are slaves to *dunyā*. We are running after work, after *dunyā*.

ʿIndamā tatajarrad min ṭabiʿati nafsak al-ḥaywānīyya. When you strip from yourselves your animal characteristics and *wujūd al-imkāni*, "the possibilities of your existence," then you can come to *al-wujūd al-jamʿi*, "the collective existence" of *awlīyā* and prophets in the Divine Presence. The existence of possibilities has no value. The Divine Existence is a very precious ocean with endless depth. You can dive and dive, and still it is as if you didn't dive at all!

That is why recitation of *"lā ilāha illa-Llāh"* takes you to *wujūd ilāhī,* the Real Existence. If you say, *"lā ilāha illa 'anā,* there is no god except me," which our actions support, that will not take you anywhere; *dunyā* will become your master and you will become a slave to *dunyā.* When you say, *"lā ilāha illa-Llāh",* then *dunyā* will become a slave to you. Say it with sincerity and Allāh will open to your heart.

May Allāh ﷻ forgive us and may Allāh bless us.

Wa min Allāhi 't-tawfiq, bi ḥurmati 'l-ḥabīb, bi ḥurmati 'l-Fātiḥah.
And with Allāh is success. For the sake of the Beloved, for his sake we recite the opening chapter of Holy Qur'an.

Shari`ah Protects the "Fruit of Islam", Tasawwuf

Aʿūdhu billāhi min ash-Shayṭān ir-rajīm. Bismillāhi' r-Raḥmāni 'r-Raḥīm. Nawaytu 'l-arbāʿīn, nawaytu 'l-ʿitikāf, nawaytu'l-khalwah, nawaytu 'l-ʿuzlah, nawaytu 'r-riyāḍa, nawaytu 's-sulūk, lillāhi Taʿalā fī hādhā 'l-masjid. Atiʿ ūllāh wa atiʿū 'r-Rasūl wa ūli 'l-amri minkum. (4:59)

O Believers! Followers and students of Mawlana Shaykh Nazim al-Haqqani ق! The Prophet ﷺ said, *kalimatān khafīfatān ʿalā al-lisān thaqīlatān lir-Raḥmān. Aʿūdhu billāhi min ash-Shayṭān ir-rajīm. Bismillāhi' r-Raḥmāni 'r-Raḥīm.*

As Mawlana Shaykh Nazim ق says, "O our Attenders!" Students of Mawlana Shaykh Nazim ق, we are followers of Āhlu 'l-Sunnah wa 'l-Jamaʿah! Therefore, we must behave likewise, not like people with no discipline. Discipline is what leads you to the love of Allāh and of Prophet ﷺ. If Sayyīdinā Muḥammad ﷺ said something, it is to be followed. He left behind his *sunnah,* which is to be followed, to guide us not to be careless about how we behave and act. We have to behave well, and to behave well is to follow the footsteps of Prophet ﷺ. If you follow Prophet ﷺ, you will be happy in this life and the Next.

Prophet ﷺ said, "Don't be like roosters and chickens when you pray, as that prayer is not accepted." He saw someone praying, going quickly up and down, and when that person made *salām,* he told him to repeat his prayer. *Ṭarīqah* is not only *māʿrifatullāh;* although that is important, you cannot leave *dhāhir ash-sharʿah,* the external (practices) of Sharīʿah or then it will be as if you didn't pray. Don't say, "My prayer is accepted, I have a shaykh." No! Your shaykh will not help you when you come against Sharīʿah. Prophet ﷺ said:

kalimatān khafīfatān ʿalā al-lisān thaqīlatān fī 'l-mīzān.
Two words that are very light on the tongue, but very heavy on the Scale.

There are different *aḥadīth* on that. One of them says, "These words are *SubhānAllāh wa biḥamdihi,*" and according to another *hadīth*, it is the *shahadah,* which Prophet ﷺ said it is to say, *Ash-hadu an lā ilāha illa-Llāh wa ash-hadu anna Muḥammadun Rasūlullāh.*

When you say, "I am *muwwāḥid*," you have to implement the meaning of *tawḥīd*, which is *sajdah*. That is what Allāh ordered Iblīs to do and he refused. Whether it is a *sajdah* of worship or of respect to the light of Prophet ﷺ in Adam ؑ, when you make *sajdah* you must keep its requirements. What are they? To say, *Subhāna Rabbī al-ʿalā wa biḥamdih,* not to say it like a parrot, (very fast). You have to meditate on it, *al-ʿalā*. The secret of that Name will reach you when you ponder it. "Allāh is High and the rest are slaves to Him!" When you say, *Subhāna Rabbī al-ʿalā wa biḥamdih,* Allāh will dress you with that dress, that *baraka,* when you say it three times in each *sajdah*. Don't allow Shayṭān to exhaust you by pecking the ground like a cock or a chicken.

Who says, *"Subhāna Rabbī al-ʿalā wa biḥamdih"* completely? Some say, *"Subhāna Rabbī al-ʿalā,"* they don't continue saying "*wa biḥamdih*." So when we are not giving all the rights to our prayers, which is a kind of worship that Allāh ordered everyone to do, should we expect we will not have problems? You will have problems in *dunyā* and in *ākhirah*! What is the benefit of *taṣawwuf* when we are dropping Sharīʿah? We are Muslim first, Shafiʿī or Hanafi (or following another) school of thought. Then we follow a *ṭarīqah,* a Way. So we have to learn Sharīʿah first, and then enter *taṣawwuf*. If we don't know Sharīʿah, we should not attend *taṣawwuf* classes!

In the previous years, students were not allowed to attend *taṣawwuf* classes at all before being checked in Sharīʿah completely, as it is not simple. In the time of Sayyīdinā ʿAbdul-Khāliq al-Ghujdawāni ق, one of the shaykhs of the Golden Chain, the grand mufti of that time came to him. He said, "*Yā* ʿAbdu 'l-Khāliq, I want to be in that path," because it is the fruit for *ʿulamā*. Sharīʿah is the shell that saves the fruit. They know the importance of the fruit. I remember when all my uncles studied in Azhar ash-Sharīf, you could not graduate except by being in a Sufi Order. Today you can graduate by being an *ʿālim,* but previously you had to have Sharīʿah (law) and *taṣawwuf*.

Imām Malik ق had 300 teachers of Sharīʿah and 600 of *taṣawwuf*. Do you think they taught him to pray like a chicken? We don't understand! Islam accommodates every century, time, culture, and moment in the lives of human beings. We cannot say we have to "Arabinize, Pakistanize, or Americanize" Islam. Anyone who is saying that is considered *kāfir* (unbeliever)! Did Allāh say that whenever someone comes they can change Islam? No! But He said:

Bismillāhi' r-Raḥmāni 'r-Raḥīm, al-yawma akmaltu lakum dīnakum wa atmamtu ʿalaykum niʿmatī wa radītum lakumu 'l-Islāmu dīna.

This day I have perfected your religion for you, completed My favor upon you, and have chosen Islām as your religion. (Sūrat al-Mā'idah, 5:3)

"Today I have perfected and completed," meaning, "There are no additions after I have completed, and I have given you with My satisfaction of my religion." So we can say we want reform Muslims, but we cannot say Islam needs reform; you cannot reform what Allāh made perfect! Muslims are mistaken, not following *sharī'atullāh,* and not understanding the taste that Allāh gave in His Sharī'ah! When they don't have taste they think, "We have to change Islam," and that is not true. Islam cannot be but what it is. No addition, no subtraction, no multiplication, and no division. Sharī'ah is clear, *al-halālu bayyin wal-ḥarāmu bayyin.* But extremists are doing different things, coming with verses of Holy Qur'an (which they misinterpret). Why blame Islam for the wrong understanding of one person? Blame that person, not the religion!

Imām Malik ق said, *man tafaqaha wa lam yatasawwaf faqad tafasaq,* "The one who studied Sharī'ah without learning the spiritual side will become corrupt." Sharī'ah is the trunk and inside is the *lubb* of the tree. When deer come in the winter and can't find anything to eat, they scrape the bark of the tree and eat the sap. The bark is Sharī'ah and the sap is *taṣawwuf.* So they take Sharī'ah and hold it, then they reach the inside; that means you need both.

That is why he said, "Who studied Sharī'ah and left *taṣawwuf* is corrupt, and whoever studied *taṣawwuf* without Sharī'ah, is a heretic." You cannot be a Sufi and not pray, but you can pray and not be a Sufi. So the first one is, to follow Sharī'ah without *taṣawwuf.* There is no taste; therefore, you are cheating and deceiving, you do what you like. But whoever studied *taṣawwuf* without Sharī'ah is also dangerous as it leads you to be a heretic. Today they say, "We are Sufis." No! You are only hiding behind the name of Sufism, but in reality doing all things that are wrong! Have you seen these big conferences? They speak on *taṣawwuf* and never on Islam.

When we came in 1991 and spoke about *taṣawwuf,* they acted like they never heard of it. How is it possible that Pakistanis, Indians, or Arabs never heard of *taṣawwuf?* Where did you throw Maqām al-Iḥsān? There are tons of books by thousands of scholars! Imām Malik ق said that you have to study both, the shell and the fruit: the shell saves the fruit, just as the cup saves the water. If there is no cup, there is no water. Where will you put it, in your pocket? No, it will run off and leak. The cup preserves the water.

So the shaykh came to 'Abdul-Khāliq al-Ghujdawāni ق and said, "I want to be your student."

He said, "I have too many students."

The shaykh said, "I have Sharī'ah, but I need to taste the sweetness of the fruit."

It is not like *dunyā* fruits; can you have more than a hundred kinds of fruit? Every moment you will be offered different heavenly fruits with a different taste. And each heavenly fruit is different from the other. So there is an infinite number of different types of fruit. As when Sayyīdinā Zakariyya ؏ entered the *mihrab* of Sayyida Maryam ؏, he found there provisions of fruit and each time the fruits were new and different. Heavenly fruit never repeats.

The shaykh said, "I don't want knowledge of papers, I want the real taste, *dhawq*."

So 'Abdul-Khāliq al-Ghujdawāni ق said, "Since you are insisting, I will give you the taste of *taṣawwuf*, some sweet fruit."

The shaykh said, "Yes, that is what I want!" He thought that Sayyīdinā 'Abdul-Khāliq al-Ghujdawāni ق will open a book and explain to him some secrets, because he is an *'ālim* (scholar) and that is how he learned. So he waited and saw the shaykh bringing a donkey, an axe, and a rope.

'Abdul-Khāliq said, "Shaykh al-Islam, you want to learn *taṣawwuf*?"

"Yes, I want to sit with you and learn from you"

He said, "No, you will sit with my donkey!"

People come to Mawlana Shaykh Nazim ق and say, "We want to sit with you." What do you mean? You are nothing; you need to fight with your ego first and then come! These are sulṭāns; come to them as such!

So he said, "Go, cut wood, and bring it. That is your job." They were in Merv, where it is very cold in the winter. And he added, "Go up to that mountain and use this road to get there." So how will Shaykh ul-Islam take the donkey up the mountain and bring back wood, as someone might see him. 'Abdul Khāliq al-Ghujdawāni ق wants to teach him humbleness. "Go and get yourself straightened out."

At one street, people saw him in the village. Children began to throw stones at him. People leave their children, especially in the West. If the children break the whole mosque, it is no problem. Now they made the child the shaykh and adults are their *murīds*! If children are not disciplined in childhood, you cannot later control them when they are older. It is better to give a little bit of discipline when the child is still young, because they will forget you disciplined them. If not, they will grow up and become gangsters and join gangs. How many children around the world are joining gangs? You cannot bring them back.

So the children were running behind him throwing stones, saying, "Shaykh ul-Islam has a donkey!"

He came back and asked ʿAbdul-Khāliq al-Ghujdawāni ق, "Can I change the route and go through the back roads?"

ʿAbdul-Khāliq said, "You want to change something? How dare you even ask me!"

Today Mawlana Shaykh Nazim ق is very soft. He doesn't say anything to people. You should have seen him twenty or thirty years ago! ʿAbdul Khāliq al-Ghujdawāni ق said, "Since you asked, now you have to go through the main roads of the city."

He wants to give him *shawāriq al-anwār,* manifestations of Heavens. One comes, the other goes, and each is different in color. But first, you have to get the key. As Sayyīdinā Mūsā ﷺ objected to Sayyīdinā Khiḍr's ﷺ actions, likewise, Shaykh ul-Islam complained.

At the first level, he said, "Can I go through the road where no one see me?" and ʿAbdul Khāliq al-Ghujdawāni ق said, "No, you go through the main roads now." And as he was going, more children and many people behind him were saying, "Shaykh ul-Islam is crazy."

So he came back, complaining, "O! That original road was better. Can you put me back on that road? They are bothering me on this one too much."

Sayyīdinā ʿAbdul-Khāliq al-Ghujdawāni ق said, "You are saying this, so give me back my donkey, my rope, and my axe. Now go and clean the toilets of the city."

Ṭarīqah is not easy; through it they bring all difficulties to your nose. "Go and clean what people don't." That is why the *khadim* (servant) of the *masjid* is the first to enter Paradise, not the *imām* or the *muʿazzin*. Even if the *imām* memorized the entire Qur'an and *hadīth,* the one cleaning the restrooms will be sent to Paradise first. Allāh looks at sweet people, ones who don't raise their heads, especially who are cleaning the *masjid;* they don't complain that someone asked them to clean the *masjid*. The person who is cleaning is carrying the waste of those who are arrogant. They don't care. They don't say, "We have to volunteer and come to clean the *masjid*." No, they are not caring.

Sayyīdinā ʿAbdul Khāliq al-Ghujdawāni ق said, "You go and clean the city restrooms."

Shaykh ul-Islam knew that he is not giving difficulty to him, but to his ego. So he did as the shaykh said. Forty days later, he came back and the shaykh said, "Now you can receive your trust." Sayyīdinā ʿAbdul Khāliq al-Ghujdawāni gave him his *amānah.*

So Sharīʿah is first, but you have to combine it with *ṭarīqah.* Or else, you will feel arrogant. Therefore, you need to say, *"Yā Rabbī,* I don't know and they don't know. Whatever you inspire to my heart, that is what I need and they need." May Allāh keep us on the track of Ahl as-sunnah wal-Jamaʿah, or else we will be falling on the ways of Shayṭān and never coming out.

Today, unfortunately we are falling into this problem; we don't accept advice. If someone tells you something, don't say, "Who are you?" Listen, you may benefit. When Shaykh Sharafuddīn ق was asked, "Why are you giving so much attention to that young one (Grandshaykh ʿAbdAllāh)," he said, "My nephew? If a child now will go to his house and say, 'Your shaykh is telling you to go to Madinah or to Mecca,' he will not *yatarajā,* hesitate. Without any doubt and without asking anything, without even saying farewell to his wife and children, he will open the door and start walking to Mecca or Madinah. He will not question or say, 'I need a ticket or a camel or a donkey, or provisions.' He will go forward, not backward!"

Not even say *salām* to his wife. Who can do that now? *Taṣawwuf* is belief in what the shaykh says, or you believe, "When someone says something to me I do it, knowing my shaykh might be making that person speak."

May Allāh ﷻ forgive us!

Wa min Allāhi 't-tawfiq, bi ḥurmati 'l-ḥabīb, bi ḥurmati 'l-Fātiḥah.
And with Allāh is success. For the sake of the Beloved, for his sake we recite the opening chapter of Holy Qur'an.

Awliyaullah Teach Tawhid by Example

A'ūdhu billāhi min ash-Shayṭān ir-rajīm. Bismillāhi' r-Raḥmāni 'r-Raḥīm. Nawaytu 'l-arbā'īn, nawaytu 'l-'itikāf, nawaytu'l-khalwah, nawaytu 'l-'uzlah, nawaytu 'r-riyāḍa, nawaytu 's-sulūk, lillāhi Ta'alā fī hādhā 'l-masjid. Ati' ūllāh wa ati'ū 'r-Rasūl wa ūli 'l-amri minkum. (4:59)

A*llāhu Akbar*! This small instrument (smart phone) has a picture of a microphone, and the phone is recording everything; taking pictures, recording sound, and storing it for whenever you need it. This is a *dunyā* innovation. Allāh's Creation is more and more advanced. Why is there competition? Allāh's Creation is much more able to take this knowledge and store it, and whenever we need it we can access it. Allāh ﷻ cannot leave his servant in the hands of Shayṭān, so He gave us ammunition and said, "Use it." How should we use it? By performing *'ibadah.*

Allāh said in Holy Qur'an:

Ma khalaqta al-jinna wa 'l-ins illa li-ya'budūn. mā urīdu minhum min rizqin wa mā urīdu an yuṭ'imūn.

And I created not the jinns and ins (humans) except they should worship Me (Alone). I seek not any provision from them, nor do I ask that they should feed Me. (Sūrat adh-Dhāriyāt, 51:57)

There might be a lot of *jinn* sitting here; if we can see, we see them. "I didn't create *jinn* and *ins* except to worship Me." This means there are *jinn* among us, sitting and listening. I don't know if they are sitting now and listening, but for sure *mu'min jinn* will sit and listen wherever Allāh's Name is mentioned. So what does Allāh want from them? Worship. He didn't create them to work. "I don't want any *rizq* from them, to provide themselves. I will provide for them." But people today are greedy, they want too much. So Allāh ﷻ is saying, "Okay, if you want too much, struggle for it. I gave some people too much because it is My will and no one can object. To some people I gave a little bit; that is My will and no one can object."

It is said that Allāh ﷻ has given His *awlīyā* their needs, without them running or struggling, as they struggled enough on Allāh's Way, and now Allāh gives to them for the benefit of His servants, to help them. One duty is *ash-shukr,* to thank Him. *Awlīyā* are thanking him, and we are forgetting. We thank Him when someone recovers from a sickness; then you say, "*Yā Rabbī,* thank you!" Then you remember. (An attendee entering the assembly stumbles.) Just now Allāh gave an immediate sign to confirm what we are saying: someone tripped. Allāh doesn't want anything from us. He wants us to remember Him, *bis-shukri tadūm an-niʿam,* by thanking Him, His provisions continue to you.

Awlīyāullāh's provision is endless. They offer a tray for ten to fifteen people and they all eat with their hands. In past times, all shared the same tray, not like today where everyone has a plate and we are wasting money. There was one plate for ten to fifteen people and everyone takes his share. That plate has endless *barakah* given to *awlīyāullāh's* food. They never run out. They are thanking for the food in front of them and Allāh keeps giving without you seeing.

For some of them, Allāh puts the *barakah* in the food, so that food increases more and more. That is a sign of the *aqṭāb awlīyā,* (a *quṭb*): Budalā, Nujabā, Nuqabā, Awtād, and Akhyār. Some people come to them needing money; for some Allāh sends angels, by His Wish, angels, that put like this under that *walī's* prayer rug whatever they need. When he doesn't have, he puts his hand under his prayer rug, takes from there and gives to others.

Did you see that in your life, someone taking money from under his carpet and give? That is rare; it is only for certain *awlīyā.* I saw it. Once in Damascus, in the eighties, there was someone who had to pay money to an official institution, a government loan had to be repaid and it was very crucial or he would go to jail. It was a big amount of money. I witnessed that. So he collected that money and put it in a bag, it was over one million, and they don't deal with checks there so he was carrying cash. He was on his way to pay, when there was an airstrike on Damascus. That car was blown up, the money was gone, but that person was safe! All that money burned and disappeared, but the government didn't care and told him, "You still have to pay!"

Where could he go to get the money? He had heard that on the mountain there is someone who is a *walī,* so he went to him. He drove up the mountain with three or four Mercedes Benz sedans, and his security detail, going up the mountain to that *walī's* house. People were running from all over the mountain to see that. They had never seen black cars with dark tinted glass and security. They all wondered, who are these people

That man got out of the car to see the *walī.* These are from *karamāt* al-Awlīyā. He stepped down and went down directly to that tiny house that was standing just through *barakah;* it may be if you shake one of its wooden pillars the house will go into *sajdah*! He came in, and that *walī* welcomed him. He came and sat there and didn't talk.

Then he said, "O my shaykh! Pray for me."

That *walī* said, "I was praying for you before you came here, you don't recall that you were saved? I was there."

Immediately he kissed the shaykh's hand. That person was from Āhlu 'l-Bayt and was very well-known. There was war in the streets. I was sitting there.

He said, "*Yā Sayyīdī*! I am in a big problem; I have to deliver that money to that institution, and it's gone. I need your help." He looked at the shaykh and said, "At least I can postpone that payment until you can help me. I am ready to take this one down with me to speak with the officials to tell them the money is coming!" And he looked at *me*!

I said, "How we can go during all this bombardment?"

He answered, "Don't worry, I can bring a military tank here to take you down to speak with them."

That *walī* said, "No need. We have people to speak to. Come tomorrow."

I said to that *walī* (Mawlana Shaykh Nazim), "You are promising him, but where will you get that money?"

He said, as usual, "Don't worry: *mā 'urīdu minhum min rizqin wa mā 'urīdu 'an yuṭʿimūn.* "I seek not any provision from them nor do I ask that they should feed Me. (I only want them to worship Me.)" (51:57)

What! Not to worry? That was thirty years ago and it is like today, still people worry too much. I was at that time in my early thirties. These people to whom he had to give the money are not normal people, they are mafia types, very dangerous. So he came the next day and brought lots of food in cooking pots, maybe forty trays of rice and meat, brought on something like a truck. Mawlana called the whole district to come and eat. All lined up and came to eat that food that, with Mawlana's *barakah*, never finished. They ate and prayed Dhuhr, then ʿAṣr, and then they wanted to go. Mawlana put his hand under his carpet and brought out a piece of paper. I looked. That man was shocked.

He said, "These people need cash!"

Mawlana said, "Take this piece of paper and don't talk, don't tell me anything, just take it and go!"

Sometimes Mawlana is very serious, so the man took the paper. I was very curious to see what was on the paper. Written on it, like a check, "Take this paper and deposit it." And usually they never accept paper to deposit. But the man took the paper and deposited it. The next day he came and kissed Mawlana's feet and said, "O Mawlana! They took the paper." Even though they never accept checks, and in three or four days that money was in that man's account! You cannot imagine that, but I saw it.

And *awlīyā* provide for Āhlu 'l-Bayt; so many poor homes of Āhlu 'l-Bayt are living from that one's generosity. *Awlīyā* don't turn away the Āhlu 'l-Bayt; they help them and that is a miracle and *wa khalaqAllāhu ʿalā sajādatihi aw khalwatihi darāhim.* "Those who are on Allāh's Way, Allāh will not put them down." He will create under their carpets money to help the needy!

So we have to learn, for *dunyā,* if you want a lot of money, struggle. No problem; work hard and get it. But, if you want a normal life you don't need to struggle. Because Allāh ﷻ will make *dunyā* a slave for you. Today anyone who goes to visit Mawlana Shaykh will never leave without something in his hand, and Mawlana is sitting on his couch and not working. He just goes and opens the drawer, and the drawer is always full. You didn't see the drawer where he is sitting? Where is the drawer? Near his feet, anyone could come, open it and take.

Allāh ﷻ provides for them as they provide for the *ummah.* Now those people want the fruit, they don't want only the shell. Sharīʿah (law), *Ḥaqīqat* (reality), *dhahir* (remembrance), and *batin* (the hidden) are important for them. They have to go side by side, parallel to each other. You cannot take one and leave the other or the scale is not in balance.

Sayyīdinā ʿAbdul Qadir Jilani said, "*ʿIsma kalāmī!*" They are strong and not playing with their *murīds.* If you have sincerity in your heart, and what is on your tongue is also what you show in your actions—not that what you show on your tongue is not what you have in your heart, not if they are something else—that sincerity will *yudfiʿ nāru ṭabaʿk,* put out the fire of your ego. The ego has been raised since childhood. The *walī* has been raised, Allāh made his father and mother raise him in a straight way, and they have pure parents who raise their children well. It depends on how you raise your child, as you reflect on him good or bad characteristics.

That is why we say, *an nafs at-tiflatil-madhmūmah,* "the spoiled-child ego." That is called *tabaʿ,* "imprinted character" from mother and father and the environment around you. So if the environment is *Shayṭānic* then what will come? It is the same for the child. So if your environment is sincere, it will put out the fire of your *nafs* and break the arrogance of your self, that you think you are so important that you don't want anyone to say anything to you.

But you should know that if someone says bad things to you, if they curse you and you keep quiet, you get rewards. If you don't keep quiet and you lose your temper, then you are fighting back and you lose the reward. So don't show your anger, that will break your arrogance and your temper will come down. That anger comes with arrogance. And you don't go to a place if you know there will be a fight; if you go to involve yourself, you are losing. If you let your feet take you to a place where there is a problem, you are destroying the house of your religion.

Nafs, dunyā, hawā', Shayṭān: these are the four things destroying your religion. *Nafs,* the self, and *dunyā,* the world; the head of every sin is love of the world and Shayṭān is pushing you to go there. They take your religion and your world. Don't listen to those *munafiqīn,* hypocrites, who are fake and decorate themselves with all kinds of importance. Because *at-taba*ʿ, the self, has grown on the kind of characteristic that always like to listen to *kalām muzakhkhraf,* ornamented, fancy words.

That is why, and I am sorry to say, scholars have fancy words in their presentations. As you go in to their talks, you come out the same (without benefit), because there is no *barakah.* They are not *awlīyā* and they cannot dress you in what they are speaking. *Awlīyā* have very simple language.

Like Ibn Muqafa ﷺ, who used a language called *as-sahil al-muntani*ʿ, "the easy language," but no one else can do it. *Mumtani*ʿ means, "difficult." He was most famous for that. It is very simple language, but very hard to imitate. *Awlīyā* have that kind of language, that is so simple, but it goes to the heart.

Their language is so simple but so strong. Scholars cannot do that. They describe to you, but Allāh didn't give them the authority to dress you with what they are saying. Some give you fancy words but cannot dress you with what they say, and others speak very simply but can dress you with the realities. Fancy words are like dough that has not been cooked well and has no salt (taste); it is still raw and when you eat it your stomach becomes upset. When you sit in the presence of these scholars, you feel okay as they are making the dough, but when you go out you have darkness coming on you, because their words have arrogance. You can be a scholar but know your limits, and when you stand at the door of a *walī* you must respect what the *walī* says.

During his *ṣuḥbah* Mawlana said to someone, "Sayyid, come," and it is rare that Mawlana stops his *ṣuḥbah.* It means, "Come and sit near me," as that one was sitting on the floor. That was Habib ʿAlī Jafri, who said, "O my shaykh! Give me *ijāzah* on *dhikr*." That means, "Give me a *wird* to use for *barakah*."

That is how they show they know the level of *awlīyā,* and in what relationship they stand. So he knows this one, although Mawlana speaks a simple language, and they respect it because they are real *ʿulamā,* and he showed respect to Mawlana. If you show respect to *awlīyā,* Allāh gives you more. From that visit ʿAlī Jafri is going to be higher, as he humbled himself to visit Mawlana.

So the difference is, when *awlīyā* make the dough it is cooked well and there are no upset stomachs. When they put the dough in the fire, know that the shaykh is cooking your dough, your ego. He has to cook it very well and sometimes he might burn it because it is too much and not a normal dough that will be fixed with heat. He has to burn your ego completely so you can receive. When your ego is finished then you can see all these manifestations. And *awlīyāullāh* know when you are ready.

Once we were coming to Grandshaykh's house, where you have to go through a narrow alley about two meters wide, and on one side is the house and on the other side is the mosque, and you pass under the window. As we were passing under it, we heard Grandshaykh ق shouting and shouting and shouting. That was in 1969; time is passing. We were mesmerized and could not move, because if he sensed our presence we may have entered that problem, that fire! We didn't know who was in there. Grandshaykh was shouting all kinds of words, I will not repeat them now. And at the end he said, "Go! I don't want to see you here!"

From his house you leave through an alley, and we saw Mawlana Shaykh Nazim coming out, smiling!

We said, "Mawlana! How can we go up, already you had a shower."

He said, "Go up."

So you go up the stairway and then in the hallway, and the door for Grandshaykh's room is there, and we heard him shouting for us by name, "Come, come, come." We thought, "O no! He saw us," not with normal sight, but he knew. Me and my brother, Shaykh Adnan, entered there trembling, and Grandshaykh ق looked at us, smiling.

He said, "That Nazim Effendi, however much I shout at him, his love never changes. I was shouting at him by order of Prophet ﷺ and I never saw in him any change, in his eyes or in his face."

Awlīyā are happy with that. We knew that was not a test, but a sign that you are put in a situation that he shouts at you to know how much you are progressing. Then he offered us tea and began a big *ṣuḥbah*. His *ṣuḥbah* is not for forty minutes, it is hours long, depending on how much *tajallī* is coming. *Awlīyāullāh* know you, and know the ego, and attack it to take away anger!

Today Mawlana cannot speak to any *murīd* like that, because they will not come back if he shouts at them. You must be careful and be happy when he shouts at you, as he is lifting away your sicknesses! When a doctor says you have an infection, *Yā Allāh*, they inject you with antibiotics at a dose more than the level of infection, to eat it. Similarly, *awlīyā* are eating your ego and *sayyi'at* when they shout at you, so be happy! Then they are taking responsibility and liability for you, and they will be asked in front of Prophet ﷺ, then you are free.

At that time, Grandshaykh ق said to us, "Don't put me in a position of shame in front of Prophet, when I present you in *sajdah* after Ṣalāt an-Najāt."

That is their responsibility and the reason Allāh gave them sainthood. May Allāh keep us under their wings to be saved in *dunyā* and *ākhirah.*

Ash-Shādhilī ؓ, *imām* of the Shādhilī Order, said, "*At-tawḥīd sīrrullāh,* that Divine Oneness is the secret of Allāh's knowledge, *was-sidqu sayfullāh,* and by saying the truth and being trustworthy you become Allāh's sword. *Wa madadu sayfī bismillāh,* and the support of this sword is by *Bismillāhi' r-Raḥmāni 'r-Raḥīm.*" That sword will be moving and we will discuss this tomorrow.

You see, look outside and take *ḥikmah,* wisdom. It is seven o'clock and still dark, but yesterday it was seven o'clock and sunny. What happened? Today the clouds hide the sun, but the sun is there. So the heart is a sun on which Allāh manifests His Beauty, on the hearts of human beings, but if there is cloud you cannot see, it is dark. So Shayṭān tries to put veils. *Awlīyā* say there are 70,000 veils between us and Prophet ﷺ. You need a shaykh to burn them. So sometimes they let you do something in order to shout at you, and that works out nicely (as when they shout, they lift the bad character that veils you). So that cloud is covering the sun of your heart. If we do not make sure Shayṭān is not taking over our hearts then the veils becomes very thick, like in Antarctica, it is snowing and snowing, and for thousands of years ice has been building up into an iceberg or "ice shelf" that doesn't melt.

Today they sell dry ice, which doesn't melt easily and lasts longer. Regarding the ice of the heart, the *Shayṭānic* veils on the heart are so thick, it becomes so difficult to dissolve them. As doctors today use lasers to take a stone from the bladder, your shaykh is your laser and he can shoot those thick veils and, *Allāhu Akbar,* what happens? It dissolves them completely. That is what we need, a "laser shaykh," not a "flashlight shaykh." (laughter) He shoots his laser and destroys the veils completely and immediately. It disseminates, takes the knots away completely and shows you your reality.

These meetings under Mawlana Shaykh's name are taking away the veils like a laser treatment, but leaving the common veil, *hijab al-awām*. It is very thick, and they keep it until you are ready for them to take it away. May Allāh take away our veils, so that we see the reality of our shaykh and the reality of Prophet ﷺ!

Wa min Allāhi 't-tawfiq, bi ḥurmati 'l-ḥabīb, bi ḥurmati 'l-Fātiḥah.
And with Allāh is success. For the sake of the Beloved, for his sake we recite the opening chapter of Holy Qur'an.

The Secret of the Name "Allah"

A'ūdhu billāhi min ash-Shayṭān ir-rajīm. Bismillāhi' r-Raḥmāni 'r-Raḥīm. Nawaytu 'l-arbā'īn, nawaytu 'l-'itikāf, nawaytu'l-khalwah, nawaytu 'l-'uzlah, nawaytu 'r-riyāḍa, nawaytu 's-sulūk, lillāhi Ta'alā fī hādhā 'l-masjid. Ati' ūllāh wa ati'ū 'r-Rasūl wa ūli 'l-amri minkum. (4:59)

Whatever we have spoken about this month on issues of *dhikrūllāh* and the best characters, it is the description of how *awlīyāullāh* lived their lives through *dhikrūllāh* and Maqām al-Iḥsān. They are not like regular people; they live in a regular life, but Allāh gave something special to their hearts, as the Prophet ﷺ said, "Allāh has given to Abū Bakr aṣ-Ṣiddīq, *shay'in waqara fī qalbihi,"* something that took root in his heart, beyond description. The *Ṣaḥābah* ﷺ were wondering about that and later they knew it was *dhikrūllāh.* He was always remembering Allāh ﷻ on his tongue and in his heart.

Once the Prophet ﷺ made his famous *ḥadīth, Allāhumā lā takilnī ila nafsī ṭarfata 'aynun wa lā aqal,* "O Allāh! Don't leave me to my ego for the blink of an eye or less." The eye blinks twenty to thirty times per minute, maybe more. Prophet ﷺ said, "O Allāh! Don't leave me to myself for the blink of an eye." He wants to express in that in such a short moment, two or three seconds, "If I rely on my ego I might fall down."

The Seal of Messengers ﷺ is *ma'ṣūm,* infallible, and he is saying, "O Allāh! Don't leave me to myself for the blink of an eye or less." What is less? How much less? It might be a lot less. He knew, since Allāh ﷻ gave him knowledge that in a fraction of a second, time disappears. Scientists recently discovered that if you go 10^{-22} of a second, it becomes energy only and time disappears. It means, "O Allāh! Don't ever leave me to myself."

What about us? When he heard this *ḥadīth,* look how Sayyīdinā Abū Bakr aṣ-Ṣiddīq reacted. It is completely different than what we do. For us, we hear hundreds of thousands of *ḥadīth.* So what will we have? We never change. Can a donkey be changed? Its ears are always long; it might be we are donkeys with long ears. We never change; we hear, we hear, we hear, and it is the same, *ṭaba',* as what you have been raised on. That is your photocopy, your print. We are a photocopy of ourselves. However we were raised from childhood, that is what we are. So don't spoil your children from childhood. Don't give them what they like, but give them what they don't like. Today everyone gives their children what they like. Just now we were speaking and we jumped up out of anger. This is our character, all of us.

So immediately, Sayyīdinā Abū Bakr aṣ-Ṣiddīq ؓ jumped up and disappeared. He went and took a stone and put it in his mouth, and went inside the Ka'aba and wept. They were looking for him but not finding him, and Prophet ﷺ knew where he was.

He found him and said, "O, where were you? For seven days you did not come."

Abū Bakr was crying and Prophet ﷺ put his hand between his shoulders and calmed him down, like when Allāh ﷻ made the fire of Sayyīdinā 'Ibraḥīm ؑ to be a cool breeze, around 69 degrees Fahrenheit, and he was very happy inside that boiling fire. When the Prophet ﷺ put his hand on Abū Bakr, all the fire that was in his heart from crying was extinguished.

Prophet ﷺ said, "Why are you crying?"

He said, "*Yā Rasūlullāh*! I know you are the Seal of Messengers and Allāh gave you *shafā'a* to intercede for believers on the Day of Judgment. You are infallible, and still you said, 'O my Lord! Don't leave me to my self for the blink of an eye.' What then will happen to me, if I leave myself to my ego for the blink of an eye?" Two seconds. Count it. It is so quick! How many times does Shayṭān come to our heart in a second or less?

Sayyīdinā Muḥammad ﷺ said, "*Yā* Abū Bakr! Allāh mentioned you in Holy Qur'an two times, when He said:

> *Illa tanṣu Rūḥu faqad naṣarahu 'Llāh. Idh akhrajahu 'Lladhīna kafarū thānīya ithnayni idh humā fī 'lghār. idh yaqūlū li-ṣāḥibhi lā taḥzan inna 'Llāha ma'nā fa-anzal 'Llāhu sakīnatahu 'alayhi wa ayyadahu bi-junūdin lam tarawhā wa ja'ala kalimat 'Lladhīna kafarū as-suflā wa kalimatu'Llāhi hīya 'l-'ulyā wa'Llāhu 'Azīzun Ḥakīm.*
>
> *If you help him not, still Allāh helped him when those who disbelieve drove him forth, the second of two; when they two were in the cave, when he said to his comrade, "Grieve not. Lo! Allāh is with us." Then Allāh caused His Peace of Reassurance to descend upon him and supported him with hosts you cannot see, and made the word of those who disbelieved the lowest, while Allāh's Word became the highest. Allāh is Mighty, Wise.*
>
> (Sūrat at-Tawba, 9:40)

He is "the second of two." He and the Prophet ﷺ were together in Ghāri Thawr, when they emigrated from Mecca to Madinah. "He made you my friend. No one took that honor but you." Sayyīdinā Abū Bakr ؓ was older than Prophet ﷺ. "And He called you aṣ-Ṣiddīq al-Akbar, 'the greatest ṣiddīq.' Whatever I said, you would say, 'It is the truth, yā Rasūlullāh.' He made you Ṣādiq and ṣiddīq."

Sayyīdinā Abū Bakr ؓ said, "Yā Rasūlullāh! On Judgment Day, if Allāh calls me and says, 'I made you ṣiddīq and I made you Ṣādiq and I made you second in the cave,' and then He says, 'Now I am changing it,' can anyone object or complain? No. So whatever He said about me, on Judgment Day He can change it. Then what will happen?" That also means, "Yā Rasūlullāh! Allāh gave you shafā'a but if He changes it, He changes it."

That will never happen, as Allāh will never change His grant! But Prophet ﷺ heard this and began to cry with him. Grandshaykh ق always told this story to let us know that if Allāh will change something, then what will happen? We will be in a gray area with our 'amal, and for sure we will go to Hellfire, but with Allāh's mercy we are in Paradise! So they were both crying, and there were rivers of tears coming from their eyes. Why did they cry? Each tear that came from the eye of Prophet ﷺ represents a human being, and the Prophet cried on all human beings of Ummat an-Nabī until Sayyīdinā Jibrīl came and said, "Stop!"

Those individual drops represent one human being, and all of them are under the shafā'a of Prophet! Allāh said it in Holy Qur'an:

walladhīna ma'ahu ashiddāu 'alā al-kuffāri ruḥamā'u baynahum.
Muḥammad is the Messenger of Allāh, and those who are with him are severe against disbelievers, and merciful among themselves.   (Sūrat al-Fatḥ, 48:29)

Here kuffār may mean "the self." You cannot be loose on your ego and tough on others; you must be loose on others and strict on your ego! And Allāh gave the same for the People of the Book, those believing in the Injīl (New Testament), and those believing in the Torah of Mūsā (Old Testament).

So Sayyīdinā Abū Bakr ؓ was crying and crying, and by Allāh's order he stopped. When he cried, each tear that fell represents one Naqshbandi follower, and each will be under safety! Then Sayyīdinā Jibrīl ؑ came and said, "Allāh sends His salām and says, 'As much as my Lordship, I am not changing! They have a certificate of bara'ah, innocence." Do we have something like that? If so, be happy and keep smiling and laughing all your life! If not, we have to remain worried about what will happen to us. So it is not only reading; we read hundreds of *ḥadīth,* and what changed in us? Nothing.

How can you change? If you are sick, if your body is infected, you take injection of antibiotics, or you take pills or whatever there is, and the only remedy is an injection from outside you; it is not coming from within you. You cannot swallow tablets without putting your hand on your tongue. You cannot have an injection with holding your hands together. That injection has to come from outside, then it has an effect, but if from inside it has no effect.

Sometimes they give not only antibiotics, but anti-inflammatories and Cortisone, if the illness is severe. So who can prescribe what you need? You need a doctor. So Sayyīdinā Abdul Qadir al-Jilani said, *ʿālim yukhadh min afwāhir-rijāl lā min aṣ-ṣuḥuf.* That injection has to "come from the mouth of men who reached manhood (sainthood)." Also ladies reached sainthood; we cannot say no.) So anyone who reached the level of sainthood is able to diagnose your sickness and prescribe what you need, an injection that has to come from outside you, not from within you.

That is why he said, *al-ʿilm yukhadh min afwāhir-rijāl lā min aṣ-ṣuḥuf,* "It cannot be taken from papers, it has to be taken from their mouth or their eyes, and they send on you ʿIlmu 'l-Yaqīn (Knowledge of Certainty), ʿAynu 'l-Yaqīn (Eye of Certainty), and Ḥaqqu 'l-Yaqīn (Reality of Certainty). They give you an injection that gives you knowledge and raises you up, first to the level of *ʿilm,* knowledge, then to the level of *ʿayn,* vision. With another deadly injection, they raise you to the level of *ḥaqq,* the reality, where there is no more question about *tawḥīd.* Your understanding is certain, in your heart and mind, then you know that everything in this life points to the Creator. There is no more hesitation or doubts, finished! That has many levels, which we might discuss in the future.

So he said, don't take from papers. *Awlīyā* can use papers to teach you, but they have to sit with you, diagnose you, and prescribe the unique medicine for you. That is why they came through the *awrād.* The different *ṭarīqahs* have different *awrād,* each shaykh has his way and they might not intersect. Each *ṭarīqah* has its own *awrād* and techniques. In the Naqshbandi Way we have to follow from shaykh to shaykh, and in the *silsilah,* chain, the *awrād* may change; as time changes, they may change.

I mentioned many times that Grandshaykh ق never gave *bayaʿ* to anyone and now Mawlana Shaykh gives everyone *bayaʿ*, even on the phone or through the Internet! It depends on the time. So don't take from papers, but take it from mouth of *awlīyā,* as they will guide us.

Who are these "men"? *man hā ulai'-rijāl.* Sayyīdinā Abdul Qadir al-Jilani ق is telling his students in the famous work, al-Faid ar-Rabbani, "They are the men of truth; *al-muttaqūn,* they are sincere, they have *taqwā; at-tārikūn,* those who left *dunyā,* they let it down; *al-wārithūn,* inheritors of the Prophet; *al-ʿarifūn, man ʿarafa nafsahu faqad ʿaraf rabbah,* those who reached level of knowing Allāh; *al-mukhlisūn,* the sincere ones; *mukhlis,* who are straight on the Straight Path; *al-ʿāmilūn,* never changing from what Allāh made them to be (not like us, sometimes Mawlana says something and we don't act on it); *rijālun sadaqū mā 'ahad Allāhu ʿalayh,* men who are true to their promise, they never changed.

We change all the time, *lā ḥawla wa lā quwatta illa billāhi 'l-ʿAlīyyi 'l-ʿAẓīm*! We are changing every time and getting older and getting worse! Sayyīdinā Abū Yazīd ق said, "I respect the elder and I respect the younger. The young have less sins and the older has more worship." Now it is rare to find someone of the same age in a city; with globalization you find many people born at the same time.

So choose: men who kept their promises with Allāh, *wa mā badalū tabdīla,* they never changed throughout their lives and they are waiting for the time they will go to Allāh; whatever they are on, they are on. Are we changing? (Yes.)

Sayyīdinā Abdul Qadir ق continues, "And whatever else we have described is *hawwas* (hallucination) and *bātil* (false)." It is obsession: you want something, you need it and you don't want to let it go. You don't want to let *dunyā* to go. Who wants *dunyā* to go? No one. You want *dunyā,* then you are obsessed by *dunyā;* when you are obsessed by *dunyā* that is *bātil.* So what he said? *al-wilāyatu li 'l-muttaqīn,* "If it is not obsession and it is true, then it is right." M*uttaqīn* means "God-fearing," those who are conscious of their Lord. So those who keep their promises are those to whom Allāh ﷻ gave *dunyā* and *ākhirah.*

Allāh said, *Rabbanā ātinā fi 'd-dunyā ḥasānatan wa fi 'l-ākhirati ḥasanat,* to ask good in this life and Next. That is first level of being a true one, then you go higher and you want *ākhirah* only, then you go higher and you want only Allāh ﷻ. There are people who dropped *dunyā* completely, even non-Muslims, monks in shrines. What will Allāh do with them? We leave that judgment to Allāh. There are people who left *dunyā* and they want to be truthful to what they believe. We have to keep our truth to them in order to be saved. *Allāhumā ṣalli ʿalā Muḥammad*! That is why he said, *abʿad nafsaka ʿani 'sh-shubuhāt, wa 'sh-shahawāt,* "Don't go near gray areas from bad desires," *a'wadh nafsaka 'alā akal al-ḥalāl* "and make your ego to eat from what is *ḥalāl*."

Sayyīdinā Abdul Qadir al-Jilani ق is not speaking of meat; it means, "eat from your sweat, work!" Allāh doesn't like people who are lazy. Are you working? (No, I lost my job.) Okay, I have a job for you. Go to the *masjid* and clean the toilets. Don't sit at home like a chicken; show *'amal* and work! Like in Europe, they grant government aid to those who have children and no work. So what are they doing? They are becoming manufacturers of children; they reproduce child after child and take money! That is a business, keeping themselves busy and not lazy! (laughter)

(A baby cries.) That baby is confirming what we said. Don't be lazy, waiting for a job to open! Show Allāh that you are working, even by selling something at cost (without profit). Show Allāh that you want to eat from your sweat! Otherwise, do *'ibādah*. Do something instead of sitting all day watching TV, eating steaks and hamburger!

W 'aḥfaẓ bāṭinaka bi 'l-murāqabah, "Protect your inner self by doing *murāqabah*." Don't say meditation doesn't exist: Ghawth al-'Adham, 'Abd al-Qādir al-Jīlānī ق is mentioning it! Keep *bāṭin*, your inner self, working. If you have no work, then place a sheet over your head and for eight hours, as you normally work eight hours, do eight hours of meditation and *'ibādah* in addition to the worship you must do. Then make an account of what you did; that is for the inside, that no one sees (internal worship).

For the outside (external) that you can see, follow the *sunnah* of the Prophet ﷺ, who said, "If you love Allāh, follow me (my *sunnah*), then Allāh will love you." If Allāh loves you, you will be lucky. Then you get correct inspirations: you will hear and see. Don't say, " I am in *ṭarīqah* 25 years and not seeing anything." You reached a limit and if you break through it, then it will open for you. Don't want the shaykh to break it for you! They want you to break it, because then you will go up very high, but if shaykh breaks it you only stop at that level. So you have only one chance in life to break it. Take that chance! Then you will have right inspiration and it will hit right on target.

At that time you will be granted *mari'fatullāh*, allowed to reach heavenly divinely knowledge. May Allāh guide us! That is why Imām Shādhilī ؓ said, *at-tawḥīd sirullāh*, "(To make *dhikr* by *tawḥīd*) *lā ilāha illa-Llāh* is the Secret of Allāh." *Qul Hūw Allāhu 'Āḥad*, "Say, 'He is the One Who is unique and He is known by the Name "Allāh".'" That concept is the Secret of Allāh! *wa 'ṣ-ṣidqu sayfullāh*, "To say the truth is the sword of Allāh," to fight the ego, not to go and fight and blow up people. Kill your self, the ego, first! And the support for the sword is by reciting, *Bismillāhi' r-Raḥmāni 'r-Raḥīm.*

May Allāh bless us and support us, and give our shaykh long life to see Sayyīdinā Mahdī ﷺ and Sayyīdinā ʿĪsā ﷺ, and give us long life!

Wa min Allāhi 't-tawfiq, bi ḥurmati 'l-ḥabīb, bi ḥurmati 'l-Fātiḥah.
And with Allāh is success. For the sake of the Beloved, for his sake we recite the opening chapter of Holy Qur'an.

Series Conclusion: Characters, Powers & Responsibilities of the Ghawth & His Aqtab

Aʿūdhu billāhi min ash-Shayṭān ir-rajīm. Bismillāhi' r-Raḥmāni 'r-Raḥīm.
Nawaytu 'l-arbāʿīn, nawaytu 'l-ʿitikāf, nawaytu'l-khalwah, nawaytu 'l-ʿuzlah,
nawaytu 'r-riyāḍa, nawaytu 's-sulūk, lillāhi Taʿalā fī hādhā 'l-masjid.
Atiʿ ūllāh wa atiʿū 'r-Rasūl wa ūli 'l-amri minkum. (4:59)

Awlīyāullāh, as we have described through these 29 days or less, have different levels and knowledges they carry in their lives. They have a strong willpower and never stop until they reach their goal and then they continue more. And it is said:

Awliyāī tahta qibābī lā yaʿlamahum ghayrī.
My awlīyā are under My domes; no one knows them except Me.
(*Ḥadīth Qudsī*)

Which saints are not known? Allāh knows them, and He knows how much they have achieved and rewarded! And we described through different sessions about their levels and what they have done. There is the *ghawth,* and under him the five *quṭbs:* Quṭb, Quṭb al-Bilād, Quṭb al-Aqtāb, Quṭb al-Irshād, Quṭb al-Mutaṣarrif. And under them are five different *awlīyā*: Budalā, Nujabā, Nuqabā, Awtād, and Akhyār. All are taking from Prophet ﷺ through their connection and their lineage, and we have mentioned that. The only one we have not described is the *ghawth.*

He takes from heart of Prophet ﷺ directly and he is *fardu 'l-jamīʿ al-waḥid,* he is the unique one to whom Allāh ﷻ gave the power of keeping all *awlīyā* together. Everything goes back from him to Prophet ﷺ. He is the one that Allāh looks at seventy thousand times daily and sends on him manifestations of His Beautiful Names and Attributes, and daily these manifestations change. The *ghawth* is the one about whom Allāh ﷻ said:

mā wasiʿanī arḍī wa lā arḍī wa lākin wasiʿanī qalbi ʿabdī al-muʾmin.
Neither Earth nor Heavens contained Me, but the heart of the believer contained Me.

The *ghawth* can carry *an-Nūr al-Ilāhī,* the Heavenly Light Allāh sends. He can carry all the rest of the ummah and whatever they receive depends on their level, if they can pull it or not. He has four other sides to know: one, he takes from the heart of and carries the secret from (archangel) Sayyīdinā Azrā'īl ﷺ, who is described as *"amadat ul-ikhsas."* Allāh gave him a specialty from the "material of life and feelings," which is the secret Allāh put in every Creation to appear. The appearance is in the heart of Sayyīdinā Isrāfīl ﷺ (Archangel Rafael). When he blows the trumpet, He will pull life out from every Creation and they will die. Then another time he will blow the trumpet and give them that sensation of the reality of life, and they will come back.

The *ghawth* takes from that knowledge, and he also takes from Sayyīdinā Jibrīl ﷺ (Archangel Gabriel), the secret of "the talking self," the ability of talking through *nashāṭun insānīyyah.* It begins when the child or creature begins talking in his own language that Allāh gave him. Human beings have a language they all know, one universal language through which Allāh ﷻ made everyone communicate.

That language is in the reality of Sayyīdinā Jibrīl ﷺ, because he was the one who revealed the message to all prophets in one language that all of them understood. What he gave to Sayyīdinā Adam ﷺ was in the same language as what he gave to Sayyīdinā Ibrāhīm ﷺ, Sayyīdinā Nūḥ ﷺ, Sayyīdinā Mūsā ﷺ, Sayyīdinā ʿĪsā ﷺ, and Sayyīdinā Muḥammad ﷺ! It is the language that the heart understands and all human beings know it.

A contemporary example is, you have many languages in technology, but all can communicate in the same language. So that is the language the heart understands, but it is veiled. The *ghawth* carries that reality.

Then he takes from Sayyīdinā Mikā'īl ﷺ (Archangel Michael), because Allāh gave him power to shower rain on human beings.

Wa jaʿalna mina 'l-ma'ī kulla shay'in ḥayy.
We have made from water every living thing. (Sūrat al- Anbīyā, 21:30)

Life may come through that. The *ghawth* knows that secret of life from the heart of Sayyīdinā Mikā'īlﷺ; he takes from that and moves them. And then he takes from Sayyīdinā Isrāfīl ﷺ the power of taking people from life to death; he has the power to bring back people as Allāh wishes. He is always looking when Allāh will order him to go and take the souls of people. It means that *ghawth* takes the bad characters from people and gives them good characters on their hearts without you knowing he is doing that, by the secret that Sayyīdinā Azrā'īl ﷺ is carrying in his heart. These are the specific functions of *al-ghawthīyyatu 'l-kubra,* the greatest *quṭbīyyah,* also known as *ghawthīya quṭbīyyah.*

Ghawth means *"yughīth,"* who gives *madad* and support. He is carrying from these four angels and taking from the heart of Sayyīdinā Muḥammad ﷺ. He is the one who is able to take whatever he needs for his job, and that is not a normal job, it is a heavenly reality that has been thrown in the heart of that *ghawth.* And he has *lahu imāman,* two *imāms* or two helpers, one on the right, one on the left.

The one on the right is always looking at what is needed to get from heavenly powers, and he is the center of receiving heavenly and spiritual support. And the one who is on his left looks at all Creation and supports them with heavenly sources directly. He is responsible for everything that Allāh created, to send to them power so they will be feeling their existence on Earth. If that *walī* pulls out, everything will faint and fall down; there will be no power!

These two *imāms* have eight characteristics: four are *ẓāhir* (apparent) and four are *bāṭin* (hidden). The apparent characteristics are: they are *az-zuhhād,* ascetics; they are *dhu 'l-warʿa,* always active in doing good things and doing what Allāh ﷻ likes; *al-amr bi 'l-mʿarūf wa 'n-nahīyy ʿani 'l-munkar,* they call people for good, and prohibit them from doing wrong. But their hidden knowledge, that they don't reveal, is *aṣ-ṣidq,* they keep their covenant with Allāh ﷻ, and they don't change, they stay on their promise. They have *ikhlāṣ,* sincerity, *ḥayā,* shyness, and they are always in *murāqaba,* meditation.

The *ʿabdāl* are under them. They are *hum Āhlu 'l-faḍl wa 'l-kamāl,* "people of honor and perfection." *W 'astiqāma wa 'l-ʿitidāl,* they stay on the right path and are always in the middle, on moderation, not too much on the right or the left. Allāh took removed imagination and doubt from them. They are the ones mentioned by Prophet ﷺ in his holy *ḥadīth:*

> *If you are in a desert or a jungle and you are feeling fear, call on rijālAllāh; they will come to you and support you.*

Then there are "al-Budalā." It is said they range in number from 40 to 300. Then are "al-Nujabā," they are from 40 to 70 in number. Budalā support people in their fears or difficulties, and grant things to them in *dunyā* matters, while Nujabā do things for their *ākhirah* matters. Their work is to carry all the heaviness of bad character, *asqal al-ʿibād,* the burdens of people. They don't look anywhere except at the Divine Presence, through the five *quṭbs*, to the *ghawth*, and then to Prophet ﷺ. Their orders come from there directly, and that is what Muḥammad al-Busayrī ق knew.

He described the realities of these *awlīyā* as, *wa kullum min rasūlullāhi multamisun*, "Everyone is taking from Prophet ﷺ, asking for support and *madad*." They are well known for *kathrat al-ʿibādah*, they are always in worship. And they are always in *muhasaba* and *wa tafakkur*, analyzing the accounts of human beings; if low, they recite *ṣalawāt* and give that to the human being.

That is why human being's level rise up, and instead of remaining negative it becomes positive. If they see someone falling down on the negative side, they push them to the positive side. It is their job to keep everyone on the positive side and they don't allow anyone to go negative. One of their characters is *at-tafakkur*, they remain in concentration. They do not give an ear to this *dunyā*. They are always perfect.

Then are the Nuqabā. Allāh ﷻ gave them a different power, that they are able to reach human beings without saying anything. They keep quiet, they don't talk except through their hearts. That is why *awlīyāullāh* have one or two hours in meditation, because the strength of the heart is more than the strength of the tongue. They are very well known for *aṣ-ṣamt*, silence, and to keep awake at nights *as-sahr*, and *al-juʿ* and they are always hungry, as Prophet ﷺ said:

> *Naḥnu qawman lā nākul ḥattā najuʿ, wa idhā akalnā lā nashbʿa.*
> *We are people who don't eat until we are hungry, and we don't eat until we are full.*

Nuqabā remain hungry and their stomachs are always grumbling; that keeps them awake. They are in complete *ʿuzlah*, they seclude themselves. They have their own *imām* who leads them to the presence of Prophet ﷺ. They are *qad tahaqaqu bi ʿism al-bātin*, certain about what is hidden, and *ashrafu bi batin an-nās*, able to observe what is hidden in people, and *fastakhrajū kashaif ad-damāir*, they extract the hidden aspects of the subconscious mind. For them all veils are taken away.

Today we see that with psychiatrists; you begin to speak to them and they ask you questions and through your answers they analyze your problems. Nuqabā don't need that as they go directly to the subconscious and to the heart, and pull that out of the heart. So to pull all that from people, the psychiatrists need psychiatrists! So don't go to psychiatrists, go to Nuqabā. With Allāh's support, they know what is hidden and by that the people are cured, as Nuqabā are not veiled and can see.

The hidden aspects of the subconscious have three characteristics. First is *an-nufūs al-ʿalīyya fa hiya haqāiqul-amrīyya,* the highest level of the subconscious; when you are in a good way, you establish that high level in the subconscious and that is the certainty and reality of heavenly orders. Their eyes are on that, as it is highest level and they will come to heavenly orders.

In each day there are 24 hours and all information of what will happen is written in the Preserved Tablets. Whatever you have to do is written there, and they can see that. For everyone else that is veiled, but for them it is not veiled and they pass it to you. Then you can get this information to your heart, or your shaykh keeps it for you. That is *nufūs al-ʿaliyya.*

The second characteristic is *nufūsun suflīyya,* the subconscious that is connected with evil, it is the lowest of realities. First is positive and second is connected to Iblīs and Shayṭān, and all that is connected to the subconscious, the inner lower conscious where all these bad gossips come to the heart. The third characteristic is *nufūs al-wa satīyya,* the reality of human nature. It is in the middle level. In all the three levels, Allāh ﷻ has put a chip or implanted there all heavenly secrets that concern that person.

These heavenly secrets are 360. Why 360 secrets? Because in the body there are 360 points that you can press and activate, and every point has its secret and every point on human beings or creatures has a pressure button to activate a certain language to know what is needed in 24 hours. So these *awlīyā* are able to get that information and if you are on the right path with your *awrād,* then this information is sent to you by *awlīyā*. Then, if your power is strong, the power of these points is sent to you as inspiration.

If you are not on the right path, then *nafs as-suflīyya* will be activated, giving you bad information. If you drop both of them, then you activate *an-nafs al-ʿulwiyya;* that higher self that is always there in presence of Prophet ﷺ, in the Divine Presence. If you are able to connect to all three, these veils will be taken; if you are unable, then Nuqabā will bring these matters to you.

Al-awtād are not too many: they are four in the east, four in the west, four in the south, and four in the north. *Awtād* are like tent pegs that stabilize the tent, which has four sides, so you have four stakes. *Awtād* are the stakes of this world, the poles that keep everything strong in the east and west, north and south. They are responsible for every group in those four regions.

Allāh gave them eight different actions they must do. The apparent actions are *kathratus-siyām,* they fast excessively; *qiyam ul-layli wan-nāsu niyam,* they are awake all night and always vigilant of what is going to happen; *wa kathratul-imtithal,* they are always submitting and they say, *samiʿna wa ataʿna,* "We hear and we obey," and they never say, "no" or use their minds, and whatever is sent to them, they accept; and the fourth apparent action is, they are always in *istighfār* when people are sleeping.

That is what we can see from them. What we cannot see are their hidden actions: *hum al-mutawakilūn ʿalā Allāh,* they always put their trust in and depend on Allāh and Prophet ﷺ, they have strong trust, *thiqah;* and they are always in *taslīmiyya,* perfect submission. Then there are many of their characters we have described in these lectures.

Al-Akhyār are the last type of *aqṭāb,* and are those who have been honored, picked up, and selected. Not everyone can be from that group and it is very limited. Akhyār are directly under the five *quṭbs* and they are *akmal ahl al-arḍ,* "the most perfect of the people of Earth."

You see no difference from their physical appearance and their hidden appearance; they have balanced them. You see them as normal people. They don't have beads in their hands (to indicate piety). They go here and there, and people say they are not *awlīyā,* so why are they going there? They go for a certain reason, which you don't know. They act normally, but they are the most perfect of the people of Earth.

They never let the right hand to know what left is doing and they never put in their hearts to do any bad action or take revenge; they have no bad intent and always take everything with good intent. They know you are Allāh's servant and they cannot criticize Allāh's servants, they have to cover them. Their arteries are saturated with the taste of sincerity. They have no other taste, but the taste of sincerity throughout their physical and spiritual bodies.

They have love to everyone and no criticism. They don't like anyone to know about them. They move through the *ummah* wearing what normal people wear; they don't say, "We need a *jubba;*" they wear normal clothes. Physically and spiritually, they look like us, so trust them! They look normal, if they look different then you will know them.

Grandshaykh ق said, "These type of *awlīyā* are there every 24 hours. Even if someone is living by himself on the peak of a mountain with no humans around, in every 24-hour period there must be one of these *awlīyā* visiting him or passing by, because they give their support to everyone. These are the ones who appear. Allāh gave them the ability to appear to every person physically, or spiritually through dreams."

પ્ર ଓ

This is the conclusion of "Ramadan Series 2010". May Allāh ﷻ grant Shaykh Nazim al-Haqqani long life and good health, and may Allāh bless us to be with him, to see Sayyīdinā Mahdī ؏!

Wa min Allāhi 't-tawfīq, bi ḥurmati 'l-ḥabīb, bi ḥurmati 'l-Fātiḥah.
And with Allāh is success. For the sake of the Beloved, for his sake we recite the opening chapter of Holy Qur'an.

Islamic Calendar and Holy Days

The Islamic calendar is lunar-based, with twelve months of 29 or 30 days. A lunar year is shorter than a solar year, so Muslim holy days cycle back in the Gregorian (Western) calendar. This is how Ramaḍān is celebrated at different times of the year, as the annual Islamic calendar is ten days shorter than the Gregorian calendar.

Four Islamic months are sacred: Muharram, Rajab, Dhūl-Qʿadah and Dhūl-Hijjah. Holy months include "God's Month" (Rajab), "Prophet's Month" (Shaʿbān) and the "Month of the People" (Ramaḍān), in which pious acts are rewarded more generously.

Months of the Islamic Calendar

Muḥarram	Rajab
Safar	Shaʿbān
Rabīʿ ul-Awwal (Rabīʿ I)	Ramaḍān
Rabīʿ uth-Thāni (Rabīʿ II)	Shawwāl
Jumāda al-Awwal (Jumādi I)	Dhū'l-Qʿadah
Jumāda uth-Thāni (Jumādi II)	Dhū'l-Hijjah

al-Hijrah

The 1st of Muharram marks the beginning of the Islamic New Year, chosen because it is the anniversary of Prophet Muḥammad's ﷺ historic *hijrah* (migration) from Mecca to Madinah, where he established the first, preeminent Muslim community in which he introduced unprecedented social reforms, including civil law, human and women's rights, religious tolerance, taxation to serve the community, and military ethics.

ʿAshura

On 10th Muharram, ʿAshūra commemorates many sacred events, such as Noah's ark coming to rest, the birth of Abraham, and the building of the Kaʿbah in Mecca. ʿAshūra is a major holy day, marked with two days of fasting, on the $9^{th}/10^{th}$ or on $10^{th}/11^{th}$ based on a holy tradition (*hadīth*) of Sayyīdinā Muḥammad ﷺ.

Mawlid

Mawlid al-Nabī, 12th Rabiʿ al-Awwal, commemorates Prophet Muḥammad's birth in 570. Mawlid is celebrated globally throughout this month in huge communal gatherings in which a famous poem "Qasīdah al-Burdah" is recited, accompanied by drummers, illustrious poetry recitals, religious singing, eloquent sermons, gift giving, feasts, and feeding the poor. Most Muslim nations observe Mawlid as a national holiday.

Laylat al-Isra wal-Mi'raj

Literally, "the Night Journey and Ascension;" 27th of Rajab is when Sayyīdinā Muḥammad ﷺ physically traveled from Mecca to Jerusalem, ascended in all the levels of Heaven from a rock in the Dome of the Rock, and returned to Mecca—while his bed was still warm. In the Night Journey, Islam's five daily prayers were ordained by God. Sayyīdinā Muḥammad ﷺ also prayed with Abraham, Moses, and Jesus in Jerusalem's al-Aqsa Mosque, signifying that Muslims, Christians, and Jews follow one god. This holy event designated Jerusalem as the third holiest site in Islam, after Mecca and Madinah.

Laylat al-Bara'ah

The "Night of Freedom from Fire" occurs on 15th Shaʿbān. On this night God's Mercy is great; hence, the night is spent reciting Holy Qurʿan and special prayers, as well as visiting the deceased.

Ramadan

Many regard Ramaḍān, the 9th month of the Islamic calendar, the holiest month of the year. Muslims observe a strict fast and participate in pious activities such as charitable giving and peace making. It is a time of intense spiritual renewal for those who observe it. Fasting is meant to instill social awareness of the needy, and to promote gratitude for God's endless favors. The fast is typically broken in a communal setting, and hence Ramaḍān is a highly social month. At night, a special Ramaḍān prayer known as "Tarawīh" is offered in congregation, in which one-thirtieth of the Holy Qurʿan is recited by the *imām* (prayer leader); thus the entire holy book of 6,000 verses is recited in this month.

Eid al-Fitr

"Festival of Fast-Breaking" marks the end of Ramaḍān and is celebrated the first three days of Shawwāl. It is a time for charity and celebration with family and friends for completing a month of blessings and joy. In the Last Days of Ramaḍān, each Muslim family gives "Zakāt al-Fitr"(charity of fast-breaking) which consists of cash and/or food, to help the poor. On the first early morning of Eid, Muslims observe a special congregational prayer, such as Christmas/Easter Mass or the High Holy Days. After Eid prayer is a time to visit family and friends, and give gifts and money (especially to children). Many specialty foods and sweets are prepared solely for Eid days. In most Muslim countries, the entire three days of Eid is a national holiday.

Yawm al-Arafat

"Day of ʿArafat," the 9th Dhul-Hijjah, occurs just before the celebration of Eid al-Adha. Pilgrims on Hajj assemble for the "standing" on the plain of ʿArafat, located outside Mecca, where they contemplate the Day of Standing (Resurrection Day). Muslims elsewhere in the world fast this day, and gather at a local mosque for prayers. Thus, those who cannot perform Hajj that year still honor the sacrifice of Abraham.

Eid al-Adha

The "Feast of Sacrifice," celebrated from the 10th-13th Dhul-Hijjah, marks Prophet Abraham's willingness to sacrifice his son Ismāʿīl on God's order. To honor this event, Muslims perform Hajj, the pilgrimage to Mecca that is incumbent on every mature Muslim once in their life if they have the means. Celebrations begin with an animal sacrifice to commemorate Sayyīdinā Abraham's sacrifice. In Islam, he is known as *Khalilullāh*, "God's friend." Many consider him the first Muslim and a premiere role model, for his obedience to God and willingness to sacrifice his only child without even questioning the command.

Glossary

ʿabd (pl. *ʿibād*): lit. slave, servant.
ʿAbdAllāh: Lit., "servant of God"
Abū Bakr aṣ-Ṣiddīq: the closest Companion of Prophet Muḥammad; the Prophet's father-in-law, who shared the *Hijrah* with him. After the Prophet's death, he was elected the first caliph (successor); known as one of the most saintly Companions.
Abū Yazīd/Bayāzīd Bistāmī: A great ninth century *walī* and a master of the Naqshbandi Golden Chain.
adab: good manners, proper etiquette.
adhān: call to prayer.
SubḥānAllāh: the Hereafter; afterlife.
al-: Arabic definite article, "the"
ʿalāmīn: world; universes.
Alḥamdūlillāh: praise God.
ʿAlī ibn Abī Ṭālib: first cousin of Prophet Muḥammad, married to his daughter Fāṭimah; the fourth caliph.
alif: first letter of Arabic alphabet.
ʿAlīm, al-: the Knower, a divine attribute
Allāh: proper name for God in Arabic.
Allāhu Akbar: God is Greater.
ʿāmal: good deed (pl. *ʿamāl*).
amīr (pl., *umarā*): chief, leader, head of a nation or people.
anā: first person singular pronoun
anbīyā: prophets (sing. *nabī*).
ʿaql: intellect, reason; from the root *ʿaqila*: lit., "to fetter."
ʿArafah, ʿArafat: a plain near Mecca where pilgrims gather for the principal rite of Hajj.
ʿarif: knower, Gnostic; one who has reached spiritual knowledge of his Lord.
ʿĀrifūnʿ bil-Lāh: knowers of God.
Ar-Raḥīm: The Mercy-Giving, Merciful, Munificent, one of Allāh's ninety-nine Holy Names.
Ar-Raḥmān: The Most Merciful, Compassionate, Beneficent; the most repeated of Allāh's Holy Names.
ʿarsh, al-: the Divine Throne.
aṣl: root, origin, basis.
astāghfirullāh: lit. "I seek Allāh's forgiveness."
Awlīyāullāh: saints of Allāh (sing. *walī*).
āyah/āyāt (pl. *Ayāt*): a verse of the Holy Qur'an.
Āyat al-Kursī: "Verse of the Throne,"a well-known supplication from the Qur'an (2:255).
ʿAzraʿīl: the Archangel of Death.
Badīʿ al-: The Innovator; a divine name.
Banī Adam: Children of Adam; humanity.
Bayt al-Maqdis: the Sacred Mosque in Jerusalem, built at the site where Solomon's Temple was later erected.
Bayt al-Mā'mūr: much-frequented house; this refers to the Kaʿbah of the Heavens, which is the prototype of the Kaʿbah on Earth, circumambulated by the angels.
bayaʿ: pledge; in the context of this book, the pledge of initiation of a disciple (*murīd*) to a shaykh.
Bismillāhi'r-Raḥmāni'r-Raḥīm: "In the name of the All-Merciful, the All-Compassionate"; introductory verse to all chapters of the Qur'an, except the ninth.
Dajjāl: the False Messiah (Anti-Christ) will appear at the end-time of this

world, to deceive Mankind with false divinity.
dalālah: evidence.
dhāt: self / selfhood.
dhawq (pl. *adhwāq*): tasting; technical term referring to the experiential aspect of gnosis.
dhikr: remembrance, mention of God in His Holy Names or phrases of glorification.
ḍīyā: light.
Diwān al-Awlīyā: the nightly gathering of saints with Prophet Muḥammad in the spiritual realm.
du'ā: supplication.
dunyā: world; worldly life.
'Eid: festival; the two major celebrations of Islam are 'Eid al-Fitr, after Ramaḍān; and 'Eid al-Adha, the Festival of Sacrifice during the time of Hajj, which commemorates the sacrifice of Prophet Abraham.
farḍ: obligatory worship.
Fātiḥah: Sūratu 'l-Fātiḥah; the opening chapter of the Qur'an.
Ghafūr, al-: The Forgiver; one of the Holy Names of God.
ghawth: lit. "Helper"; the highest rank of all saints.
ghaybu' l-muṭlaq, al-: the Absolute Unknown; known only to God.
ghusl: full shower/bath obligated by a state of ritual impurity, performed before worship.
Grandshaykh: generally, a *walī* of great stature. In this text, where spelled "Grandshaykh,"refers to Mawlana 'Abd Allāh ad-Daghestani (d. 1973), Mawlana Shaykh Nazim's master.
hā': the Arabic letter ه
ḥadīth Nabawī (pl., *aḥadīth*): prophetic *ḥadīth* whose meaning and linguistic expression are those of Prophet Muḥammad.
Ḥadīth Qudsī: divine saying whose meaning directly reflects the meaning God intended but whose linguistic expression is not divine speech as in the Qur'an.
ḥaḍr: present
Hajj: the sacred pilgrimage of Islam obligatory on every mature Muslim once in their life.
ḥalāl: permitted, lawful according to Islamic Sharī'ah.
ḥaqīqah, al-: reality of existence; ultimate truth.
ḥaqq: truth
Ḥaqq, al-: the Divine Reality, one of the 99 Divine Names.
ḥarām: forbidden, unlawful.
ḥasanāt: good deeds.
hāshā: God forbid.
ḥarf: (pl. *ḥurūf*) letter; Arabic root "edge."
Ḥawā: Eve.
ḥaywān: animal.
Hijrah: emigration.
ḥikmah: wisdom.
ḥujjah: proof.
hūwa: the pronoun "he,"made up of the Arabic letters *hā'* and *wāw* .
'ibādu 'l-Lāh: servants of God.
'ifrīt: a type of Jinn, huge and powerful.
iḥsān: doing good, "It is to worship God as though you see Him; for if you are not seeing Him, He sees you."
ikhlāṣ, al-: sincere devotion.
ilāh: (pl. *āliha*): idols or gods.
ilāhīyya: divinity.
ilhām: divine inspiration sent to *awlīyāullāh.*
'ilm: knowledge, science.
'ilmu 'l-awrāq: knowledge of papers.
'ilmu 'l-adhwāq: knowledge of taste.
'ilmu 'l-ḥurūf: science of letters.

ʿilmu ʾl-kalām: scholastic theology.
ʿilmun ladunnī: divinely inspired knowledge.
imān: faith, belief.
imām: leader of congregational prayer; an advanced scholar followed by a large community.
insān: humanity; pupil of the eye.
insānu ʾl-kāmil, al-: the Perfect Man, *i.e.*, Prophet Muḥammad.
irādatullāh: the Will of God.
irshād: spiritual guidance.
ism: name.
isma-Llāh: name of God.
isrāʿ: night journey; used here in reference to the night journey of Prophet Muḥammad.
Isrāʿfīl: Archangel Rafael, in charge of blowing the Final Trumpet.
jalāl: majesty.
jamāl: beauty.
jamaʿa: group, congregation.
Jannah: Paradise.
jihād: to struggle in God's Path.
Jibrīl : Gabriel, Archangel of revelation.
Jinn: a species of living beings created from fire, invisible to most humans. Jinn can be Muslims or non-Muslims.
Jumuʿah: Friday congregational prayer, held in a large mosque.
Kaʿbah: the first House of God, located in Mecca, Saudi Arabia to which pilgrimage is made and to which Muslims face in prayer.
kāfir: unbeliever.
Kalāmullāh al-Qadīm: lit., Allāh's Ancient Words, *viz.* the Holy Qur'an.
kalīmat at-tawḥīd: lā ilāha illa-Llāh: "There is no god but Al-Lah (the God)."
karāmat: miracles.
khalīfah: deputy.
Khāliq, al-: the Creator, one of 99 Divine Names.
khalq: Creation.
khāniqah: designated smaller place for worship other than a mosque; *zāwiyah.*
khuluq: conduct, manners.
Kirāmun Kātabīn: honored Scribe angels.
lā: no; not; not existent; the particle of negation.
lā ilāha illa-Llāh Muḥammadun Rasūlullāh: there is no deity except Allāh, Muḥammad is the Messenger of Allāh.
lām: Arabic letter ل.
al-Lawḥ al-Maḥfūẓ: the Preserved Tablets.
Laylat al-Isrāʿ waʾl-Miʿrāj: the Night Journey and Ascension of Prophet Muḥammad to Jerusalem and to the Seven Heavens.
Madīnātu ʾl-Munawwara: the Illuminated city; city of Prophet Muḥammad; Madinah.
mahr: dowry, given by the groom to the bride.
malakūt: divine kingdom.
Malik, al-: the Sovereign, a divine name.
Mālik: Archangel of Hell
maqām: spiritual station; tomb of a prophet, messenger or saint.
maʿrifah: gnosis.
Māshā'Allāh: as Allāh Wills.
Mawlānā: lit. "Our master" or "our patron,"referring to an esteemed person.
maẓhar: place of disclosure.
miḥrāb: prayer niche.
Mikāʿīl: Michael, Archangel of rain.
mīzān: the scale that weighs our deeds on Judgment Day.
mīm: Arabic letter م.

minbar: pulpit.
Miracles: of *awlīyā*, known as *karamāt*; of prophets, known as *muʿjizāt* (lit., "That which renders powerless or helpless").
miʿrāj: the ascension of Prophet. Muḥammad from Jerusalem to the Seven Heavens.
Muḥammadun rasūlu ʾl-Lāh: Muḥammad is the Messenger of God.
mulk, al-: the World of dominion.
Muʿmin, al-: Guardian of Faith, one of the 99 Names of God.
muʿmin: a believer.
munājāt: invocation to God in a very intimate form.
Munkir: one of the angels of the grave.
murīd: disciple, student, follower.
murshid: spiritual guide; *pir*.
mushāhadah: direct witnessing.
mushrik (pl. *mushrikūn*): idolater; polytheist.
muwwāḥid (pl. *muwāḥḥidūn*): those who affirm God's Oneness.
nabī: a prophet of God.
nāfs: lower self, ego.
Nakīr: the other angel of the grave (with Munkir).
nūr: light.
Nūḥ: the prophet Noah.
Nūr, an-: "The Source of Light"; a divine name.
Qādir, al-: "The Powerful"; a divine name.
qalam, al-: the Pen.
qiblah: direction, specifically, the direction faced by Muslims during prayer and other worship, towards the Sacred House in Mecca.
Quddūs, al-: "The Holy One"; a divine name.
qurb: nearness
quṭb (pl. *aqṭāb*): axis or pole. Among the poles are:
Quṭbu ʿl-Bilād: Pole of the Lands.
Quṭbu ʿl-Irshād: Pole of Guidance.
Quṭbu ʿl-Aqṭāb: Pole of Poles.
Quṭbu ʿl-Aʿdham: Highest Pole.
Quṭbu ʿl-Mutaṣarrif: Pole of Affairs.
al-quṭbīyyatu ʾl-kubrā: the highest station of poleship.
Rabb, ar-: the Lord.
Raḥīm, ar-: "The Most Compassionate"; a divine name.
Raḥmān, ar-: "The All-Merciful"; a divine name.
raḥmā: mercy.
rakaʿat: one full set of prescribed motions in prayer. Each prayer consists of a one or more *rakaʿats.*
Ramaḍān: the ninth month of the Islamic calendar; month of fasting.
Rasūl: a messenger of God.
Rasūlullāh: the Messenger of God, Muḥammad ﷺ.
Raʿūf, ar-: "The Most Kind"; a divine name.
Razzāq, ar-: "The Provider"; a divine name.
rawḥānīyyah: spirituality; spiritual essence of something.
Riḍwān: Archangel of Paradise.
rizq: provision; sustenance.
rūḥ: spirit. *Ar-Rūḥ* is the name of a great angel.
rukūʿ: bowing posture of the prayer.
ṣadaqah: voluntary charity.
Ṣaḥābah (sing., *saḥābi*): Companions of the Prophet; the first Muslims.
ṣaḥīḥ: authentic; term certifying validity of a ḥadīth of the Prophet.
ṣāim: fasting person (pl. *ṣāimūn*)
sajdah (pl. *sujūd*): prostration.
ṣalāt: ritual prayer, one of the five obligatory pillars of Islam. Also, to invoke blessing on the Prophet.

Ṣalāt an-Najāt: prayer of salvation, offered in the late hours of night.
ṣalawāt (sing. *ṣalāt*): invoking blessings and peace upon the Prophet.
salām: peace.
Salām, as-: "The Peaceful"; a divine name. *As-salāmu ʿalaykum:* "Peace be upon you." (Islamic greeting).
Ṣamad, aṣ-: Self-Sufficient, upon whom creatures depend.
ṣawm, ṣiyām: fasting.
Sayāt: bad deeds.
sayyid: leader; also, a descendant of Prophet Muḥammad.
Sayyīdinā: our master (fem. *sayyidunā; sayyidatunā*: our mistress).
shahādah: lit. testimony; the testimony of Islamic faith: *Lā ilāha illa ʾl-Lāh wa Muḥammadun rasūlu ʾl-Lāh,* "There is no god but Allāh, the One God, and Muḥammad is the Messenger of God."
Shah Naqshband: Muḥammad Bahauddin Shah Naqshband, a great eighth century walī, and the founder of the Naqshbandi Ṭarīqah.
shaykh: lit. "old Man,"a religious guide, teacher; master of spiritual discipline.
shifāʾ: cure.
shirk: polytheism, idolatry, ascribing partners to God
ṣiffāt: attributes; term referring to Divine Attributes.
Silsilat adh-dhahabīyya: "Golden Chain"of spiritual authority in Islam
sohbet (Arabic, *suḥbah*): association: the assembly or discourse of a shaykh.
subḥānAllāh: glory be to God.
sulṭān/sulṭānah: ruler, monarch.
Sulṭān al-Awlīyā: lit., "King of the *awlīyā*; the highest-ranking saint.
Sūnnah: Practices of Prophet Muḥammad in actions and words; what he did, said, recommended, or approved of in his Companions.
sūrah: a chapter of the Qur'an; picture, image.
Sūratu ʾl-Ikhlāṣ: Chapter 114 of Holy Qur'an; the Chapter of Sincerity.
ṭabīb: doctor.
tābiʿīn: the Successors, one generation after the Prophet's Companions.
tafsīr: to explain, expound, explicate, or interpret; technical term for commentary or exegesis of the Holy Qur'an.
tajallī (pl. *tajallīyāt*): theophanies, God's self-disclosures, Divine Self-manifestation.
takbīr: lit. *"Allāhu Akbar,"*God is Great.
tarawīḥ: the special nightly prayers of Ramaḍān.
ṭarīqat/tarīqah: lit., way, road or path. An Islamic order or path of discipline and devotion under a guide or shaykh; Sufism.
taṣbīḥ: recitation glorifying or praising God.
tawāḍaʿ: humbleness.
ṭawāf: the rite of circumambulating the Kaʿbah while glorifying God during Hajj and ʿUmra.
tawḥīd: unity; universal or primordial Islam, submission to God, as the sole Master of destiny and ultimate Reality.
Tawrāt: Torah
tayammum: Alternate ritual ablution performed in the absence of water.
ʿubūdīyyah: state of worshipfulness. Servanthood
ʿulamā (sing. *ʿālim*): scholars.
ʿulūmu ʾl-awwalīna wa ʾl-ākhirīn: knowledge of the "Firsts"and the "Lasts"refers to the knowledge God

poured into the heart of Prophet Muḥammad during his ascension to the Divine Presence.
ʿulūm al-Islāmī: Islamic religious sciences.
Ummāh: faith community, nation.
ʿUmar ibn al-Khaṭṭāb: an eminent Companion of Prophet Muḥammad and second caliph of Islam.
ʿumra: the minor pilgrimage to Mecca, performed at any time of the year.
ʿUthmān ibn ʿAffān: eminent Companion of the Prophet; his son-in-law and third caliph of Islam, renowned for compiling the Qur'an.
walad: a child.
waladī: my child.
walāyah: proximity or closeness; sainthood.
walī (pl. *awlīyā*): saint, or "he who assists"; guardian; protector.
wasīlah: a means; holy station of Prophet Muḥammad as God's intermediary to grant supplications.
wāw: Arabic letter و
wujūd, al-: existence; "to find,""the act of finding,"as well as "being found."
Yʿaqūb: Jacob; the prophet.
yamīn: the right hand; previously meant "oath."
Yawm al-ʿahdi waʾl-mīthāq: Day of Oath and Covenant, a heavenly event before this Life, when all souls of humanity were present to God, and He took from each the promise to accept His Sovereignty as Lord.
yawm al-qiyāmah: Day of Judgment.
Yūsuf: Joseph; the prophet.
zāwiyah: designated smaller place for worship other than a mosque; also *khāniqah*.
zīyāra: visitation to the grave of a prophet, a prophet's companion or a saint.

Other Publications / www.isn1.net

Mawlana Shaykh Nazim Adil al-Haqqani

- The Sufilive Series, Vols 1-4 (2010)
- Breaths from Beyond the Curtain (2010)
- In the Eye of the Needle
- The Healing Power of Sufi Meditation
- The Path to Spiritual Excellence
- In the Mystic Footsteps of Saints, 2 volumes
- Liberating the Soul, 6 volumes

Shaykh Hisham Kabbani

- The Sufilive Series (2010-11)
- Cyprus Summer Series (2 vols)
- The Nine-fold Ascent
- Who Are the Guides?
- Illuminations
- Banquet for the Soul
- Symphony of Remembrance
- The Healing Power of Sufi Meditation
- In the Shadow of Saints
- Keys to the Divine Kingdom
- The Sufi Science of Self-Realization
- Universe Rising: the Approach of Armageddon?
- Pearls and Coral (2 volumes)
- Classical Islam and the Naqshbandi Sufi Tradition
- The Naqshbandi Sufi Way
- Encyclopedia of Islamic Doctrine (7 volumes)
- Angels Unveiled
- Encyclopedia of Muḥammad's Women Companions and the Traditions They Related

Hajjah Amina Adil

- Muḥammad: the Messenger of Islam
- The Light of Muḥammad
- Lore of Light / Links of Light
- My Little Lore of Light (3 volumes)

Hajjah Naziha Adil Kabbani

- Secrets of Heavenly Food (2009)
- Heavenly Foods (2010)

www.ingramcontent.com/pod-product-compliance
Lightning Source LLC
LaVergne TN
LVHW040137080526
838202LV00042B/2940
* 9 7 8 1 9 3 0 4 0 9 7 9 8 *